# Software Verification and Validation

## Realistic Project Approaches

**Prentice-Hall Series in Software Engineering**
Randall W. Jensen, editor

# Software Verification and Validation
## Realistic Project Approaches

**Michael S. Deutsch**
*Hughes Aircraft Company*

**Prentice-Hall Inc.**
*Englewood Cliffs, NJ 07632*

*Library of Congress Cataloging in Publication Data*

DEUTSCH, MICHAEL S.
    Software verification and validation.

    (Prentice-Hall series in software engineering)
    Bibliography: p. 315
    Includes index.
        1. Computer programs—Verification.
2. Computer programs—Validation.    I. Title.
II. Series.
QA76.6.D48        001.64'24'0287        81-12133
ISBN O-13-822072-7                      AACR2

Editorial/production supervision
and interior design by Kathryn Gollin Marshak
Cover design by Edsal Enterprises
Manufacturing buyer: Gordon Osbourne

Printed in the United States of America

10  9  8  7  6  5  4  3

ISBN 0-13-822072-7

Prentice-Hall International, Inc., *London*
Prentice-Hall of Australia Pty. Limited, *Sydney*
Prentice-Hall of Canada, Ltd., *Toronto*
Prentice-Hall of India Private Limited, *New Delhi*
Prentice-Hall of Japan, Inc., *Tokyo*
Prentice-Hall of Southeast Asia Pte. Ltd., *Singapore*
Whitehall Books Limited, *Wellington, New Zealand*

# Contents

# Preface

The development of software systems involves a series of production activities in which the opportunities for interjection of human fallibilities are enormous. Errors may begin to occur at the very inception of the process when the objectives of the software system may be erroneously or imperfectly specified, as well as during the later design and development stages when these objectives are mechanized. The basic quality goal for software is that it performs its functions in the manner that was intended by its architects. In order to achieve this quality, the final product must contain a minimum of mistakes in implementing their intentions as well as being void of misconceptions about the intentions themselves. Because of human inability to perform and communicate with perfection, software development is accompanied by a verification and validation activity. The importance of verification and validation to the software project continues to amplify as data processing interacts in more and more critical areas, such as health and transportation, where a software failure could have a castastrophic effect on life and property.

The terms *verification* and *validation* are proliferated through the literature of the software community with varying expressed or implied definitions. Although no authority exists to ascribe absolute meanings to this terminology, a preponderance of usage does emerge from a survey of the literature. Verification refers to an activity that assures that the results of successive steps in the software development cycle correctly embrace the intentions of the previous step. Validation has a more global connotation; its goal is to ensure that the software end item product functions and contains the features prescribed by its requirements specification.

We are constantly reminded that we are in the midst of a "software crisis." The software crisis is associated with the vastly increased complexity of data processing systems coupled with the inability of software practices to deal with this complexity. The record over the past ten to fifteen years reflects this deficiency; few major systems have been delivered within original costs, schedules, and performance specifications. Verification and validation is intimately involved with the software crisis. Some inadequate verification and validation practices have contributed to the crisis, and improved verification and validation technology is a major component of solutions to the crisis. Although we are not as yet in the concluding stage of this software trauma, some positive feedback from actual software projects that have applied modern software engineering techniques is beginning to occur. Improved verification and validation methodologies are among the key software engineering ingredients that have achieved positive results.

The main thrust of this book is to describe verification and validation approaches that have been used successfully on contemporary large-scale software projects. Methodologies are explored that can be pragmatically applied to modern complex software developments and that take account of cost, schedule, and management realities in the actual production environment. This book is intended to be tutorial in nature with a "This is how it's done in the real world" orientation. Contributing to this theme will be observations and recounts from actual software development project experiences in industry.

Verification and validation approaches that seem to have been the most successful are those that have combined technical and management merits. Indeed, it is most difficult to separate technology from management in this field. Thus, a balanced treatment of technical and management aspects of verification and validation is provided.

Verification and validation is now a continuous activity over the software life cycle. The requirements and design are subject to continual evaluation in the early phases of the life cycle well before the product is physically implemented. Nevertheless, program testing is still a fundamental and highly relied upon verification and validation mechanism for today's software projects. Accordingly, a major portion of this book deals with modern testing technology and tools; extensive treatment is given, however, to the interaction of the software project organization with a full range of verification and validation activities over the software life cycle.

This book is organized into five semi-independent parts as shown on the next page:

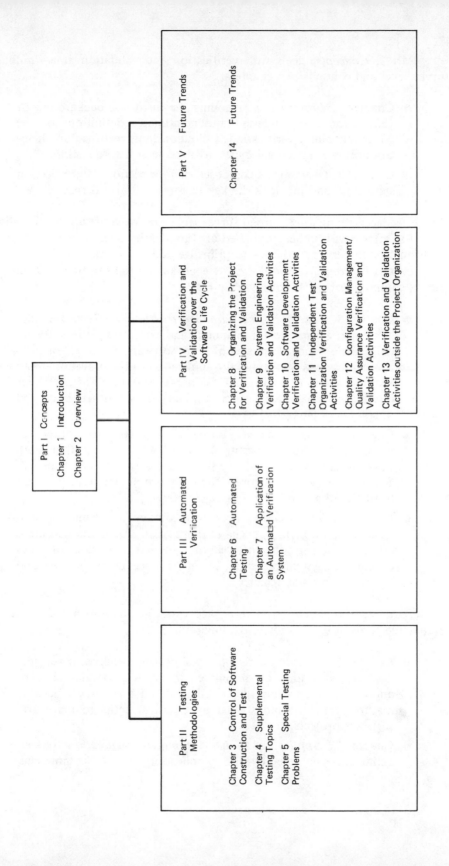

Part I Concepts

Chapter 1 Introduction

Chapter 2 Overview

Part II Testing Methodologies

Chapter 3 Control of Software Construction and Test

Chapter 4 Supplemental Testing Topics

Chapter 5 Special Testing Problems

Part III Automated Verification

Chapter 6 Automated Testing

Chapter 7 Application of an Automated Verification System

Part IV Verification and Validation over the Software Life Cycle

Chapter 8 Organizing the Project for Verification and Validation

Chapter 9 System Engineering Verification and Validation Activities

Chapter 10 Software Development Verification and Validation Activities

Chapter 11 Independent Test Organization Verification and Validation Activities

Chapter 12 Configuration Management/Quality Assurance Verification and Validation Activities

Chapter 13 Verification and Validation Activities outside the Project Organization

Part V Future Trends

Chapter 14 Future Trends

Part I, *Concepts,* deals with verification and validation at a summary or survey level and contains two chapters:

- Chapter 1, *Introduction,* recounts the historical background of verification and validation and investigates definitions of the terms reliability, verification, validation, and certification. It introduces the conceptual issues involved in software testing.
- Chapter 2, *Overview,* is composed of four sections. Each Section synopsizes and previews the key features of Parts II through V.

Those readers wishing only a broad survey treatment of verification and validation may stop after Part I. Others may use Part I to identify selected regions from Parts II through V to peruse further or to prioritize additional reading.

Part II, *Testing Methodologies,* is a broad tutorial on modern testing techniques composed of the following chapters:

- Chapter 3, *Control of Software Construction and Test,* describes a modern technique for planning and controlling the software construction and test phases of large software projects. An exercise is presented that shows the application of the procedure to an example software package. This chapter should be of particular interest to managers, prospective managers, and others interested in software management.
- Chapter 4, *Supplemental Testing Topics,* considers other approaches and topics pertinent to software testing that both dovetail and contrast with the procedure described in Chapter 3. Some of the views of software engineers prominent in the program testing field are included in this chapter.
- Chapter 5, *Special Testing Problems,* contains comments and considerations for certain special testing topics. The specialized areas discussed are testing of real-time systems, testing of data dominated systems, testing of microprocessor software, and testing during maintenance.

Part III, *Automated Verification,* addresses, in Chapters 6 and 7, the role of automated tools in verification and validation:

- Chapter 6, *Automated Testing,* explores the benefits to verification and validation of automated tools. A particular class of automated test tools is described in detail that are sufficiently mature to have demonstrated pragmatic benefits to real-world software projects.
- Chapter 7, *Application of an Automated Verification System,* delineates the step-by-step application of a commercial,

automated test tool to an example testing problem. This chapter discusses an automated testing discipline that provides life cycle cost advantages. Included is a commentary on a recent industrial software project that utilized this test discipline and test tools; the projected life cycle cost savings accrued on this project is presented.

Part IV, *Verification and Validation over the Software Life Cycle,* narrates the complete set of verification and validation activities performed over the software life cycle. The vehicle for this discussion is the software project organization explained in the following chapters:

- Chapter 8, *Organizing the Project for Verification and Validation,* describes the structure of a typical software project organization and delineates the events of the software life cycle.
- Chapter 9, *System Engineering Verification and Validation Activities,* details the verification and validation tasks of the system engineering organization.
- Chapter 10, *Software Development Verification and Validation Activities,* discusses verification- and validation-oriented activities performed by the software development organization.
- Chapter 11, *Independent Test Organization Verification and Validation Activities,* narrates the functions of the independent test organization over the software life cycle.
- Chapter 12, *Configuration Management/Quality Assurance Verification and Validation Activities,* explains the verification and validation activities of the configuration management and quality assurance organizations.
- Chapter 13, *Verification and Validation Activities outside the Project Organization,* addresses the roles of the independent verification and validation contractor and the independent review group.

Part V, *Future Trends,* consists of Chapter 14, *Future Trends,* which reports on prospective future directions of the verification and validation field.

This book is intended for dual utilization. It should prove useful to both technicians and managers engaged in industry or government. The book will also serve the needs of computer science students. It should be of particular interest to those students interested in what to expect in an industrial software development environment and would bridge the gap between academic and pragmatic verification and validation concepts.

## Acknowledgements

I wish to thank Mr. William R. DeHaan and associates of General Research Corporation of Santa Barbara, California for providing me with descriptive materials on the verification tools RXVP80™ and V-IFTRAN™ from which Section 6.4 (A Commercial Automated Verification System) is largely derived. The Software Workshop™, IFTRAN™, V-IFTRAN™, and RXVP80™ are registered trade marks of General Research Corporation.

At various points in this book I have used excerpts from the Verification and Validation chapter that I authored in *Software Engineering,* Jensen and Tonies, editors, a text book published by Prentice-Hall, Inc. These excerpts have been reprinted by permission of Prentice-Hall, Inc., Englewood Cliffs, N.J.

I would also like to express my appreciation to Dr. Randall Jensen, of Hughes Aircraft Co., who provided me with invaluable advice and counsel, to my wife Dotti for her work in editing and assistance in preparing the manuscript, and to Ms. Frances Christenson for her assistance in handling the wealth of correspondence that is associated with an endeavor of this kind.

*Michael S. Deutsch*

# Software Verification and Validation

Realistic Project Approaches

# Part I

# Concepts

_____Chapter 1_____

# Introduction

_____

## 1.1
## Historical Perspective of Verification
## and Validation

Over the past fifteen to twenty years software projects have developed from rather small tasks involving a few people to enormously complex undertakings that sometimes seemingly require the services of a "cast of thousands." The mentality of verification and validation has undergone a commensurate radical adjustment. Previously, verification and validation was an informal, highly individualized activity; this consisted almost entirely of the programmer exercising his code against a small set of *ad hoc* test cases. As the volume and complexity of the software increased on more contemporary projects, the fallibilities of this "craftsman"-type approach became evident in the form of unreliable products. It became clear that to fully entrust responsibility for product verification with the product developer created intellectual demands that were conflicting and overwhelming. As a result, verification and validation emerged as an activity requiring individual emphasis and technology within the software project.

The verification and validation (V & V) technology that is applied to today's complex software projects has certain characteristics which are in sharp contrast to original practices:

- V & V is now practiced over the full software life cycle.
- V & V is now highly formalized with specifically identified activities.
- Some V & V activities are performed by organization(s) independent of the software developer.

Verification and validation methodologies are now applied over the software life cycle before software testing begins. These pretesting activities typically include requirements verification, design walkthroughs, design quality measurements, interface control definition, code inspections, and formal design reviews. This broad approach has been inspired by the realization that mistakes discovered earlier in the life cycle are less costly to correct. The concept of testing has undergone significant evolutionary change. It has become a highly rigorous function involving formalized plans and procedures. The use of automated test tools has taken some error-prone operations out of human hands.

Formerly, the scope of verification and validation was almost entirely concerned with evaluation of functionality and performance. This would usually entail satisfying the following kinds of queries:

- Do the design and product contain all the required functions and have the functions been implemented correctly?
- Will the design and product produce the desired parameter accuracies, respond within the required time frame, and operate within the allocated computational resources?

These areas, of course, still remain as key focal points for verification and validation efforts. However, an aroused level of cost and quality awareness on the part of today's customers has significantly widened the scope of verification and validation. We are now equally interested in such subjects as producability, maintainability, and operability. These new areas of concern give rise to the following types of issues:

- Can the system be produced within the contracted cost and schedule constraints?
- Can the system product, once initially installed, be easily modified or extended to accommodate changing user needs?
- Can the system operate efficiently in the user's operating environment?

Intrinsic to these issues is a sensitivity to life cycle costs. Previously, customers have been preoccupied essentially with the initial costs of developing a system. There is now a more balanced interest in determining a system's cost over the full cycle of its operational life before it is built. Life cycle costs include the initial development cost plus the cost of operation and cost of maintenance. The scope of verification and validation has grown to embrace these issues.

The modern software project is composed of three basic technical line organizations—*system engineering, software development,* and the *independent test organization* (ITO). Each of these entities reports to the project manager on an equal basis. Each has certain verification and validation activities specifically allocated to it. The independent nature of the test organization has evolved to preserve objectivity and avoid possible conflicts of interest. All formal testing is normally performed by the ITO. On very large projects, the customer may employ a verification and validation contractor that is independent of the project organization.

Testing, much maligned in recent years, still remains as an important pragmatic verification and validation mechanism on the software project; this is despite certain deficiencies with regard to formal verification and validation. This book focuses first on modern testing approaches which ameliorate many of the earlier deficiencies that have resulted in unreliable software products; the scope of consideration then broadens to include a full set of verification and validation activities over the entire software life cycle.

This introductory chapter continues with an exploration of the definitions of verification and validation terminology.

## 1.2
## Definition of Terms

The terms software reliability, verification, validation, and certification fill the literature of the software community. They are used with varying expressed or implied definitions. This diversification may be traced to the individual author's need to customize a set of terminology that is appropriate and convenient for his specialized area of interest. Often the usage and definition of the terms are simply a matter of interchangeability between authors, that is, the differences are that of appearance rather than of substance.

The major purpose of the immediately forthcoming pages is to convey a general understanding of this terminology and its application by surveying previous and ongoing usage of the terms.

### RELIABILITY

Reliability of the product software is a specific measure of software quality. The achievement of high reliability in the final delivered product is the primary objective of the verification and validation process and the ambition of the total program of software development.

Schneidewind[1] defines software reliability as the probability that a program will operate successfully for at least time $t$. Shooman in Yourdon[2] defines software reliability as the probability that a program operates for some time interval without error on the machine for which it was designed, given that it is used within design limits. This is similar but more extensive than the previous definition. The key issue here is clearly the concept of successful operation over a specific time duration and the ascription of a probability to that success. This is somewhat analogous to the meantime-between-failure (MTBF) metric for hardware.

Errors or defects are uncovered as the software is exercised. The volume, frequency, and severity of errors are the inverse measures of software reliability. Each time an error is detected and successfully rectified, the reliability has improved. Nelson[3] furnishes an algorithmic measure of reliability by first defining the *execution failure probability* as the quotient of the number of inputs for which failures occur and the total number of inputs. He then defines reliability as one minus the execution failure probability.

Speaking in a quality control context, Schneidewind[4] advocates as a noble goal the establishment of reliability specifications as quantitative acceptance criteria for software. Here, the software reliability budget would be derived from the total system reliability requirement, and then this budget would be allocated to each software element. A positive reliability value judgment based solely on a very low volume of errors, however, does not consider the impact or potential adverse effect of even a single error. On a very large real-time system, even a specification that permits only a very small error tolerance for an arbitrary number of instructions could cause the system to become incapacitated at a critical moment. Such a contrived, but realistic, situation promulgates two essential points: (1) Software reliability is multidimensional; in addition to volume, error severity, as a minimum, needs also to be considered; and (2) the problem of the "single critical error" cannot be persuasively addressed by today's technology within reasonable cost constraints.

There have been substantial investigations into using error statistics collected from software executions in conjunction with a model depicting error depreciation in order to predict future reliability. Schneidewind[5] analyzed error data from nineteen programs of the Naval Tactical Data System and concluded that reliability should be predicted only on an individual program basis because of the large variations in the error depreciation profiles between programs that he encountered. He also suggests that, because of differing impacts on system operations, reliability

[1] Norman F. Schneidewind, "An Approach to Software Reliability Prediction and Quality Control," in *Proceedings of Fall Joint Computer Conference, 1972* (Montvale, N.J.: American Federation of Information Processing Societies, Inc., 1972), p. 240.

[2] Edward Yourdon, *Techniques of Program Structure and Design* (Englewood Cliffs, N. J.: Prentice-Hall, 1975), p. 245.

[3] Eldred C. Nelson, "Software Reliability, Verification and Validation," in *Proceedings of the TRW Symposium on Reliable, Cost-Effective, Secure Software* (Redondo Beach, Ca.: TRW, 1974), pp. 5-22-23, 5-28-29.

[4] Schneidewind, op. cit., p. 837.

[5] Schneidewind, op. cit., p. 846.

predictions for several severity levels of errors may be in order. Nelson[6] reports on good agreement between measured reliability and estimated a priori reliability based on program complexity and quality of documentation.

Some interesting tendencies in error statistics have been noted. Collected error data on newly installed versions of the Satellite Control Facility software system revealed that, for each version, the error rate reached a peak approximately one month after installation on the system.[7]

Except in a very general context, the term *reliability* is awkwardly applied to the software product and is not well understood by software practitioners and theoreticians. This is understandable because the initial application of this terminology to software arose as an analogy to hardware. It later became obvious that there are certain rudimentary differences between hardware and software, particularly with regard to degradation attributes; that is, software does not "wear out." There has not been a full recovery from this observed dissimilarity and, for the time being, there has not been a reconciled precise and universal definition of software reliability that is pragmatically useful.

Software reliability is primarily a function of its development history. The conditions experienced during the early life cycle phases (requirements definition, design) are highly influential in determining the probability that errors, that is, reduced reliability, are introduced. Verification and validation activities are therefore applied to all life cycle phases in pursuit of the high reliability objective.

The basic goal of verification and validation, the production of reliable software, has now been briefly explored. Next, the definitions and implications of the verification and validation terminology are examined.

## VERIFICATION, VALIDATION, AND CERTIFICATION

There appears to be a reasonable level of agreement among software engineers that the activities of verification, validation, and certification are directed both toward determining that the software performs its intended functions and ensuring reliability of the software. The definitions of these three terms are related to the formalized activities of the overall software development process. A general model of the *system* development cycle is depicted in Figure 1-1 in terms of the products or deliverable items. *System* is emphasized with the realization that data processing may be just one of several segments that comprise the total system and that the data processing system consists not only of software elements but may also include development of special hardware elements such as displays, logic chips, customized interfaces, and so on.

The system development cycle occurs in discrete steps. It may be characterized as, first, a decomposition procedure that defines, in the form of requirements and specifications, the components of the system. This begins at the system/mission

[6] Nelson, op. cit., pp. 5-22-23.
[7] E. F. Miller, Jr., *A Survey of Major Techniques of Program Validation* (Santa Barbara, Ca.: General Research Corp., 1972), RM-1731, pp. 14-15.

level. The definition process then successively branches until specifications for individual elements are produced. From these specifications the software or hardware elements are built. The end item elements are then composed in successive stages until an end item system product is assembled, delivered, and accepted by the buyer. The depth of the hierarchy shown in Figure 1-1 for any individual system development may vary, depending on system complexity, governing standards, and *ad hoc* agreements between seller and buyer. For example, the design specification activity is frequently extended to include a preliminary design specification as well as a detailed design specification; each is normally the major subject of a preliminary and of a critical design review respectively.

Referring again to Figure 1-1, the process may be geometrically viewed as consisting of two symmetrical tree-like structures, one diverging from the system to the element level and the other converging back to the system level. Each member of the converging tree has a "mirror image" analogous member in the diverging tree. For example, the data processing subsystem #1 end item (converging tree) was defined by the data processing subsystem #1 requirements (diverging tree). The requirements and specifications of the diverging tree define and induce the end item products of the converging tree. The verification–validation–certification process seeks to reflect backward and ensure the integrity of the converging tree (the product) with respect to the diverging tree (the definition of the product). Thus, the collective verification–validation–certification activities intend to guarantee that each end item properly reflects its mirror image specification/requirements document, that each step is consistent with and implements the intentions of the previous step, and that the data processing segment end item is compatible with the total system.

When viewed in the context that is represented diagrammatically by Figure 1-1, an appropriate allocation of the previous definition to the individual terms is

*Validation*—This activity ensures that each end item product functions and contains the features as prescribed by its requirements and specifications at the corresponding level.

*Verification*—This activity ensures that each step of the development process correctly echoes the intentions of the immediately preceding step.

*Certification*—This activity ensures that the data processing system (hardware and software) properly interacts within the total system and performs its specified functions within the total system context.

Reifer,[8] after a survey of the software literature, concludes somewhat similar definitions. He does, however, note a cumulative effect in that validation requires the accomplishment of all verification activities. He specifically breaks down the verification activity to consist of these components:

1. Verification that mission requirements have been correctly translated into data processing requirements

[8] D. J. Reifer, *Computer Program Verification/Validation/Certification* (Los Angeles, Ca.: The Aerospace Corp., 1974), Report No. TOR-0074(4112)-5, pp. 18-23.

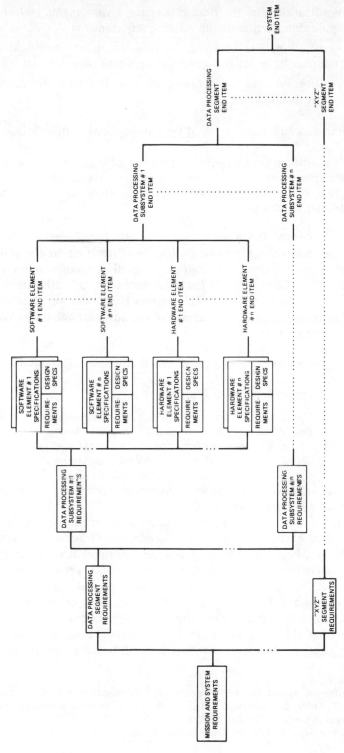

**Figure 1-1** System development model. (Michael S. Deutsch, "Verification and Validation," in *Software Engineering*, ed. Jensen & Tonies, © 1979, p. 335, fig. 5–1. Reprinted by permission of Prentice-Hall, Inc., Englewood Cliffs, N.J.)

2. Verification that the data processing requirements reflect the computer-applicable portion of the mission requirements

3. Verification that the computer program design specification represents a true translation of the computer program requirements

4. Verification that the actual code complies with the computer program design specification

Reifer also addresses the total system implication of certification:

> Certification extends the process of verification and validation to an operational (real or simulated) environment. Here, the code can be exercised to determine with some confidence whether or not the stated mission requirements are met.[9]

Hetzel[10] contributes a somewhat different definitional framework. Verification is concerned with a program's logical correctness in the test environment. Validation is directed toward a program's logical correctness in a given external environment. He defines *certification* as connotating an authoritative endorsement implying written testimony that the program is of a certain standard of quality.

Miller relates program validation to the software reliability concept with the following definition:

> Definition: Program Validation is the process of assuring that the probability of failure of a given software system on its next invocation is appropriately small, given that:
>
> 1. There is sufficient quantitative information about the past behavior of the software system (if there is a past), and
> 2. Some means of affirmation of the software system has been (or is being) applied to decrease the probability of a failure.[11]

He refers to certification as a process concluding with some statement of the degree of quality of a software system.

Definitions of validation, verification, and certification have been advanced by the author based on a geometric argument. Other views, both similar and dissimilar, have been summarized from the literature. It is generally accepted that complete validation, implying absolute correctness, is presently infeasible with any sizable program. An economically-acceptable partial validation is achieved by testing the software. It has been similarly asserted that certification of large operational programs is not attained with current practices.[12] What is achieved is a validation that the programs have passed certain tests. Despite this recognized limitation, state-of-the-art verification and validation of programs are largely ac-

[9] Reifer, op. cit., p. 25.

[10] William C. Hetzel, *Program Test Methods* (Englewood Cliffs, N.J.: Prentice-Hall, 1973) p. 9.

[11] E. F. Miller, Jr., *A Survey of Major Techniques of Program Validation* (Santa Barbara, Ca.: General Research Corp., 1972), RM-1731, p. 4.

[12] J. S. Prokop, in *Program Test Methods,* p. 31.

complished by exercising the software in a testing process. From the test results, proper functioning of the software and its reliability are inferred. Discussion of the conceptual issues involved in software testing is continued in the next section.

## 1.3
## Conceptual Issues of Software Testing

### THEORETICAL BACKGROUND

It is the purpose of verification and validation to determine that a software product performs according to the intentions of its architects. One community asserts that the ideal manner in which to accomplish this involves viewing the program as a theorem. A formal proof may then be constructed to establish the correctness of the theorem (and program). These techniques are not presently developed enough to be economically viable in practice. There is skepticism that this avenue represents the final answer to the problem regardless of economic considerations. A more practical immediate approach is to develop confidence in a program through accumulated experience of its use on a set of test cases.

Thus, *testing* is defined as the controlled exercise of the program code in order to expose errors. When, according to preestablished criteria, the number and severity of errors fall below a specified threshold, it is normally concluded that *proper operation* of the software has been demonstrated. The accuracy of this conclusion depends heavily on the framework in which *proper operation* is defined. A complete testing approach would ideally consist of demonstrating successful traversal of all possible paths through a program. Figure 1–2[13] helps explain the futility of such a goal. There are about $10^{20}$ different paths through the flow chart, and several

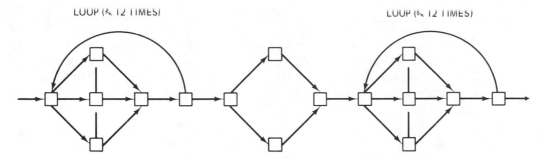

**Figure 1-2**   How many different paths through this flowchart? (Barry W. Boehm, *Some Information Processing Implications of Air Force Space Missions: 1970–1980,* 1970, RM-6213-PR, p. 24. Reprinted by permission of the Rand Corporation, Santa Monica, CA.)

[13] Barry W. Boehm, *Some Information Processing Implications of Air Force Space Missions: 1970–1980* (Santa Monica, Ca.: The RAND Corp., 1970), Memorandum RM-6213-PR, pp. 23–25.

thousand years of computer time would be required to check all paths. An analogous view of comprehensive testing is to test a program for all possible input cases to see if the correct outputs are generated. In considering a hypothetical program with two independent integer input variables, it was calculated that fifty billion years of computing time would be required to complete the test.[14] Clearly, this is prohibitive, and more pragmatic test goals need to be established. Fortunately, it is almost always the case that a much smaller number of test cases stresses a sufficient, statistically significant number of paths through the program.

Some insight into the objectives of testing can be obtained by delineating the types of errors that testing strives to expose. An extensive list of error categories has been compiled by Yourdon[15] and is summarized below:

1. Logic errors, which are the most common type of software bug

2. Documentation errors, including both technical and user documentation

3. Overload errors whereby various storage areas are stressed up to and beyond their capacities

4. Timing errors, which are of most importance to real-time systems and are frequently difficult to reproduce

5. Throughput and capacity errors that involve the amounts of computational resources (CPU utilization, various storage allocations) consumed by a program.

6. Fallback and recovery errors concerning the software response to hardware and software failures

7. Hardware errors and system software errors in the context of testing the overall system, which consists of the applications software, system software, and hardware

8. Standards errors that entail adherence to various software construction standards

Software testing consumes a significant, sometimes paramount, portion of software project budgetary expenditures. On medium- to large-scale software systems, approximately 50% of the software budget has been historically expended on testing and integration. The following expenditures expressed as a percentage of total effort have been reported for the testing of these actual spaceborne and command-control projects:[16]

| | |
|---|---|
| Sage | 47% |
| Naval Tactical Data System | 50% |
| Gemini | 47% |
| Saturn I | 44% |

[14] J. C. Huang, "An Approach to Program Testing," *ACM Computing Surveys,* 7 (1975), p. 114.
[15] Yourdon, op. cit., pp. 254–56.
[16] Boehm, op. cit., p. 36.

It is estimated that on the NASA Apollo project nearly 80% of project costs were consumed by testing.[17] As more powerful source languages are introduced, the amount of object code generated per line of source code is amplified. The relative amount of time consumed in actual programming will commensurately decrease while the time expended on software testing will probably increase beyond the present 50% rule-of-thumb figure.

It is well known that the cost of revealing and rectifying errors becomes larger with each successive step in the development cycle. For this reason, a building block approach to testing is undertaken. The initial level of testing performed is in small *chunks* of software consisting of very small groups of modules (or routines). Here, it is easier and more economical to detect and isolate errors. Also, at this level, it is possible to check more logical paths. After combination into higher level units, the task becomes less feasible and more expensive.

A definite technology void still exists in the area of test case design. Although there appears to be significant amounts of research in this area, the actual level of technology transfer into methods pragmatically useful to larger scale software projects is very small at this time. The design of functional test cases is presently an artistic process intimately related to the specific applications involved and cannot be adequately described in algorithmic terms. Some practical methodologies have been devised which allow extension of functional test cases to achieve a wider testing coverage. An extension technique and supporting tool are described in Chapters 6 and 7.

## COMPONENTS OF THE TESTING PROCESS

The testing process essentially consists of exercising the software and accumulating performance statistics on its operation. The conception, execution, and evaluation of the process are only semiscientific. The prediction of expected program performance prior to testing has a scientific orientation; the determination of what to test for, the design of specific tests, and the management of the test execution are artistic in nature.[18] There has been substantial progress in recent years toward making test engineering a more quantitative rigorous discipline. For some specific system applications, test case design and execution has taken on an algorithmic orientation. In general, however, test engineering is still subject to the craftsman type approach.

The successful engineering of a testing effort usually makes use of a great deal of accumulated software experience on the part of the participants and, thus, inexperienced beginners are likely not to make a substantial contribution if assigned to this activity. Although partly artistic in nature, testing is not a "black magic" craft, but is a systematic and disciplined activity.

An overall software testing activity would nominally include test planning, test case design, test execution, and evaluation of test results.

[17] Yourdon, op. cit., pp. 254–56.
[18] Fred Gruenberger, "Program Testing and Validation," *Datamation,* July 1968, p. 39.

The test planning task usually manifests itself in a master planning document. This is initially produced early in the development cycle or may have been generated prior to the manufacturing contract during a definition phase. It is updated through progressive stages. This plan specifies the overall test and integration philosophy, strategies, and methodologies to be employed. It traces the testing sequence from unit level tests to final acceptance test and identifies each individual test. This document will either contain or be accompanied by a "requirements/test matrix." This matrix identifies each individual requirement that is being tested and specifies the test or tests by which each requirement is to be verified. A representative form of a requirements/test matrix is depicted in Figure 1-3.

Each test indicated in the master test plan is given individual engineering attention; that is, each test is designed and documented in test specifications. For each test, a test plan, test procedure, and a test report are produced. These documents are prepared by the developer (or integrator) and may require customer concurrence or approval.

The test plan will contain the test objectives, a test description, a description of the test environment, including required hardware and software, a delineation of the requirements being verified, and an evaluation plan. The evaluation plan will consist of the acceptance criteria and a description of the techniques to be used in analyzing the test data in order to determine compliance with the acceptance criteria.

The test procedure will describe the test sequence, the test input data, and the data base; identify the software configuration; and identify the required test per-

| SPEC PARAGRAPH \ TESTS | CPCI Test #1 | CPCI Test #2 | CPCI Test #3 | ... | CPCI Test #n | Subsystem test #1 | Subsystem test #2 | Subsystem test #n | System test #1 | System test #2 | Acceptance test | Analysis |
|---|---|---|---|---|---|---|---|---|---|---|---|---|
| 1.0 | X | | | | | X | | | | X | X | |
| 1.1 | | | | | | X | | | | X | X | |
| 1.2 | X | | | | | | | | X | X | X | |
| 2.0 | | X | | | | | | | | | | |
| 2.1 | | X | | | | | | | | | | |
| 2.2 | | X | | | | | | | | | | |
| 2.3 | | | | | | | | | X | X | | |
| 2.4 | | | | | | | | | | | | X |

**Figure 1-3**  Representative requirements/"where verified" matrix.

sonnel and their functions. The test is executed in accordance with the script and environment stated in the individual test specification. The test is typically witnessed by customer and quality assurance personnel. Any observed irregularities are noted and considered later in the evaluation stage. Output data from the test is captured for subsequent evaluation. A test report is issued, describing the test results in light of the objectives of the test. The results of the analysis of the test data are detailed and any anomalies are noted.

Observations of the test itself and evaluation of the test output constitute the basis on which it is determined whether the test objectives have been met, the pertinent requirements verified, and the acceptance criteria satisfied. The evaluation of the output data, if performed manually, is likely to be a tedious, time-consuming, and error-prone process for all but the most elementary of tests. This has been one of the major motivations for the development of automatic test tools whose utility and necessity are becoming increasingly paramount. Hetzel[19] notes that automation requires at least a semialgorithmic process. He attributes possible limitations on the success of automation to the fact that testing is not currently such a process.

Disciplined control of the testing effort is maintained by emphasizing comprehensive and precise definition of test plans, evaluation of test achievement against the test plan at periodic checkpoints, and quantitative measurement and expression of testing extent at checkpoints.[20] Except for very simple programs, utility of automatic test tools is practically a necessity in order to maintain this discipline. Automatic test tools are the subject of Chapters 6 and 7.

[19] Hetzel, op. cit., p. 25.

[20] William R. Elmendorf, "Controlling the Functional Testing of an Operating System," *IEEE Transactions on Systems Science and Cybernetics,* SSC–5 (1969), p. 284.

# Chapter 2

# Overview

This chapter provides a summary of the key concepts and methodologies that are presented in detail in the body of this book.[1] The sections of this chapter are delineated in the following list and essentially parallel Parts II through V.

- *A modern testing methodology*—A formal procedure for the control of software construction and test that is visibly correlated with requirements is described.
- *Automated verification*—This section explains the application of automated verification systems that will expose errors early in the development cycle that would otherwise have gone undetected until some later time.
- *Verification and validation over the software life cycle*—Verification and validation activities over the full span of the software life cycle are summarized and allocated to the key organizations of the software project.

[1] Portions of this chapter are extracted from Michael S. Deutsch, "Software Project Verification and Validation," *Computer,* April, 1981 © 1981 IEEE.

- *Future trends*—This section projects into the future to scope the expected developments in the dynamic software verification and validation field.

There are two alternate perspectives from which the reader may choose to view this overview material. This chapter can serve as a further more involved introduction to verification and validation approaches. Alternatively, the reader might elect to use this overview as a survey from which to identify certain portions of the book to be read further or to prioritize continued reading.

## 2.1
## A Modern Testing Methodology

This section describes a method of software construction and test that segments a complex software development into more manageable functional elements and maintains a strong visible connection between testing and requirements. The approach described here was originally developed at Computer Sciences Corporation and has undergone refinement in its application at Hughes Aircraft Company. This concept has a powerful effect on ordering the software construction/test process because of its combined technical and management merits.

Figure 2-1 depicts the basic approach to a software test procedure that is visibly connected to the requirements. The process is driven by a tool called the *system verification diagram* (SVD) derived directly from the software requirements specification. The SVD consists of stimulus/response elements (threads) that are associated with both an identifiable function and specific requirements. Each stimulus/response element can be mapped into the design to identify the specific software modules which, when executed, perform the function of that thread. A relationship now exists at a detailed level between the functional requirements (the threads) and the design (the modules). This relationship is the primary means by which the software development can be accurately defined and closely controlled.

The next step is to allocate specific threads to specific builds. Each build represents a significant subset of the functional capabilities of the system. Each incremental build demonstration is a partial dry run of the Final Acceptance Test. Each successive build demonstration regression tests the capabilities of the previous builds. Thus, the demonstration of the full system is a natural culminating step of integrating the final build into the accumulation of previous builds. The tools and various facets of this approach are described in the following paragraphs, beginning with the SVD.

The tool employed for defining the threads is the SVD. The objective of the SVD is the representation of the software requirements in a complete, consistent, and testable manner. The SVD represents these requirements as a series of stimulus/response pairings. Inconsistencies, redundancies, and omissions may be revealed while developing these stimulus/response pairings. An effective approach is to draft a SVD immediately upon availability of each draft of the software requirements specification. This provides maximum opportunity for feedback and incorporation of findings into the next release of the specification. It may also

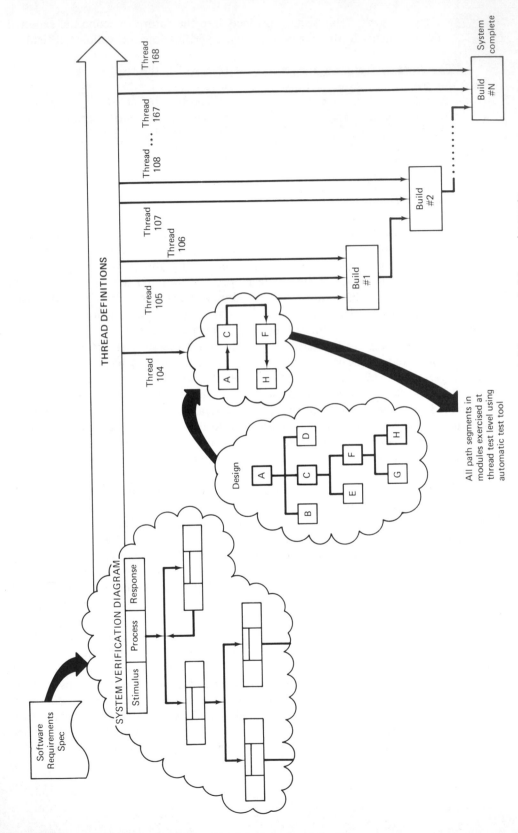

**Figure 2-1** Software test/construction procedure visibly connected to requirements.

highlight the need for consultations with the customer on heretofore unrecognized open requirements issues. Thus, the SVD is also an informal requirements verification tool.[2]

Each stimulus consists of one or more inputs plus any conditional qualifiers; each response consists of one or more outputs plus conditional qualifiers generated as a result of the input event.[3] Each stimulus/response element represents an identifiable function or microfunction and is also called a *thread*. Each thread has a direct relationship to one or more software requirements (usually several) and can later be associated with the modules in the software design architecture that will implement the thread. The SVD is normally generated from the requirements specification before the software architecture is designed.

Figure 2–2 shows an example of the derivation of a thread from requirements specifications.[4] One of the objectives illustrated here is to define a transfer function that coalesces two or more functionally related requirements that may possibly reside in physically separate areas of the requirements specification. The test procedure that verifies the software modules that implement this thread also validates the requirements associated with the thread, paragraphs 3.7.1.1.4 and 3.7.3.1.5 in this example.

The entire requirements specification can be represented by a set of threads that are logically connected to each other by arrows that denote sequence. Quite often, a conditional qualifier associated with the input event of a thread is the successful completion of the function represented by the previous thread in the sequence. Complete functional testing of the software is attained if all paths through the SVD are traversed during the test program.[5]

Detailed test planning can begin when the software architecture defining the structure of the modules is available. This normally occurs, in software developments sponsored by the Department of Defense, by the time of the *preliminary design review* (PDR). This test/construction approach requires a modular software architecture developed from structured design precepts; otherwise the positive effect is diluted. Experience shows that the technique works well with a structure granularity of, on the average, 100 higher-order-language source lines per module (which later may be subdivided further into subroutines).

In this concept, software test and construction are intertwined; they do not occur separately and sequentially. The order in which the software is coded, tested, and synthesized is essentially determined by the SVD that defines the test procedure. The SVD has segmented the system into demonstrable functions called *threads*. The development of the threads are calendarized. The modules associated with each thread are coded and tested in an order that is commensurate with this calendarization. The threads are synthesized into higher order sections called *builds;* each build incrementally demonstrates a significant partial functional

[2] Robert Carey and Marc Bendic, "The Control of a Software Test Process," *Proceedings Computer Software and Applications Conference 1977* (New York: IEEE), IEEE Catalog No. 77CH1291-4C.

[3] Carey and Bendic, op. cit.

[4] Carey and Bendic, op. cit.

[5] Carey and Bendic, op. cit.

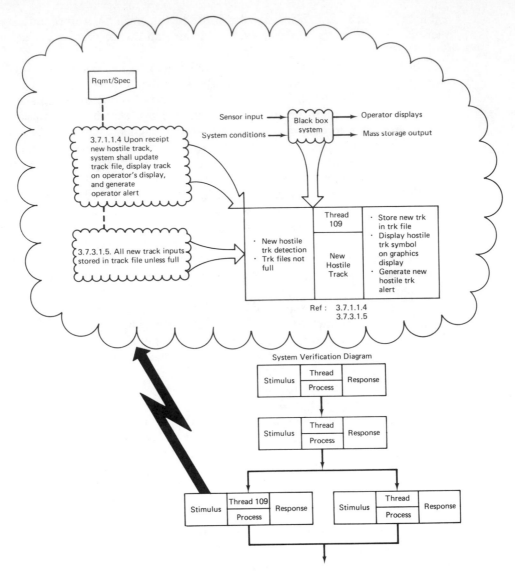

**Figure 2-2** Defining the system verification diagram.

capability of the system. This culminates in a demonstration of the full system, which occurs as a natural concluding step of integrating the last build to the accumulation of previous builds. This approach provides an orderly means of segmenting a complex software development into smaller, functionally oriented sections.

A convenient mechanism to record the relationships between the thread, requirements, and modules which implement the thread is the Thread Functional

Allocation Chart contained in Figure 2-3.[6] The column head *Complexity Units* represents an estimation on a linear scale from 1 to 5 of the person-effort required to code, checkout, test, and integrate each thread. A rating of 5 is the most complex and 1 is the simplest. This subjective measure is based on the volume of code to be constructed, code complexity, and complexity of the interface with other threads that have already been integrated. Application at Hughes Aircraft Company largely supports the Computer Science Corporation experience that this estimation parameter is useful and linear.

The next step is to assign threads to builds and designate completion points over the schedule period. Two considerations are paramount in this process: (1) It would normally be in the interest of the project to implement the threads which comprise the highest technical risk early; and (2) a logically complete system, although not functionally complete, should be the objective as early in the buildup schedule as possible.[7] This is basically an implement-to-schedule strategy. If, despite the best efforts of all concerned, the entire system has not been completed by the scheduled date, there will still exist the nucleus of a system that performs

| REQUIREMENT ID'S | THREAD ID | THREAD TITLE | COMPLEXITY UNITS | MODULE ID'S |
|---|---|---|---|---|
| | | | | |
| | | | | |
| | | | | |
| | | | | |
| | | | | |
| | | | | |
| | | | | |
| | | | | |
| | | | | |
| | | | | |
| | | | | |

**Figure 2-3**  Thread functional allocation chart.

[6] For military standard software developments, these charts will satisfy the information content requirements of Type C-5 Specification paragraph 3.1.1 *Functional Allocation*.
[7] Carey and Bendic, op. cit.

functions which are demonstrable and operationally useful. The customer will undoubtedly be displeased. However, it is presumed that the extent of his displeasure will be far less with this situation than with a less organized approach which may have completed the same volume of code consisting of diverse software units not yet orderly sequenced into operational functions.

The results of the planning effort described above are displayed on a *Build Plan* diagram. This Build Plan provides an overall calendarized view of the sequence of construction/test events, including

- The sequence of the builds
- The relationship of the builds to each other
- The allocation of threads to builds
- The sequence of the threads

An example Build Plan from a recent software development is contained in Figure 2–4. Implementation of an end-to-end data flow is achieved at Build 6.0, which occurs less than halfway into the scheduled implementation period; this constitutes a logically complete system for this project. Builds 7.0 to 15.0 add additional functions which supplement the basic data transformations and provide operator interactive control over the processing sequence. Each build adds new functions (threads) to the system and, to the extent indicated by the connecting arrows on the Build Plan, contains the cumulative capabilities of previous builds. Each build demonstration tests the new capabilities, and regression tests the capabilities accumulated from previous builds. The final acceptance test of the total system occurring at Build 15.0 is merely a natural culminating event of this succession.[8] Because each thread is directly linked to software modules, the Build Plan also defines the order of construction of the modules.

Because by their very nature threads represent useful operational functions, a measure of thread completion also represents a measure of project completion. By using the number of complexity units assigned to each thread, the Build Plan may be summarized into a *Thread Production Plan,* shown on Figure 2–5 for the same software development. The solid line represents the planned production rate against which the actual production rate may be plotted in dashed lines. Thus, the Thread Production Plan provides an easily understood means of reporting actual progress versus planned progress.

The benefits of the thread testing approach may be summarized as

- Allows testing and analysis in digestible quantities
- Provides early demonstration of key functional capabilities
- Forces the early availability of executable code
- Provides a meaningful measurement of project progress that is easily understood

[8] Each thread is also tested informally. The build demonstration tests may be viewed as natural culminating events in a succession of thread tests.

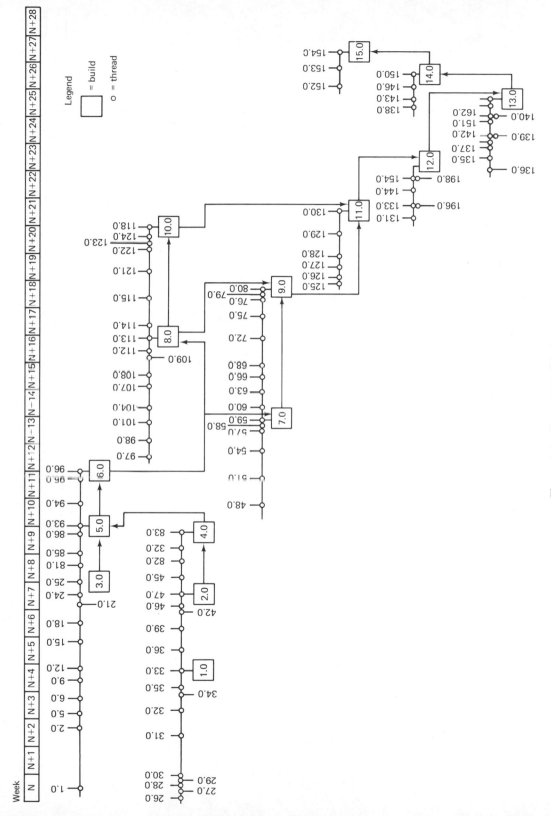

**Figure 2-4** Example build plan.

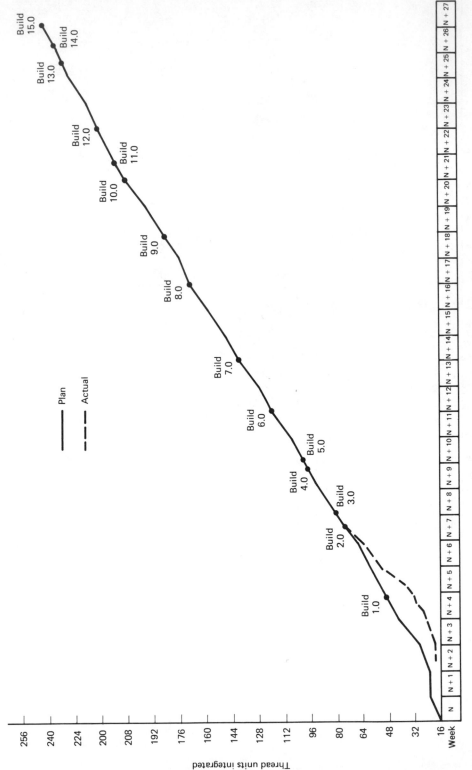

**Figure 2-5** Example thread production plan.

- Defines module construction sequence and serves as a basis for allocating personnel resources
- Brings a degree of formality to software project verification and validation by validating that the end item satisfies requirements and by verifying that the end item implements the design.
- Because of the analogy of threads/builds to operational functions, mission analysts can interact earlier in the testing process to scrutinize performance results

To some extent, the description of this approach has understated the complexity of modern software development projects by addressing a software system as a single development entity. Many software projects are too large and the schedule too short to manage in this fashion. The software system is decomposed into structural elements that are developed in parallel and are eventually integrated to recompose the system; on military standard software developments, this element is referred to as the *computer program configuration item* (CPCI). The software construction and test process that has been described here is an effective approach both at the CPCI and software system levels. Procedures for testing and integration at the system level may be prescribed by defining system level threads. These high-level threads would be correlated with CPCIs or sub-CPCIs in lieu of modules.

## 2.2
## Automated Verification

### *MOTIVATION FOR AUTOMATION*

The basic approach to software construction and testing, summarized in Figure 2-1, prescribed that testing of each thread include the exercise of all path segments in the associated modules. This is an ambitious goal and perhaps costly to attain. In this section, the motivation for this objective is explored and a tool which will help achieve this end is demonstrated. In addition, certain quantitative data from contemporary project experiences are presented which explain the benefit of this approach to earlier detection of software errors.

As software systems have grown to immense proportions in both size and complexity, the effort required to test these systems has grown more than proportionately. The need for a mass application of human resources has risen. This has been both costly and not particularly effective in terms of the reliability produced. Despite expenditures of up to one half of software development budgets for testing, significant numbers of errors remain in delivered software that often severely deter normal system operations. This situation has inspired the development of automatic test tools that assist in the production of effective tests and analyze the test results. In essence, much of the time-consuming, mechanical aspects of testing is taken out of human hands.

Automatic test tools provide the following attributes that are not as easily attainable by manual testing approaches:

- Improved organization of testing through automation
- Measurement of testing coverage
- Improved reliability

Automatic tools furnish machine amplification of human capability and relieve test personnel of routine time-consuming chores. Routine tasks such as manual error-checking are preferably removed from human hands. This is because manual error-checking itself is an error-prone process performed more reliably through automation. Budget and schedule considerations foreclose on the slow, tedious process of manual testing with the result that volume of testing is often insufficient. Relief is available through utilization of automated tools.

The complex content of large software systems requires the application of many test cases to thoroughly exercise the code. The generation of the test cases and analysis of the paths exercised in order to determine the extent of the resulting testing coverage would quickly exceed human capacity. Testing aids can instrument the code, measure the coverage provided by a test case, and furnish a report that shows the number of times each statement and sequence of statements was executed.

Improved reliability results when potential sources and avenues of errors are more closely investigated; this occurs as more experience in the use of the software is accumulated through carefully directed testing. Automatic tools enable a higher volume of testing than would be attainable manually for the same cost.

Almost all aspects of the software development process can be assisted by some form of automation and a complete spectrum of tools exists in various states of development. Particularly advanced, and of demonstrated utility to real-world industrial software projects, is a class of automated test assistance tools called *automated verification systems* (AVS). The following paragraphs describe Automated Verification Systems and illustrate an example application of an AVS to a sample program.

AVSs provide facilities for measuring the performance of the software and effectiveness of test cases. Such tools derive their information from the source text of the program that is being analyzed and tested. There are five basic functions performed by the AVS:

1. Analysis of source code and creation of a data base
2. Generation of reports based on static analysis of the source code that reveal existing or potential problems in the code and identify the software control and data structures
3. Insertion of software probes into the source code that permit data collection on code segments executed and values computed and set in storage
4. Analysis of test results and generation of reports

5. Generation of test assistance reports to aid in organizing the testing and deriving input sets for particular tests

The elements of a typical AVS that perform these functions are diagrammed in Figure 2-6.

The static analysis module analyzes the static structure of the code. Typically, this analysis would consist of: (1) partitioning each routine into path segments which support an evaluation of test thoroughness; and (2) analyzing the invocation structure of the program. This information is captured in a data base file and also formatted for output as a printed report.

The instrumentation module acts as a preprocessor by inserting additional statements within the original source code. During execution, these additional

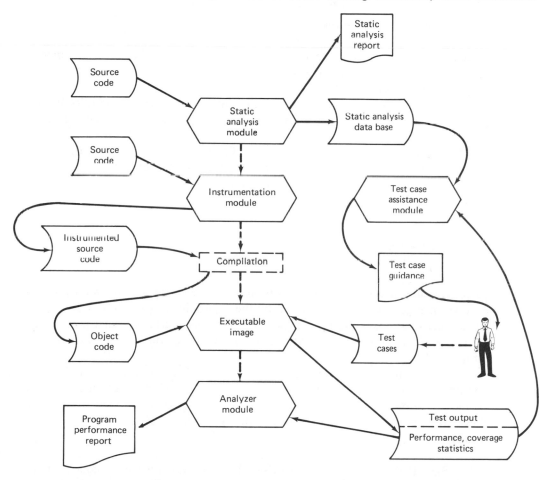

**Figure 2-6** Typical elements of an automated verification system. (Adapted from Michael S. Deutsch, "Verification and Validation," in *Software Engineering*, ed. Jensen & Tonies, © 1979, p. 361, fig. 5-12. Reprinted by permission of Prentice-Hall, Inc., Englewood Cliffs, N.J.)

statements or *probes* intercept the flow of execution at key points and record program performance statistics and signals in an intermediate file. The instrumented source code is compiled, an executable image is built, and the image is executed.

The analyzer module functions as a postprocessor after the program execution. It formats and edits data recorded in an intermediate file during program execution and provides a printed report. The report furnishes information on testing coverage, including

- Statements executed and frequency; percentage of statements executed
- Statement sequences traversed; percentage of sequences traversed; listing of sequences not traversed
- Data ranges of variables
- Assertion violations

The analyzer module may also compare anticipated test-case output augmented by any user-supplied evaluation criteria (prestored in a file) with actual output and list resulting discrepancies.

The test case assistance module aids testing personnel in the selection of test inputs that will economically attain comprehensive testing goals. The module uses the static analysis data base and the coverage data recorded during executions to guide the testers in the preparation of additional test cases. These, then, exercise paths in the program not executed by previous test cases. An algorithm detects statements and branches not exercised and indicates conditions necessary to traverse that path.

## TYPICAL APPLICATION
## OF AN AUTOMATED TEST TOOL

The sequence of events in the software testing procedure with the aid of an AVS is shown in Figure 2-7 as exemplified by the capabilities of the RXVP80™ System.[9] The individual boxes define complete steps in the operation, each producing outputs that feed subsequent operations either directly or through updates to the central data base.

The complete operation shown in Figure 2-7 covers the five AVS functions outlined previously. In the discussion, each step identified is described in terms of some of the outputs generated and the purpose of those outputs in the testing process. In describing these operations, the subroutine SOLVE is the subject of analysis.

STEP 1: BUILDING THE DATA BASE   The system reads source code as its input. Simple commands are also supplied as a separate input file to direct the operations.

The system first derives its data base from the source code. Line numbers are

[9] RXVP80™ is a FORTRAN/IFTRAN™ Source Text Analysis System built and marketed by General Research Corporation of Santa Barbara, Ca.

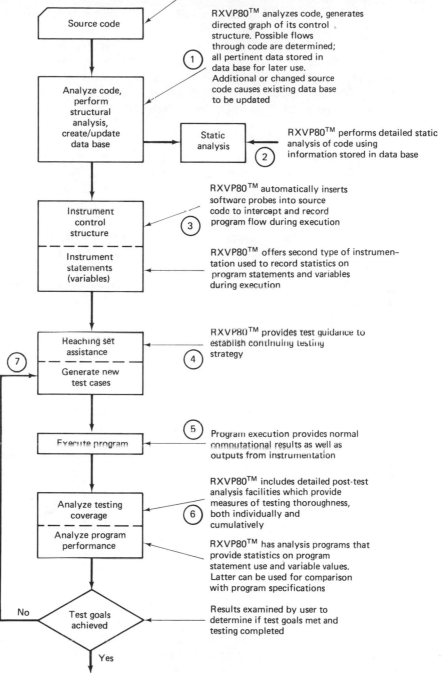

FORTRAN (or IFTRAN) source code is input for processing and analysis

Source code

RXVP80™ analyzes code, generates directed graph of its control structure. Possible flows through code are determined; all pertinent data stored in data base for later use. Additional or changed source code causes existing data base to be updated ①

Analyze code, perform structural analysis, create/update data base

Static analysis

RXVP80™ performs detailed static analysis of code using information stored in data base ②

Instrument control structure

RXVP80™ automatically inserts software probes into source code to intercept and record program flow during execution ③

Instrument statements (variables)

RXVP80™ offers second type of instrumentation used to record statistics on program statements and variables during execution

Reaching set assistance

RXVP80™ provides test guidance to establish continuing testing strategy ④

⑦ Generate new test cases

Execute program

⑤ Program execution provides normal computational results as well as outputs from instrumentation

Analyze testing coverage

RXVP80™ includes detailed post-test analysis facilities which provide measures of testing thoroughness, both individually and cumulatively ⑥

Analyze program performance

RXVP80™ has analysis programs that provide statistics on program statement use and variable values. Latter can be used for comparison with program specifications

Test goals achieved

Results examined by user to determine if test goals met and testing completed

No

Yes

**Figure 2-7**  Application of RXVP80™ in software testing. (Adapted from Michael S. Deutsch, "Verification and Validation," in *Software Engineering,* ed. Jensen & Tonies, © 1979, p. 366, fig. 5-13. Reprinted by permission of Prentice-Hall Inc., Englewood Cliffs, N.J.)

assigned to each line of text; the control structure and symbols are identified; and a directed graph model of the control structure is built. The resulting information is stored in the data base, which becomes the controlled copy of module text as well as the source of all outputs generated in later steps.

The control structure of a module is defined in terms of the sequence of statements lying between the outcome of a decision up to and including the next decision. This sequence is immediately executable, once the initial decision outcome has been evaluated, and is the basic logical segment of the control structure. The sequence is called a Decision-to-Decision Path (*DD-Path*).

STEP 2: PRODUCING DOCUMENTATION REPORTS  After the data base is created, the documentation reports are generated. These reports provide information that will be used to document the code and to aid the test group in understanding code organization. These include several reports delineating the invocation hierarchy of the modules and the module text. A full set of documentation reports is presented in Chapter 7.

The module text is shown in Figure 2–8. The text of a module as stored on the data base is the source of this report. The left-most column is the statement number, and adjacent to that in parentheses is a nesting level number that identifies nesting depth for the structured languages. The statement is printed, indented consistent with nesting level, and then, for each statement that starts a DD-path, the path number is printed. This module text printout is the basic module description report that gives the statement numbers that are referred to in other reports, identifies all of the DD-paths, and lists the full module text.

STEP 3: MODULE INSTRUMENTATION  Collection of program flow statistics is facilitated by the instrumentation of the program control structure. The system examines the code and automatically inserts a call to a data collection routine that is invoked each time a control branch is taken. When the instrumented code is executed, the collection routine notes the module and code section executed and builds up a data file from which the test analyzer generates its reports.

If more detailed performance statistics are desired, another form of instrumentation provides data collection calls for each executable statement, permitting a complete record of the values stored during execution. This level of instrumentation would normally only be applied to selected modules with which the more detailed information is needed to ensure that testing covers a proper range of computational results.

STEP 4: TEST ASSISTANCE  Testing is now ready for a set of test cases. It is assumed that some form of prior testing has produced a set of working test cases. At the first cycle of testing these existing cases are executed with the instrumented code. After these initial tests are analyzed and the reports examined, this step will entail generation of new or modified test cases as needed to achieve testing goals. Before discussing the extension of test cases (Step 7), the reports generated by analyzing the initial test case will be examined.

```
STMT NEST LINE  SOURCE...

 1         1    SUBROUTINE SOLVE(ARRAY,SOLUTN,ORDER,EPS,ITER,CONVRG)
           2  C ROUTINE TO COMPUTE SOLUTION TO A SYSTEM OF SIMULTANEOUS
           3  C EQUATIONS BY THE GAUSS-SEIDEL METHOD
           4  C
           5  C DESCRIPTION OF VARIABLES
           6  C ARRAY  - COEFFICIENT ARRAY FOR SYSTEM (INCLUDES R.H. SIDE)
           7  C SOLUTN - SOLUTION VECTOR
           8  C ORDER  - ORDER OF SYSTEM
           9  C EPS    - CONVERGENCE TOLERANCE
          10  C CONVRG - CONVERGENCE FLAG
          11  C RESID  - SOLUTION ERROR
          12  C DEBUG  - DEBUG OUTPUT FLAG
          13  C LUNIN  - LOGICAL INPUT UNIT
          14  C LUNOUT - LOGICAL OUTPUT UNIT
          15  C
          16  C
          17  C
                                                        ** DDPATH   1  IS  PROCEDURE ENTRY

 2        18    COMMON /MISC/ DEBUG
 3        19    COMMON /UNITS/ LUNIN, LUNOUT
 4        20    DIMENSION ARRAY(80,81)
 5        21    DIMENSION SOLUTN(80)
 6        22    INTEGER ORDER,COUNT
 7        23    LOGICAL CONVRG, DEBUG
 8        24    INITIAL ( .ALL. I .IN. (1,ORDER)( SOLUTN(I) .EQ. 0.0))
 9        25    IF (DEBUG)
                                                        ** DDPATH   2  IS  TRUE BRANCH
                                                        ** DDPATH   3  IS  FALSE BRANCH

10   1    26  .   WRITE (LUNOUT,910) ITER
11        27    ENDIF
12        28    CONVRG=.TRUE.
          29  C
          30  C SET RESIDUAL TO VERY LARGE NUMBER
          31  C
13        32    RESID= 1.E20
          33  C
          34  C CALCULATE SYSTEM SOLUTION
          35  C
14        36    DO (COUNT=1,ITER)
15   1    37  .   IF (RESID .GT. EPS)
                                                        ** DDPATH   4  IS  TRUE BRANCH
                                                        ** DDPATH   5  IS  FALSE BRANCH

16   2    38  .    .   RESID=0.0
17   3    39  .    .   DO (I=1,ORDER)
18   3    40  .    .    .   SUM=0.0
19   3    41  .    .    .   DO (J=1,ORDER)
20   4    42  .    .    .    .   IF (I .NE. J)
                                                        ** DDPATH   6  IS  TRUE BRANCH
                                                        ** DDPATH   7  IS  FALSE BRANCH
```

Figure 2-8   Module text with DD-paths annotated.

SUBROUTINE SOLVE(ARRAY,SOLUTN,ORDER,EPS,ITER,CUNVRG)

```
STMT NEST LINE  SOURCE...                                              ...SOURCE TAB
==================================================================================

 21   5   43    . . . . .  SUM= SUM + ARRAY(I,J) * SOLUTN(J)
 22   4   44    . . . .  ENDIF
 23   3   45    . . .  ENDDO                                  ** DDPATH  8 IS LOOP ESCAPE
                                                              ** DDPATH  9 IS LOOP AGAIN

 24   3   46    . . .  TEMP=(ARRAY(I,ORDER+1) - SUM)/ARRAY(I,I)
 25   3   47    . . .  TEMPX=ABS(SOLUTN(I)-TEMP)
 26   3   48    . . .  RESID=AMAX1(RESID,TEMPX)
 27   3   49    . . .  SOLUTN(I)=TEMP
 28   2   50    . .  ENDDO                                    ** DDPATH 10 IS LOOP ESCAPE
                                                              ** DDPATH 11 IS LOOP AGAIN

 29   2   51    . .  IF (DEBUG)                               ** DDPATH 12 IS TRUE BRANCH
                                                              ** DDPATH 13 IS FALSE BRANCH

 30   3   52    . . .  IF (MOD(COUNT,10) .EQ. 0)              ** DDPATH 14 IS TRUE BRANCH
                                                              ** DDPATH 15 IS FALSE BRANCH

 31   4   53    . . . .  WRITE (LUNOUT,900) COUNT, (SOLUTN(I), I=1,ORDER)
 32   3   54    . . .  ENDIF
 33   2   55    . .  ELSE
 34   1   56    .  GO TO 20
 35   2   57    . .  ENDIF
 36   1   58    .  ENDDO
 37   1   59    ENDDO                                         ** DDPATH 16 IS LOOP ESCAPE
                                                              ** DDPATH 17 IS LOOP AGAIN

 38   20  60    CONTINUE
 39       61    ASSERT (RESID .LE. EPS)
          62 C  ----------------------------------------------------------------------
          63 C  TEST ITERATION COUNT FOR CONVERGENCE
          64 C  ----------------------------------------------------------------------
 40       65 C  IF (COUNT .GE. ITER)                          ** DDPATH 18 IS TRUE BRANCH
          66 C                                                ** DDPATH 19 IS FALSE BRANCH
          67 C  SET NONCONVERGENCE SWITCH
          68 C  ----------------------------------------------------------------------
 41   1   69    . CONVRG=.FALSE.
 42       70    ENDIF
 43       71    IF (DEBUG)                                    ** DDPATH 20 IS TRUE BRANCH
                                                              ** DDPATH 21 IS FALSE BRANCH
```

**Figure 2-8** continued

```
44   72        .       WRITE (LUNOUT,920) COUNT
45   73        ENDIF
46   74        FINAL (.SOME. I .IN. (1,ORDER)(SOLUTN(I) .NE. 0.0))
47   75        RETURN
     76   C
48   77   900  FORMAT(5X,I4,8E15.3)
49   78   910  FORMAT(5X, 20HENTER SOLVE, ITER=   ,I4)
50   79   920  FORMAT(5X, 20HEXIT SOLVE, COUNT=   ,I4)
51   80        END
```

**Figure 2-8** *continued*

STEP 5: TEST EXECUTION   While the instrumented code is running, it produces its normal outputs and also invokes the data collection routine. In its simplest form the data collection routine merely writes a trace file that records the sequence of DD-paths executed or the sequence of variable values assigned. More extensive data collection routines can perform some analysis and summarizing during execution to reduce the amount of data collected.

STEP 6: TEST ANALYSIS   The function of the post-test analyzer is to supply the reports that can be evaluated against testing goals. A DD-path coverage analysis reports execution counts by module and DD-path as well as summary data on testing progress. The statement probe analyzer reports the maximum, minimum, first, last, and average value of numeric variables; for logical expressions it reports times true, times false, and final value of the expression.

*Coverage Summary* (Figure 2–9). The top-level view of testing progress is depicted in this report. For each module, the number of DD-paths, number of invocations, number of DD-paths traversed, and percent coverage are shown. These same parameters are also depicted for the accumulation of all the modules. This information is presented for each test case and for the accumulation of all the test cases.

*DD-Paths Not Hit* (Figure 2–10). This report tells the tester which DD-paths were not executed by each test case and which remain untested after all tests are accumulated. The report also displays single test and cumulative test information. This information guides the tester as to potential targets for the next test case.

*DD-Path Execution Counts* (Figure 2–11). This report gives the finest detail on DD-path execution for each test case. For each DD-path, an entry is made under NOT EXECUTED where execution count is zero. For execution counts greater than zero, the bar represents the count as a percent of the maximum number of executions for a single path. The exact number of path executions is entered under NUMBER OF EXECUTIONS. This report shows where the most execution time is being spent in a module in addition to the module summary line at the bottom. The report also shows more graphically than the list of numbers where there are large segments of code that are not being tested.

*Statement Probe Analysis* (not shown). The more detailed variable trace analyzer produces a report which is keyed directly to the source statements. Three types of reports are given. If the statement has no value computed (e.g., a CONTINUE, WRITE, READ, CALL, or assignment of a constant), then only the execution count is printed. Statements that test logical expressions report times true, times false, and final value of the logical expression. Statements that compute a numeric value (e.g., assignment, arithmetic IF, or DO) report initial, final, maximum, and minimum values.

STEP 7: TEST ASSISTANCE   Figure 2–10 shows that a number of DD-paths remain untested. The objective of continued testing is to generate test cases that will include at least one execution of the untested DD-paths. This testing goal should be

SUMMARY -- THIS TEST | CUMULATIVE SUMMARY

| TEST CASE | MODULE NAME | NUMBER OF DD-PATHS | NUMBER OF INVOCATIONS | D-D PATHS TRAVERSED | PER CENT COVERAGE | NUMBER OF TESTS | INVOCATIONS | TRAVERSED | COVERAGE |
|---|---|---|---|---|---|---|---|---|---|
| 1 | LINEAR | 3 | 1 | 2 | 66.67 | 1 | 1 | 2 | 66.67 |
| | GETSYS | 7 | 1 | 4 | 57.14 | 1 | 1 | 4 | 57.14 |
| | FORM | 15 | 1 | 11 | 73.33 | 1 | 1 | 11 | 73.33 |
| | VALID8 | 13 | 1 | 10 | 76.92 | 1 | 1 | 10 | 76.92 |
| | SOLVE | 21 | 1 | 15 | 71.43 | 1 | 1 | 15 | 71.43 |
| | OUTPUT | 7 | 1 | 4 | 57.14 | 1 | 1 | 4 | 57.14 |
| | SSALLSS | 66 | | 46 | 69.70 | 1 | | 46 | 69.70 |

**Figure 2-9**  Coverage summary for one test case.

35

| MODULE NAME | TEST NUMBER | PATHS NOT HIT | LIST OF DECISION TO DECISION PATHS NOT EXECUTED | | | | | |
|---|---|---|---|---|---|---|---|---|
| <LINEAR > | 1 | 1 | 1 | 3 | | | | |
|  | CUMUL | 1 | 1 | 3 | | | | |
| <GETSYS > | 1 | 3 | 3 | 5 | 7 | | | |
|  | CUMUL | 3 | 3 | 5 | 7 | | | |
| <FORM > | 1 | 4 | 3 | 5 | 8 | 15 | | |
|  | CUMUL | 4 | 3 | 5 | 8 | 15 | | |
| <VALID8 > | 1 | 3 | 3 | 8 | 13 | | | |
|  | CUMUL | 3 | 3 | 8 | 13 | | | |
| <SOLVE > | 1 | 6 | 3 | 13 | 14 | 16 | 18 | 21 |
|  | CUMUL | 6 | 3 | 13 | 14 | 16 | 18 | 21 |
| <OUTPUT > | 1 | 3 | 3 | 5 | 7 | | | |
|  | CUMUL | 3 | 3 | 5 | 7 | | | |

**Figure 2-10**  DD-paths not hit (one test case).

```
RECORD OF DECISION TO DECISION (DD PATH) EXECUTION

MODULE SSOLVE s        TEST CASE NO.    1

DD PATH I NO. NOT EXECUTED I  NUMBER OF EXECUTIONS -- NORMALIZED TO MAXIMUM   I            I NUMBER OF
NUMBER  I                  I.-------2).------40.------60.------80.------100.  I            I EXECUTIONS
        I                  I                                                  I            I
   1    I                  I                                                  I  1    I     1
   2    I                  I                                                  I  2    I     1
   3    I     3    00000   I                                                  I       I
   4    I                  I XXXX                                             I  4    I     5
   5    I                  I                                                  I  5    I     1
   6    I                  I XXXXXXXXXXXXXXXXXXXXXXXXXXXXXXXXXXXX              I  6    I    60
   7    I                  I XXXXXXXXXXXXXX                                    I  7    I    20
   8    I                  I XXXXXXXXXXXXXX                                    I  8    I    20
   9    I                  I XXXXXXXXXXXXXXXXXXXXXXXXXXXXXXXXXXXX              I  9    I    60
  10    I                  I XXXX                                             I 10    I     5
  11    I                  I XXXXXXXXXXX                                      I 11    I    15
  12    I                  I XXXX                                             I 12    I     5
  13    I    13    00000   I                                                  I       I
  14    I    14    00000   I                                                  I       I
  15    I                  I XXXX                                             I 12    I     5
  16    I    16    00000   I                                                  I       I
  17    I                  I XXXX                                             I 17    I     5
  18    I    18    00000   I                                                  I       I
  19    I                  I                                                  I 19    I     1
  20    I                  I                                                  I 20    I     1
  21    I    21    00000   I                                                  I       I

                                                    TOTAL NUMBER OF DD PATH EXECUTIONS =    205

TOTAL OF  6  NOT EXECUTED      EXECUTED 15/ 21      PERCENT EXECUTED =    71.43
```

**Figure 2-11** DD-paths execution counts.

considered a minimum level of testing in which all statements are executed at least once and each decision is exercised through all possible outcomes. Although this is far from a complete test that exercises all logical paths through the program, it is more comprehensive than is generally achieved by tests that sample only selected values in the input space. Furthermore, the process of generating new test cases focuses attention on the source code of the program and frequently reveals errors that would go undetected when looking only at execution results.

Using the DD-paths not hit report (Figure 2–10) and the module text with DD-paths annotated (Figure 2–8), we see that three of the untested DD-paths of module SOLVE (3,13,21) are controlled by the variable DEBUG. DEBUG is provided to SOLVE in a common block. Through a documentation report called *common matrices* (not shown) it can be determined that DEBUG is set as an input parameter in the module LINEAR. Therefore, a test case can be contrived to make the input parameter DEBUG false and cover these three untested paths.

We also see from the module text that the other three missed paths are controlled by the variables COUNT and ITER. COUNT is a local variable in a module that is the loop variable of the DO loop. Thus, Path 16 will be reached if the DO loop exit is reached (as will Path 18). These conditions are achieved by a failure to converge within the allowable limits of ITER. To reach these paths, either a nonconvergent case must be supplied or the value of ITER reduced. By manual examination it can be determined that ITER is also read in the module LINEAR and can be reduced to a small number by a simple data input change.

A new test case was generated. Figure 2–12 shows the summary report as a result of adding the new test case for module SOLVE to our test set. Additional test cases may be contrived by using the methodology just described until the testing goals are attained.

RXVP80™ does offer some automated test case assistance in the form of the *reaching set* capability. This capability addresses the problem of finding a test set that involves the internal logic of a program. A reaching set report may be produced that identifies the union of all DD-path sequences that lead from one DD-path up to and including another path. The reaching set capability is demonstrated in Chapter 7.

Automated test tools are currently gaining widespread use and acceptance. They are attaining recognition as cost-effective devices that provide the ability to exhaustively test software to a level that would otherwise be cost prohibitive when using manual means. The realization of benefits derived from this approach is contingent upon the proper scope of application. This procedure when applied to large amounts of code can become overly involved and thus probably neutralize potential positive effects. Recent project experiences indicate that maximum advantage is attained when this testing approach is applied at the individual thread level; here, reasonably small chunks of code (100 to 300 source lines) are involved. Indeed, this scope of application is consistent with the overall objective of uncovering as many errors as possible early in the implementation period rather than risk encountering these errors at higher levels of integration.

| TEST CASE | MODULE NAME | NUMBER OF DD-PATHS | SUMMARY -- THIS TEST | | | CUMULATIVE SUMMARY | | | |
|---|---|---|---|---|---|---|---|---|---|
| | | | NUMBER OF INVOCATIONS | D-D PATHS TRAVERSED | PER CENT COVERAGE | NUMBER OF TESTS | INVOCATIONS | TRAVERSED | COVERAGE |
| 1 | LINEAR | 3 | 1 | 2 | 66.67 | 1 | 1 | 2 | 66.67 |
| | GETSYS | 7 | 1 | 4 | 57.14 | 1 | 1 | 4 | 57.14 |
| | FORM | 15 | 1 | 11 | 73.33 | 1 | 1 | 11 | 73.33 |
| | VALID8 | 13 | 1 | 10 | 76.92 | 1 | 1 | 10 | 76.92 |
| | SOLVE | 21 | 1 | 15 | 71.43 | 1 | 1 | 15 | 71.43 |
| | OUTPUT | 7 | 1 | 4 | 57.14 | 1 | 1 | 4 | 57.14 |
| | $$ALLSS | 66 | | 46 | 69.70 | 1 | | 46 | 69.70 |
| 2 | LINEAR | 3 | 1 | 2 | 66.67 | 2 | 2 | 2 | 66.67 |
| | GETSYS | 7 | 1 | 4 | 57.14 | 2 | 2 | 6 | 85.71 |
| | FORM | 15 | 1 | 11 | 73.33 | 2 | 2 | 13 | 86.67 |
| | VALID8 | 13 | 1 | 10 | 76.92 | 2 | 2 | 12 | 92.31 |
| | SOLVE | 21 | 1 | 14 | 66.67 | 2 | 2 | 20 | 95.24 |
| | OUTPUT | 7 | 1 | 4 | 57.14 | 2 | 2 | 7 | 100.00 |
| | $$ALLSS | 66 | | 45 | 68.18 | 2 | | 60 | 90.91 |

**Figure 2-12** Summary report after additional test cases.

It is possible to view the quantitative benefits to enhanced early error detection that result from the test strategy previously described. Experience from a recent software project at Hughes Aircraft Company, which utilized this test approach, reveals that additional errors were detected which otherwise would have gone undiscovered until some later time.

The general influence of this exhaustive testing strategy is depicted in Figure 2–13. This figure shows the comparative effects of the testing approach, which utilizes the automatic tool, in contrast to the standard test approach, which does not. The use of the automatic test tool results in higher error detection rates during the construct period. However, during subsequent periods, including operations, the detection rate of latent errors remains higher in the situation where the test tool is not used. The area under both curves, that is, the total number of errors, would be approximately equal. Of course, the cost of rectifying the same error later in the life cycle is higher than it would have been were it detected earlier.

The exhaustive testing approach on the Hughes software project consisted of first checking out each thread using a set of functionally oriented test cases. It is at this point where the traditional brand of testing would conclude. Instead, additional test cases were contrived in order to achieve a DD-path coverage of close to

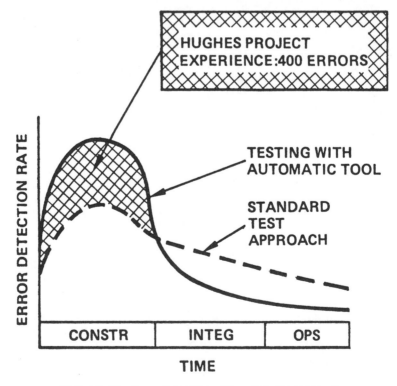

**Figure 2-13**  Error detection with automatic test tool.

100%; the expectation was that this extra test effort would expose additional errors. The actual experience on this project supported this belief. Because of these clearly demarcated testing phases, it was a simple matter to maintain a count of the errors detected by the extended testing. The accounting showed that an average of one additional error per thread was uncovered.

The influence of this error detection profile on projected life cycle costs of this project is analyzed in Chapter 7.

## 2.3
## Verification and Validation over the Software Life Cycle

It has already been observed that the approach to verification and validation on modern software projects involves activities over the entire software life cycle, not just testing. The merits of this practice include a more reliable product, lower life-cycle costs, early exposure of requirements inconsistencies, and early exposure of design errors. Statistics have been compiled that depict the escalating costs to correct errors as later stages of the development cycle are traversed.[10] This profile reveals that it is 10 to 100 times more costly to correct an error after the software is operational than it would have been if detected during the preliminary design period.

The responsibility for verification and validation is distributed among the three technical line organizations which comprise the software project—system engineering, software development, and the independent test organization.

SYSTEM ENGINEERING. This is normally the smallest of the three groups. It is responsible for prescribing the overall architecture of the system. This includes definition of system level requirements, system level design, and requirements for each computer program configuration item (CPCI). By focusing responsibility for definition and maintenance of a system's external attributes (requirements) in a single organization, it is assured that the system architecture reflects a single philosophy and a unified set of concepts. System engineering defines the system architecture at an abstract level and does not prescribe a specific implementation.

SOFTWARE DEVELOPMENT. This organization designs and implements the software product in accordance with the intentions of the architects. On large projects, software development may be divided into several or more groups. Each group develops a chunk of the system, usually a CPCI. At the conclusion of thread/build testing, the development organization hands the software product over to the independent test organization for formal qualification testing.

---

[10] Barry W. Boehm, "Government/Industry Software Management Initiatives—Status and Trends," in *Documentation from the Software Management Conference, 1978* (jointly sponsored by AIAA, TMSA, DPMA).

INDEPENDENT TEST ORGANIZATION (ITO). The ITO maintains a healthy adversary relationship with the software development organization. It is the ITO's job to scrutinize (by testing) the software product and identify discrepancies where the requirements have not been implemented correctly. The discrepancies are referred back to the developer for rectification. The ITO also integrates the individual CPCIs to form a unified system product.

The verification and validation activities which occur over the software life cycle are summarized in Figure 2–14. The V & V tasks are allocated to the three performing organizations. This is a typical life cycle and allocation. Small projects will be associated with a simpler, more compressed set of activities. Very large projects will be connected with a more complex succession of life cycle events. All three organizations are at least minimally involved with verification and validation at each life cycle stage. The intended effect is that there exists a set of checks and balances on the software project between the organizations that collaborate to produce a reliable software system product.

The last three sections have collaborated to present a "snapshot" of today's verification and validation practices on the modern software project. The next section looks into future directions in this field.

## 2.4
## Future Trends

The foregoing sections have described pragmatic verification and validation techniques presently in use on modern software projects, including a brief historical perspective. This material has suggested some trends for the future in verification and validation. Future directions and advances appear to be concentrated in these categories:

1. Improved management approaches
2. Improved implementation of proven technologies
3. Evolution of present experimental techniques

These categories are discussed individually in the following text. It should be recognized that these areas are not necessarily mutually exclusive or discrete.

In recalling the historical progression of the software project, the need for separation of system engineering, software development, and an independent test organization developed. Unfortunately, in many instances, this resulted in the deployment of separate approaches and tools by these organizations with marginal coordination. Economics and the resulting poor performance of this arrangement are bringing about its demise. A revised, more realistic approach to software development requires an overall coordinated package of tools and methodologies covering all phases of the software life cycle. This will, of course, place more of a burden on management to achieve these results. What is needed is the continued evolution of a corps of software managers who are well educated in the elements of

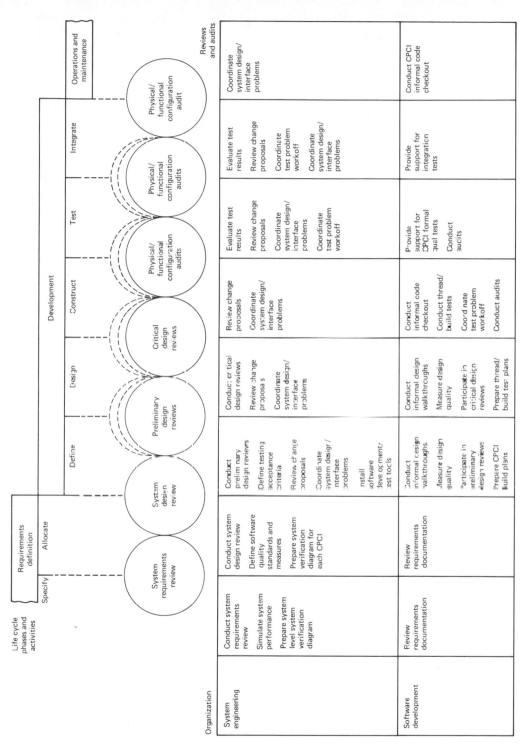

**Figure 2-14** V & V activities by organization over software life cycle. (Michael S. Deutsch, "Software Project Verification and Validation," *Computer* (April, 1981), © 1981. Reprinted by permission of IEEE.)

| Independent test organization | | | | | | | |
|---|---|---|---|---|---|---|---|
| Prepare system test requirements | Prepare CPCI test requirements | Review design documentation | Review design documentation | Prepare integration test plans | Prepare integration test procedures | Conduct system integration testing | Prepare test plans/procedures |
| Review requirements documentation | Review requirements documentation | Prepare CPCI test plans | Prepare CPCI test procedures | | Conduct CPCI formal qual tests | Prepare integration test reports | Conduct maintenance retesting |
| Prepare system integration plan | | | Prepare test data base (s) | | Prepare CPCI test reports | Manage test problem reporting | Manage test problem reporting |
| Define test software requirements | | | | | Manage test problem reporting | | |

**Figure 2-14** *continued*

*software physics,* who are committed to modern methodologies, and who will be aggressive in overcoming inertia to ensure that these approaches are implemented.

What seems to have occurred is that in the compulsion to provide individual attention to verification and validation, V & V became too detached from other activities on the software project. Management must review this separation and provide a more integrated role for verification and validation. This would involve reassimilating verification and validation such that each area of software engineering has a synergized V & V aspect while still maintaining the separate test organization.

The software development process is more accurately viewed when the technical engineering problem is considered in conjunction with the human engineering aspect of the process. The application of talented personnel should, theoretically, be a sufficient requisite on which to forecast success. However, basic human fallibilities provide the possibility for errors to occur. Engineering, scientific, and management practices are frequently corrupted by human errors of inconsistency and omission. Computer automated tools have been and will continue to be developed to implement existing proven technologies that are most prone to inconsistency and omission errors if performed manually.

Although more detailed classifications are possible, automated tools may be partitioned into two basic groups: (1) those tools that assist in the definition and design of the software, and (2) those tools that help evaluate the software once it is built. The first group of tools performs clerical functions of checking for completeness, consistency, and omission errors during requirements definition and design activities. The usefulness of such tools depends on the ability to express requirements and software design in machine-readable form. Thus, the future utility of these tools is, to a large degree, directly keyed to progress in the development and widespread use of specification languages, program design languages, and automated documentation systems.

The RXVP80™ source text analysis system, explained in a previous section, is typical of the evaluation tools. This technology is already in a highly developed state although much necessary research continues to be directed toward the automatic generation of an optimal set of test cases. Widespread use and acceptance of these tools are presently hampered by (1) the reluctance of management to forsake traditional manual methods that have been previously successful on small software projects, and (2) the availability of tools only to companies that have been able to finance their development. Each of these restraints is expected to be slowly eroded in the next several years. The first problem will be overcome through an educational process, particularly with regard to cost benefits of the automated tools and the prospect of being denied contracts for large software projects if the tools are not used. The second difficulty is more acute. More companies may be willing to invest the necessary funds for automatic tool development in order to protect future business. The purchase rights to some existing tools are presently being marketed by their developers. A further possibility is that, for projects for which a government agency is the procurer, automatic test tools may be available as government-furnished equipment.

As the more prolific usage of automated tools is expected over the software life cycle from requirements definition through testing, a more complete verification and validation of the system will result. It is also expected with such approaches that errors would be detected earlier in the development cycle and lead to cost containment.

It is the forward-looking concept of some that nearly error-free programs can be constructed by applying certain organizational techniques and that the correctness of these programs can be certified in a static manner (without actual execution) by using mathematical proofs. The constructive approach to the development of programs is with us today in the form of *structured* design and programming. The static approach concerns *program proofs,* a popular subject of current research. Practical application of program proof techniques to programs of significant size may be at least a decade away.[11]

The proof concept employs the program source statements to prove mathematical theorems about program behavior. The expected program behavior is characterized by a set of assertions. The intentions of the designers are reflected in these assertions about values of variables at end or intermediate points of the programs; then, the asserted program can be converted into a theorem and the theorem proved.[12] Program proofs are intended to place verification and validation on a more sound theoretical foundation than testing which checks the performance of programs on the limited basis of a set of sample data. Major obstacles limiting wider use of proof techniques include the difficulties in developing the assertions that are to be proved and the length of the proof computations. Economic feasibility of program proofs requires further development of automatic theorem proving tools.[13]

A related subtechnology of program proofs is symbolic execution. This experimental technique is more likely to develop a practical implementation in the near future. Symbolic execution is a means of executing a program as a series of symbolic formulas which are verified against a set of predefined conditions or assertions. The practical difficulties involve generation of the assertions and the economics of the required computations. Because of these difficulties of use, symbolic execution does not now appear to be economically feasible for mass application to large software projects. Some selective application to critical software units would, however, be an advantageous use of symbolic execution when these software units could do irreparable harm if certain conditions are violated; an example application might be in spacecraft command and control in which certain combinations of commands could injure the vehicle. Such software would require maximum verification.

Presently a good environment does not exist for the introduction of new verification and validation approaches. A consolidation of present technology is needed to fill a gap between technology and the ability of management to efficiently

[11] E. F. Miller, Jr., *Methodology for Comprehensive Software Testing* (Griffiss Air Force Base, N.Y.: Rome Air Development Center, 1975), p. 17.

[12] M. R. Paige and E. F. Miller, Jr., *Methodology for Software Validation—A Survey of the Literature* (Santa Barbara, Ca.: General Research Corp., 1972), RM 1549, p. 37.

[13] E. F. Miller, Jr., *A Survey of Major Techniques of Program Validation* (Santa Barbara, Ca.: General Research Corp., 1972), RM–1731, p. 58.

apply what already exists. This consolidation is a necessary step to providing a firm baseline for the introduction of advanced methodologies.

Testing is the most visible verification and validation activity but not necessarily the most important. Testing methodologies are addressed first in Part II. However, a major intention of this book is to disclaim the notion that the traditional series of formal tests applied to software products at the end of a development constitutes effective verification and validation. Such testing, in fact, has little effect on product integrity from an effectiveness/cost standpoint. Probably the two areas with the greatest influence/cost ratio on product quality are the verification and validation activities performed by the system engineering organization (Chapter 9) and the informal development testing (Chapters 3, 6, and 7).

# Part II

# Testing Methodologies

_____Chapter 3_____

# Control of Software Construction and Test

_____

## 3.1
## Basic Approach

This chapter describes a method of software construction and test that

- Segments a complex software development into more manageable functional elements
- Demonstrates key functional capabilities early in the testing activity
- Maintains a visible connection between testing and software requirements, thus formalizing the testing process
- Forms the basis of a very effective project planning and control strategy

The approach described here is derived from a methodology developed at Computer Sciences Corporation and has undergone refinement in its application at Hughes Aircraft Company. This concept has a powerful effect on ordering the software construction/test process because of its combined technical and management merits.

Construction is defined to include software coding and informal programmer functional checkout. Test is a more formal activity that is guided by prepared plans and/or procedures. The tested product normally forms a baseline against which changes are controlled. Formality in this context does not always imply control and approval by an authority external to the developer (e.g., the customer). At the earliest levels of testing, the product developer conducts the tests and controls the baseline. Formality, in a general sense, entails the existence of predefined controls and procedures. The level of formality determines who the administrator of these controls and procedures is.

The software construction activity has traditionally constituted the *dark* period of the development cycle. During this stage, there has been a lack of adequate metrics to define the status of the project and, thus, the development has seemingly gone *underground*. The approach explained in this chapter ameliorates this deficiency by providing a rigorous means of segmenting a complex software development into small, functional chunks; the chunks, known as threads, are individually scheduled and completion status is monitored. The status is updated frequently and displayed, thus providing visibility into the condition of the project.

Figure 3–1 depicts a software test procedure that is visibly connected to the requirements. The process is driven by a tool called the system verification diagram (SVD) derived directly from the software requirements specification. The SVD consists of stimulus/response elements (threads) that are associated with an identifiable function and specific requirements. Each stimulus/response element can be mapped into the design to identify the specific software modules which, when executed, perform the function of that thread. A highly granular relationship now exists between the functional requirements (the threads) and the design (the modules). This relationship is the primary means by which the software development can be accurately defined and closely controlled. The SVD is described in more detail in the next section. Each thread will be tested individually by the development team. The modules corresponding to the thread are exhaustively tested such that each path segment is exercised at least once. The mechanisms for accomplishing this objective are explained in Chapter 6.

The next step of the planning process is to allocate specific threads to specific builds. Each build represents a significant partial functional capability of the system. Each incremental build demonstration is a partial dry run of the *final acceptance test*. Each successive build demonstration regression tests the capabilities of the previous builds. Thus, the demonstration of the full system is a natural culminating step of integrating the final build into the accumulation of previous builds.

The tools and various facets of this approach are described in the following sections, beginning with the system verification diagram. Section 3.3 explains the planning procedure and includes sample planning charts from a recent software project. An exercise is presented in Section 3.4 which develops the step-by-step application of this procedure to an example software package. Section 3.5 shows how

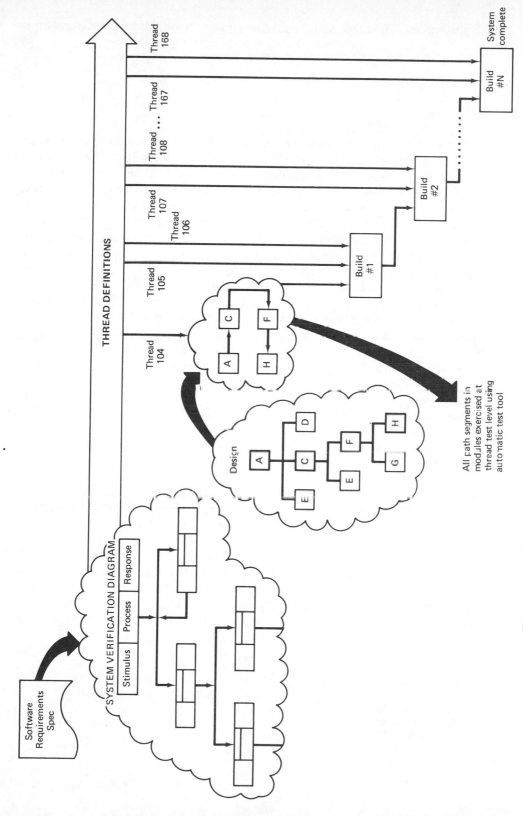

**Figure 3–1** Software test/construction procedure visibly connected to requirements.

this approach may be extended to control integration testing of large software projects.

## 3.2

## Defining the Threads

The tool employed for defining the threads is the system verification diagram (SVD). The objective of the SVD is the representation of the software requirements in a complete, consistent, and testable manner. The SVD represents these requirements as a series of stimulus/response pairings. Inconsistencies, redundancies, and omissions may be revealed while developing these stimulus/response pairings. An effective approach is to construct an SVD immediately upon availability of each draft of the software requirements specification. This provides maximum opportunity for feedback and incorporation of findings into the next release of the specification. It may also highlight the need for consultations with the customer on heretofore unrecognized open requirements issues. Thus, the SVD is also an informal requirements verification tool.[1]

Each stimulus consists of one or more inputs plus any conditional qualifiers; each response consists of one or more outputs plus conditional qualifiers generated as a result of the input event.[2] Each stimulus/response element represents an identifiable function or subfunction and is also called a thread. Each thread has a direct relationship to one or more software requirements (usually several) and can later be associated with the modules in the software design architecture which will implement the thread. The SVD is normally generated from the requirements specification before the software architecture is designed.

Figure 3–2 shows an example of the derivation of a thread from requirements specifications.[3] One of the objectives illustrated here is to define a transfer function which coalesces two or more functionally related requirements which may possibly reside in physically separate areas of the requirements specification. The test procedure which verifies the software modules that implement this thread also validates the requirements associated with the thread, paragraphs 3.7.1.1.4 and 3.7.3.1.5 in this example.

The entire requirements specification can be represented by a set of threads which are logically connected to each other by arrows which denote sequence. Quite often, a conditional qualifier associated with the input event of a thread is the successful completion of the function represented by the previous thread in the sequence. Complete functional testing of the software is attained if all paths through the SVD are traversed during the test program.[4]

The stimulus/response elements of the SVD may also be viewed as qualitative

---

[1] Carey and Bendic, in "The Control of a Software Test Process," *Proceedings Computer Software and Applications Conference 1977* (New York: IEEE), IEEE Catalog no. 77CH1291–4C.

[2] Carey and Bendic, op. cit.

[3] Carey and Bendic, op. cit.

[4] Carey and Bendic, op. cit.

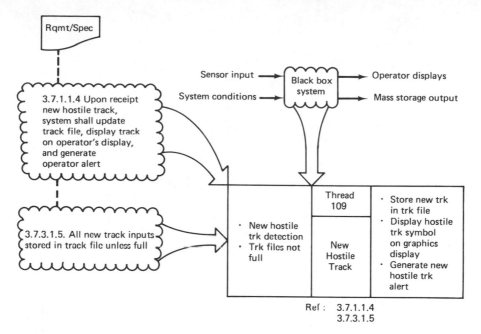

**Figure 3-2**  Identifying a thread from the requirements. (Robert Carey and Marc Bendic, "The Control of a Software Test Process," *Proceedings Computer Software and Applications Conference 1977* (New York, N.Y.: IEEE, Inc.), IEEE Catalog No. 77CH 1291-4C, © 1977 IEEE.)

assertions of system behavior. These assertions specify, in an informal language, the state of the system before and after each processing transformation. In this context, it is the objective of testing to demonstrate that actual system behavior is the same as the asserted behavior that is specified by the SVD.

The SVD is a unified depictment of the test requirements in graphical form. It can be included in the requirements specification document to identify the testing requirements. The threads represent the functions that must be tested, and the paths through the SVD are the sequences of functions that are to be tested. These test requirements can be allocated to the various levels of testing, including preliminary qualification testing, final qualification testing, integration testing, and final acceptance testing.

A portion of a SVD that was used for a recent software development is contained in Figure 3-3. This SVD addresses a set of display interactive functions in which the operator is presented a display containing a set of default initialization parameters. The operator may accept the default set of parameters or enter manual overrides for any or all of these initialization parameters. The requirement numbers that each thread satisfies are denoted below and to the left of each thread block.

Thread 1.0 begins the processing sequence by presenting a display consisting of the initialization parameters and default values. One of seven paths from thread 1.0 is possible depending on the operator input event and system condition:

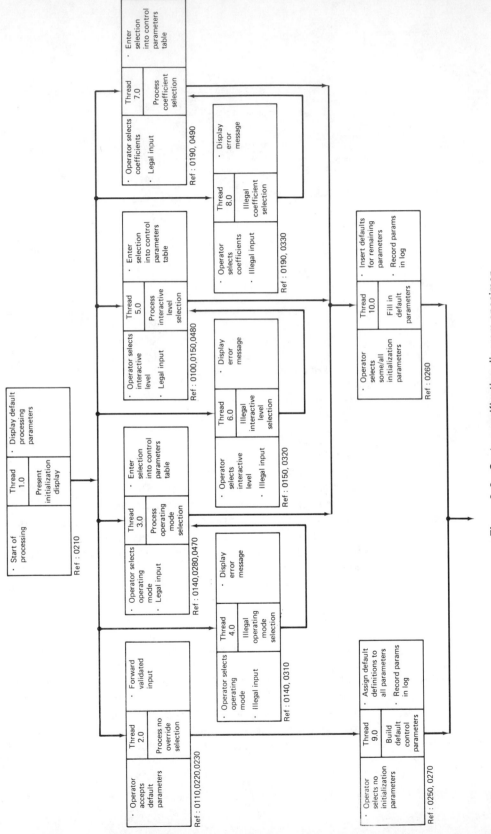

**Figure 3-3** System verification diagram specimen.

1. Thread 2.0 involves the operator accepting all the default parameters without modification. This is followed by thread 9.0, which accepts the stimulus of thread 2.0 and sets all the control parameters to default values.

2. Thread 3.0 is stimulated by the operator manually selecting a legal operating mode. The response is to set this selection in the control parameters table.

3. Thread 4.0 occurs on the condition that the operator enters an operating mode selection that is illegal. The response is to feedback an error message in the display. The eventual succeeding event is a legal operating mode selection, thread 3.0.

4. Thread 5.0 is stimulated by the operator manually selecting a legal interactive level. The response is to set this selection in the control parameter table.

5. Thread 6.0 occurs on the condition that the operator enters an interactive level selection that is illegal. The response is to feedback an error message on the display. The eventual succeeding event is a legal interactive level selection, thread 5.0.

6. Thread 7.0 is stimulated by the operator manually selecting a legal set of coefficients. The response is to set these selections in the control parameter table.

7. Thread 8.0 occurs on the condition that the operator enters one or more illegal coefficient values. The response is to feedback an error message on the display. The eventual succeeding event is a legal coefficient input, thread 7.0.

The common succeeding event of threads 3.0, 5.0, and 7.0 is thread 10.0. This thread fills in default values for these parameters not set by the operator. The paths from threads 9.0 to 10.0 then converge to another thread not shown on this example.

The example highlights the logical association of stimulus/response events derived from the functional requirements. The SVD is the key factor that subsequently drives the planning effort for test and buildup.


## 3.3

## Planning the Test and Build-Up Process

Detailed test planning can begin when the software architecture defining the structure of the modules is available. This normally occurs, in software developments sponsored by the Department of Defense, by the time of the preliminary design review (PDR). This test/construction approach requires a modular software architecture developed from structured design precepts; less organized designs of diluted modularity will reduce effectiveness because of an indistinct relationship between the threads and software modules. Experience shows that the technique works well with a structure granularity of, on the average, 100 higher-order-language source lines per module (which later may be subdivided further into subroutines).

In this concept, software test and construction are intertwined; they do not occur separately and sequentially. The order in which the software is coded, tested, and synthesized is essentially determined by the system verification diagram, which defines the test procedure. The SVD has segmented the system into demonstrable functions or threads. The development of the threads are calendarized. The modules associated with each thread are coded and tested in an order that is commensurate with this calendarization. The threads are synthesized into higher-order sections called *builds*; each build incrementally demonstrates a significant partial functional capability of the system. This culminates in a demonstration of the full system, which occurs as a natural concluding step of integrating the last build to the accumulation of previous builds. This approach provides an orderly means of segmenting a complex software development into smaller, functionally oriented sections.

A convenient mechanism to record the relationships between the thread, requirements, and modules which implement the thread is the thread functional allocation chart contained in Figure 3-4. The information contained in this chart is derived from (1) the system verification diagram (Figure 3-3), and (2) the software design architecture for these interactive functions.

The architecture of the software modules is represented by the structure diagram shown in Figure 3-5. Each module is assigned a hierarchically numbered identification located in the upper left corner of the box. The structure diagram describes this portion of the system in hierarchical terms. The diamond at the bottom of some of the boxes are alternation constructs; the subordinate modules of the construct are conditionally executed depending on the state of a parameter (or parameters) evaluated in the parent module. This structure decomposes into two basic branches—those modules which build and output the display picture to the display terminal and those modules which process the operator inputs after presentation of the display on the terminal. In a well-structured design, all of the basic processing work is done by the modules at the terminal or lowest level of the hierarchy. All of the parent modules are control modules, that is, the function of these modules is to properly invoke and sequence the subordinate modules.

The information contained on the thread functional allocation chart under the headers "Requirements IDs," "Thread ID," and "Thread Title" is transferred directly from the system verification diagram. The header "Complexity Units" represents an estimation on a linear scale from 1 to 5 of the person-effort required to code, check-out, test, and integrate each thread. A rating of 5 is the most complex and a rating of 1 is the simplest. This subjective measure is based on the volume of code to be constructed, code complexity, and complexity of the interface with other threads that have already been integrated. The threads under examination here contain a moderate volume of code, involving relatively noncomplicated interfaces. The thread complexity ratings of 2's and 3's reflect this evaluation. Application at Hughes Aircraft Company largely supports the Computer Science Corporation experience that this estimation parameter is useful and linear.

| Requirement IDs | Thread ID | Thread Title | Complexity Units | Module IDs |
|---|---|---|---|---|
| 0210 | 1.0 | Present initialization display | 3 | 1.1, 1.1.1, 1.1.1.1, 1.1.1.2 |
| 0110, 0220, 0230 | 2.0 | Process no override selection | 2 | 1.1, 1.1.2, 1.1.2.1, 1.1.2.1.2, 1.1.2.5 |
| 0140, 0280 0470 | 3.0 | Process operating mode selection | 2 | 1.1, 1.1.2, 1.1.2.2, 1.1.2.2.1 |
| 0140, 0310 | 4.0 | Illegal operating mode selection | 2 | 1.1, 1.1.2, 1.1.2.2, 1.1.2.2.2 |
| 0100, 0150, 0480 | 5.0 | Process interactive level selection | 2 | 1.1, 1.1.2, 1.1.2.3, 1.1.2.3.1 |
| 0150, 0320 | 6.0 | Illegal interactive level selection | 2 | 1.1, 1.1.2, 1.1.2.3, 1.1.2.3.2 |
| 0190, 0490 | 7.0 | Process coefficient selection | 2 | 1.1, 1.1.2, 1.1.2.4, 1.1.2.4.1 |
| 0190, 0330 | 8.0 | Illegal coefficient selection | 2 | 1.1, 1.1.2, 1.1.2.4, 1.1.2.4.2 |
| 0250, 0270 | 9.0 | Build default control parameters | 2 | 1.1, 1.1.2, 1.1.2.1, 1.1.2.1.1 |
| 0260 | 10.0 | Fill in default parameters | 2 | 1.1, 1.1.2, 1.1.2.6 |

**Figure 3-4** Thread functional allocation chart specimen.

Under the header "Module IDs" are the modules, referenced to the structure diagram in Figure 3–5, which implement each thread. For an individual thread, the serial execution of the modules listed perform the function of the thread and its associated requirements. In the case of thread 1.0, all of its modules are new and must be coded in order to implement this thread. Subsequent threads involve a combination of new and previously coded/tested modules. Usually, the higher-level control structure is implemented as a result of the first two or three threads and the subsequent threads add new modules to the structure at lower levels of the architecture hierarchy. For military standard software developments, the thread functional allocation charts will satisfy the information content requirements of Type C-5 Specification paragraph 3.1.1, *Functional Allocation.*

The serial execution sequences of the modules correlated with three threads—1.0, 3.0, and 4.0—are illustrated in Figure 3–6. All of the modules of thread 1.0 will be newly coded. For thread 3.0, module 1.1 has previously been implemented as a result of thread 1.0, and module 1.1.2 already exists courtesy of

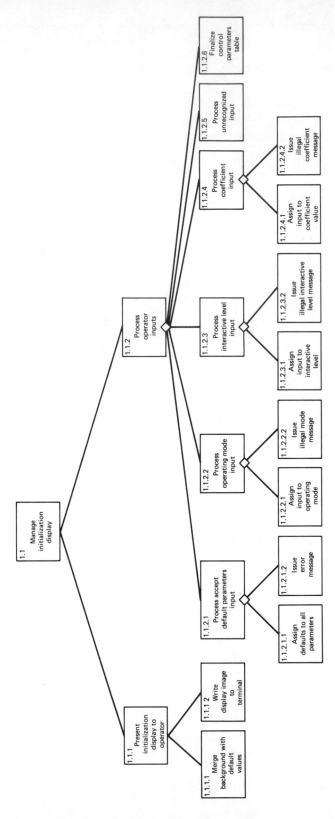

**Figure 3-5** Sample software architecture.

thread 2.0. Modules 1.1.2.2 and 1.1.2.2.1 must be coded and then integrated with modules 1.1 and 1.1.2 to form thread 3.0. In the case of thread 4.0, modules 1.1, 1.1.2, and 1.1.2.2 are existing modules. Module 1.1.2.2.2 is a new unit that must be constructed and then integrated with modules 1.1, 1.1.2, and 1.1.2.2 to constitute thread 4.0.

In order to fully test module 1.1.2.2 in thread 3.0, a complication occurs. Note in Figure 3–5 that this module acts as a control module with an alternation construct. It will direct processing of a valid operating mode input by ordering execution of module 1.1.2.2.1, or it will handle an invalid operating mode input by executing module 1.1.2.2.2 to issue an error message for the operator. The invalid input case is not within the scope of thread 3.0. Nevertheless, in order for the modules of thread 3.0 to link properly and to fully test module 1.1.2.2, some mutation of module 1.1.2.2.2 must exist. The remedy for this situation is to substitute a *stub* for module 1.1.2.2.2. A stub is a dummy component that simulates the functioning of the module in question. Stubs will have varying levels of functionality. In this case, the stub need only consist of the subroutine name and the proper termination control statements; no functional statements are necessary. Thus, the insertion of a stub for module 1.1.2.2.2 is an expediency that permits us to test thread 3.0. For thread 4.0, this stub will be replaced by the actual functional code written for this module. This is just one case in our ten-thread example in which a stub is required; there are others.

It should be observed that, with the threads approach, the order of implementation of the modules in the design structure is in execution order sequence; this has been illustrated in Figure 3–6. This implies that, for each thread, the order of construction commences at the top of the hierarchy and penetrates to the lowest level until all the modules that are required to perform the function of the thread are coded and integrated. This sequence corresponds to the order of the execution for

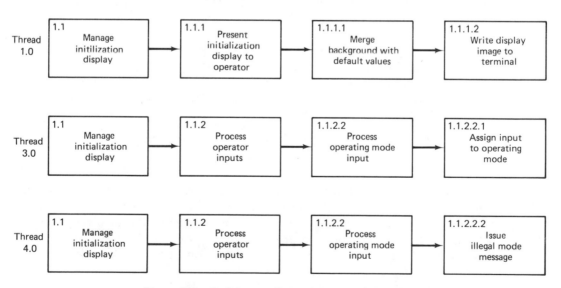

**Figure 3-6**  Serial execution sequences of threads.

the modules of the thread. This is neither top-down implementation nor bottom-up implementation. Top-down/bottom-up are strictly structural concepts without a rigorous association to functions. Top-down implements all the modules at higher levels in the invocation structure before penetrating to the lowest levels. Bottom-up, of course, proceeds from the lowest level. The threads approach is concerned with the implementation of functions; it utilizes structure only as a means of achieving that end. Thus, within the threads approach we reject the concept of top-down implementation (and bottom-up for that matter) in favor of execution-order implementation for each thread. In order to avoid any possible confusion over the use of top-down techniques, this is not an indictment of top-down design. It is assumed that this is one of the methods that have been used to formulate a structured design.

The next step is to assign threads to builds and designate completion points over the schedule period. Two considerations are paramount in this process: (1) it would normally be in the interest of the project to implement the threads which comprise the highest technical risk early, and (2) a logically complete system, although not functionally complete, should be the objective as early in the build-up schedule as possible.[5] This is basically an implement-to-schedule strategy. If, despite the best efforts of all concerned, the entire system has not been completed by the scheduled date, there will still exist the nucleus of a system that performs functions which are demonstrable and operationally useful. The customer will undoubtedly be displeased. However, it is presumed that the extent of his displeasure will be far less with this situation than with a less organized approach which may have completed the same volume of code consisting of diverse software units not yet orderly sequenced into operational functions.

One of the objectives of this strategy is to furnish management and the customer with alternatives should it become clear that the full product that has been contracted for cannot be delivered by the scheduled date, or cannot be built within the originally allocated budget, or both. The customer would like full latitude in dealing with the situation. Such latitude would consist of being able to exercise any of the following options:

1. Accept delivery on the originally scheduled date with only a subset of the required functions
2. Extend the delivery date so that the system will contain all the required functions, or a fuller subset
3. Provide more funding to obtain a fuller set of functions
4. Do both (2) and (3) if necessary (as is usually the case)

As has been previously pointed out, the customer will always be unhappy with schedule slippages and/or cost overruns. This displeasure is undoubtedly compounded if his choices to resolve the situation are strictly limited to extending the schedule and, in all likelihood, absorbing a cost overrun. A schedule slip could have far-reaching repercussions. Other systems that in some way interface with the local

[5] Carey and Bendic, op. cit.

system may be prevented from reaching operational status as a result of the delay. The customer can escape these consequences, or at least some of them, if he is able to accept, by the original date, a partially completed system that logically functions while containing a subset of the original capabilities that are operationally useful. As a result of these circumstances, the contractor's reputation will no doubt be blemished. However, by having a fallback position available for the customer, the extent of this negative image will at least be limited. There is, of course, never any substitute for on-time/on-budget performance. Yet, the contractor can still maintain a reputation for rational project management under adverse conditions with proper planning.

A logically complete system is one that can accept input data, process the data, and provide a useful set of outputs or partial outputs while applying an operationally useful subset of functions. The main thrust of this concept is attaining an overall system state that flows from front-end to back-end with, perhaps, only a subset of functions implemented in between. The approach to defining a logically complete system is highly dependent on the individual application. There are some general guidelines and considerations that are useful in a number of situations:

1. *Full system data flow*. Achieve a full system data flow, front-end to back-end, even though the flow will be through a skeleton system.

2. *Two levels of logical completeness*. Consider *logical completeness* on two levels. One level of completeness will be useful to the customer. Another level, containing even a lesser set of functions, will be pertinent internally. The internal minimal level of completeness should be an initial planning target and ease of transition should be possible to grow to the customer's level of logical completeness.

3. *Multiple contributors to file product*. Some systems produce a single file as the key product. The chronology of the processing may include a number of different functions that contribute information into the file before it is completed. Orient the planning for a logically complete system around early implementation of the functions that initialize the file and finalize the file. Add other contributing functions to the system afterward. The logically complete concept for this type of system is diagrammed in Figure 3–7a.

4. *Pipelined multiple filters*. This guideline concerns a system that contains a number of filters that reduce the bandwidth of the data with the filters arranged serially or in pipeline fashion. In this case it may be possible to implement those filters with maximum contribution to bandwidth reduction first to constitute a logically complete system. The lesser contributors are inserted into the pipeline later. Or there may be some other criterion for establishing implementation priority of the filters. This concept is shown in Figure 3–7b.

5. *Display interactive features*. Some systems, including on-line systems, have a basic, fixed, automatic processing flow supplemented by extensive man/machine interactive display capabilities that can override/reroute the processing sequence, modify control parameters, view intermediate results,

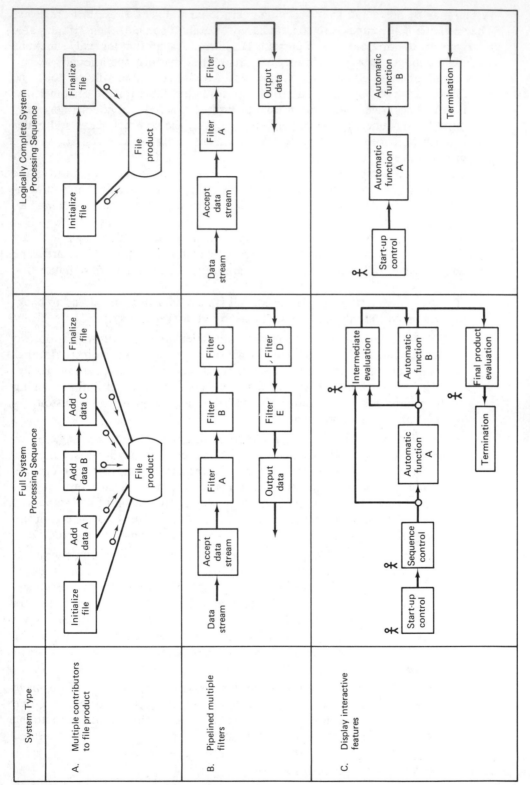

**Figure 3-7** Logically complete system concepts.

and so forth. Here, a logically complete system can comprise the basic automatic processing sequence plus the minimal display interactive capabilities to control start-up and termination. Schedule the implementation of the more powerful interactive and display features after the basic automatic processing sequence. This approach is illustrated in Figure 3–7c.

Basically, the planner or manager will have to be innovative in defining logical completeness with respect to the individual system application involved.

The results of the planning effort just described are displayed on a *build plan* diagram. This build plan provides an overall calendarized view of the sequence of construction/test events, including

- The sequence of the builds
- The relationship of the builds to each other
- The allocation of threads to builds.
- The sequence of the threads.

An example build plan from a recent software development is contained in Figure 3–8. Implementation of an end-to-end data flow is achieved at build 6.0, which occurs less than halfway into the scheduled implementation period; this constitutes a logically complete system for this project. Builds 7.0 to 15.0 add additional functions which supplement the basic data transformations and provide operator interactive control over the processing sequence. Each build adds new functions (threads) to the system and, to the extent indicated by the connecting arrows on the build plan, contains the cumulative capabilities of previous builds. Each build demonstration tests the new capabilities and regression tests the capabilities accumulated from previous builds. The final acceptance test of the total system occurring at build 15.0 is merely a natural culminating event of this succession. Because a thread is directly linked to software modules, the build plan also defines the order of construction of the modules. Each thread is also tested informally. The build demonstration tests may be viewed as natural culminating events in a succession of thread tests.

Because by their very nature threads represent useful operational functions, a measure of thread completion also represents a measure of project completion. By using the number of complexity units assigned to each thread, the build plan may be summarized into a *thread production plan,* shown in Figure 3–9, for the same software development. The solid line represents the planned production rate against which may be plotted the actual production rate in dashed lines. Thus, the thread production plan provides an easily understood means of reporting actual progress versus planned progress.

The planning efforts described thus far provide direction for defining the module construction sequence and serve as a basis for allocating personnel resources. In order to manage the construction and test effort at a detailed level, we would like to identify the order in which the modules must be coded and assign pro-

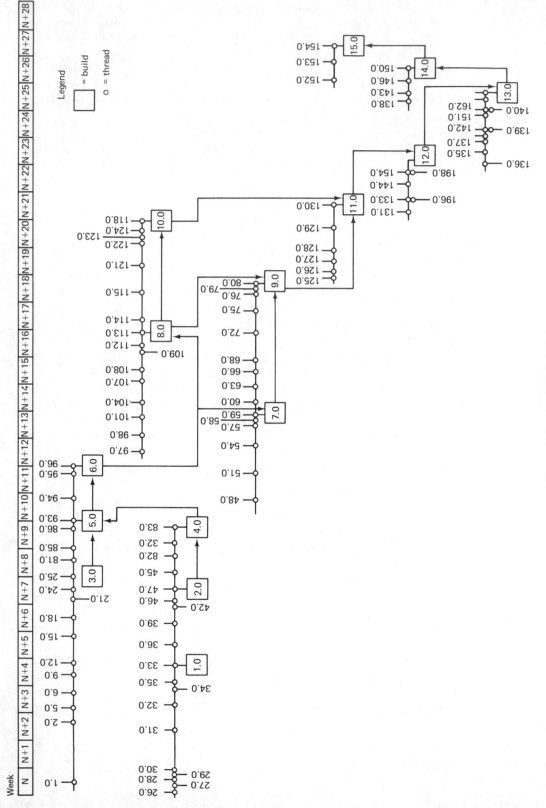

**Figure 3–8**  Example build plan.

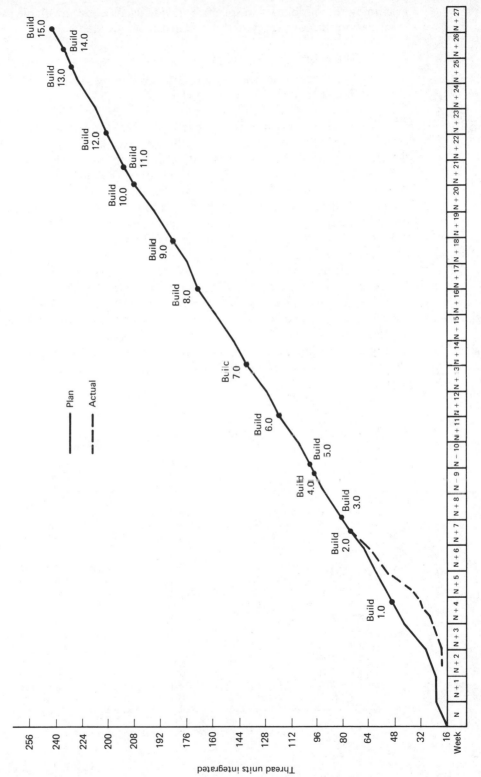

**Figure 3-9** Example thread production plan.

gramming responsibilities to specific individuals. We have available two sources of information that will support this detailed planning step:

1. The order of thread implementation defined on the build plan
2. The modules that are required to mechanize each thread defined on the thread functional allocation charts

In order to illustrate this process, the ten threads defined in the system verification diagram of Figure 3–3 will be used. We learn from the build plan contained in Figure 3–8 that the required order of implementation of these threads is 1.0, 2.0, 9.0, 3.0, 4.0, 5.0, 6.0, 7.0, 8.0, and 10.0. The modules associated with each of these threads have been identified on the thread functional allocation chart of Figure 3–4. By studying the module associations on the thread allocation chart, the order of the threads on the build plan, and the completion date for each thread on the build plan, the sequence of module construction can be defined and due dates for each module assigned.

The result of this exercise is a *programming assignments plan,* displayed in Figure 3–10. The new modules that must be coded for each thread are listed in chronological order, the associated thread is identified for reference purposes, and the due date and responsible programmer for each module are specified. Reality dictates that these assignments be regarded as tentative. As unexpected problems usually arise during the development, the manager must be prepared to realign the assignments to work around the problems and keep the effort running relatively smoothly.

| Module ID | Thread ID | Due Date | Responsible Programmer |
|-----------|-----------|----------|------------------------|
| 1.1 | 1.0 | 2 June | Person A |
| 1.1.1 | 1.0 | 3 June | Person B |
| 1.1.1.1 | 1.0 | 4 June | Person B |
| 1.1.1.2 | 1.0 | 5 June | Person C |
| 1.1.2 | 2.0 | 6 June | Person D |
| 1.1.2.1 | 2.0 | 9 June | Person D |
| 1.1.2.1.2 | 2.0 | 13 June | Person A |
| 1.1.2.5 | 2.0 | 13 June | Person B |
| 1.1.2.1.1 | 9.0 | 15 June | Person C |
| 1.1.2.2 | 3.0 | 13 June | Person D |
| 1.1.2.2.1 | 3.0 | 15 June | Person D |
| 1.1.2.2.2 | 4.0 | 18 June | Person A |
| 1.1.2.3 | 5.0 | 19 June | Person B |
| 1.1.2.3.1 | 5.0 | 21 June | Person B |
| 1.1.2.3.2 | 6.0 | 23 June | Person C |
| 1.1.2.4 | 7.0 | 22 June | Person D |
| 1.1.2.4.1 | 7.0 | 26 June | Person A |
| 1.1.2.4.2 | 8.0 | 29 June | Person D |
| 1.1.2.6 | 10.0 | 6 July | Person B |

**Figure 3–10** Programming assignments plan.

Part II   Testing Methodologies

This section has defined the planning sequence for software construction and test and has illustrated the tools and products of the process—the system verification diagram, the thread functional allocation chart, the build plan, the thread production plan, and the programming assignments plan. These tools and techniques bring rigor, visibility, and manageability to the software construction and test process.

## 3.4
## Application of the Procedure—
## The DC Network Analysis Software System

In order to further clarify the utility of the threads approach, an example application is presented. The *dc network analysis system*, a small software package, has been selected for this demonstration. The entire planning procedure is exhibited step-by-step starting with the software requirements specification. The derivation of the planning products is shown using the requirements specification and software design structure as inputs.

The dc network analysis system analyzes the input description of an electrical network and calculates the node voltages plus other electrical parameters. It is probably correct to contend that the development of a small straight forward system such as this does not require elaborate planning procedures; that is, because of the system simplicity, it is "intellectually manageable" on an informal basis. The focus of this example is intended to be on an end-to-end demonstration of the application of the technique. It is hoped that the reader has already been convinced that the approach has considerable merit with respect to organizing large complex system developments, and no further amplification of this point is intended in this section.

The functional requirements specification for the dc network analysis system is contained in Figure 3–11. The data flow diagram furnishes an overall view of the system functions and functional interfaces. Three major processing functions are specified—an input processing and control function, a central transform, and an output processing function. *Input processing and control* accepts parameters describing the requested system output products. The *central transform* determines the node voltages by calculating the element parameters, forming the elements into matrices, and computing the voltages from the matrices. *Output processing* furnishes a printout report of the node voltages and calculates/outputs certain ancillary electrical parameters if they have been requested. Section 3.0, *Requirements,* of the specification contains the processing requirements for each of these functions. In addition, a section containing capacity requirements delimits the size of the network that the system can accommodate. An identification number, indicated in parentheses, has been assigned to each requirement in order to facilitate traceability of the satisfaction of each requirement.

The requirements of this specification have been synthesized into stimulus/response elements. The resulting system verification diagram is depicted in Figure 3–12. This SVD is fairly straightforward and without complication. Some salient observations are

## 1.0 Introduction

This computer program accepts inputs describing the dc electrical network, generates the network equations, and solves the equations to determine the unknown voltages and currents.

## 2.0 Interfaces

A data flow diagram of the three major processing functions is presented here:

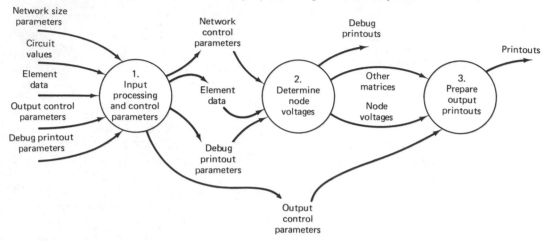

## 3.0 Requirements

## 3.1 DC Network Analysis Capacity Requirements

The system shall be able to process a network of the following size:

(C010) a. Up to twenty nodes
(C020) b. Up to fifty branches
(C030) c. Up to fifty passive elements including independent voltages and current sources
(C040) d. Up to fifty dependent current sources
(C050) e. Up to fifty dependent voltage sources

## 3.2 Requirements for Input Processing and Control Parameters Function

(I010) a. This function shall accept the following network configuration parameters as input:

(I020)  1. Number of network nodes
(I030)  2. Number of network branches
(I040)  3. Short circuit value
(I050)  4. Open circuit value
(I055)  5. Element data for each branch consisting of branch type, branch number, initial node, final node, branch element value, and branch number for dependent source

(I060) b. This function shall accept as input control parameters requests for hardcopy output of any or all of the following data sets:

(I070)  1. Node voltages
(I080)  2. Branch voltages
(I090)  3. Element voltages
(I100)  4. Element currents
(I110)  5. Branch currents

(I120)  c. It shall be possible, if requested by input control parameter, to obtain debug printouts of the following data sets:

(I130)  1. Nodal conductance matrix
(I140)  2. Equivalent current vector
(I150)  3. Nodal incidence matrix
(I160)  4. Branch conductance matrix
(I170)  5. Dependent voltage source matrix
(I180)  6. Independent voltage source vector
(I190)  7. Independent current source vector

### 3.3 Requirements for Determine Node Voltages Function

(V010)  a. The following elements shall be computed for each branch:

1. Resistance
2. Conductance
3. Capacitance
4. Inductance
5. Independent voltage source

6. Independent current source
7. Transconductance
8. Transfluence
9. Transpotential
10. Transresistance

(V020)  b. A nodal incidence matrix $A$ shall be constructed consisting of resistance, conductance, capacitance, and inductance elements for each branch.

(V030)  c. An independent voltage source matrix $E$ shall be constructed consisting of independent voltage source elements for each branch.

(V040)  d. An independent current source matrix $J$ shall be constructed consisting of independent current source elements for each branch.

(V050)  e. A branch conductance matrix $G$ shall be constructed consisting of resistance, conductance, capacitance, inductance, transconductance, transfluence, and transresistance elements for each branch.

(V060)  f. A dependent voltage source matrix $D$ shall be constructed consisting of transpotential and transresistance elements for each branch.

(V070)  g. If requested, debug printout of the nodal incidence, independent voltage source, independent current source, branch conductance, and dependent voltage sources shall be provided.

(V080)  h. A nodal conductance matrix $G_n$ shall be calculated using the following equation:

$$G_n = A (GD^{-1}) A^T$$

(V090)  i. An equivalent current source vector $J_n$ shall be calculated using the following equation:

$$J_n = A(J\text{-}GE)$$

(V100)  j. If requested, debug printout of the nodal conductance matrix and equivalent current source vector shall be provided.

(V110)  k. A solution vector $V_n$ containing the node voltages shall be calculated using the following equation:

$$V_n = G_n J_n$$

### 3.4 Requirements for Prepare Output Printouts Function

(P010)  a. A printout of the output node voltages shall be provided.
(P020)  b. If requested, a branch voltage vector shall be computed and printout provided.
(P030)  c. If requested, an element voltage vector shall be computed and printout provided.
(P040)  d. If requested, an element current vector shall be computed and printout provided.
(P050)  e. If requested, a network branch current vector shall be computed and printout provided.

**Figure 3-11**  Functional requirements specification for DC network analysis system.

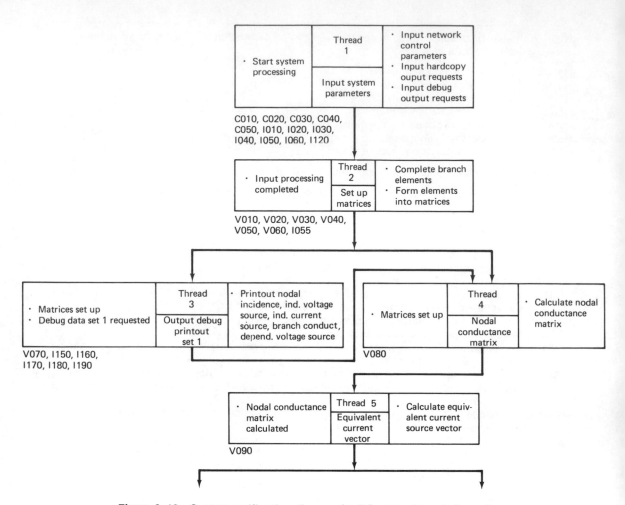

**Figure 3-12** System verification diagram for DC network analysis system.

1. Thread 3 occurs on a condition that debug data set 1 has been requested as an input parameter. This stimulus/response element combines requirements from Section 3.3 and 3.2.

2. Because both threads 3 and 4 occur on the stimulus that the matrices have been set-up, they are depicted on this diagram in parallel.

3. Thread 6 occurs on the condition that debug data set 2 was requested by an input parameter. The requirements associated with this thread have been similarly combined from Sections 3.3 and 3.2.

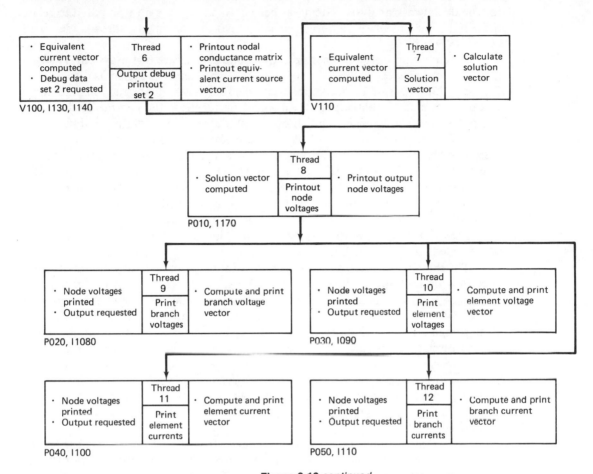

| · Equivalent current vector computed<br>· Debug data set 2 requested | Thread 6<br>Output debug printout set 2 | · Printout nodal conductance matrix<br>· Printout equivalent current source vector |
|---|---|---|

V100, I130, I140

| · Equivalent current vector computed | Thread 7<br>Solution vector | · Calculate solution vector |
|---|---|---|

V110

| · Solution vector computed | Thread 8<br>Printout node voltages | · Printout output node voltages |
|---|---|---|

P010, 1170

| · Node voltages printed<br>· Output requested | Thread 9<br>Print branch voltages | · Compute and print branch voltage vector |
|---|---|---|

P020, I1080

| · Node voltages printed<br>· Output requested | Thread 10<br>Print element voltages | · Compute and print element voltage vector |
|---|---|---|

P030, I090

| · Node voltages printed<br>· Output requested | Thread 11<br>Print element currents | · Compute and print element current vector |
|---|---|---|

P040, I100

| · Node voltages printed<br>· Output requested | Thread 12<br>Print branch currents | · Compute and print branch current vector |
|---|---|---|

P050, I110

**Figure 3-12** *continued*

4. Threads 6 and 7 are both invoked by the stimulus that the equivalent current vector is computed. They are also depicted in parallel on the diagram.

5. Threads 9, 10, 11, and 12 are stimulated by the printout of the node voltages, which occurs in thread 8. These threads will be executed in any combination based upon requests for the appropriate data sets in the input parameters. All of these threads combine requirements from physically separate portions of the specification.

With the completion of this system verification diagram, the test procedure for the dc network analysis system has been defined. We are now prepared to relate these test requirements with design elements that implement the threads identified in the SVD.

It is now appropriate to consider the module structure of the system. A structure chart defining the architecture of the dc network analysis system is displayed in Figure 3-13. The system decomposes at the first level of abstraction into three modules—a module that inputs the control parameters, the central module that computes the nodal voltages, and an output module that provides printed output of the circuit quantities. Note that this structure conforms to the classical structured design arrangement of an input branch, a central transform, and an output branch. The central transform module VOLT consists of two major functions—a module that formulates the network equations and a module that solves the network equations. Note the substructure beneath the module FORM. The sequence of this substructure—consisting of the modules READ, ELEMNT, and DEBUG1—is analogous to the input, central transform, and output branches that constitute the well-formed structure attribute.

The thread functional allocation chart for this system will now be constructed. Specific modules will be allocated to each thread, and a complexity unit rating will be assigned to each thread. This thread functional allocation chart is included as Figure 3-14. It can be seen that, in most cases, the modules relied upon for any given thread reflect capabilities of previous threads plus new modules unique to the present thread. Thus, each thread regression tests the capabilities of the previous threads in the sequence. In this example we have been able to unambiguously assign new modules to each thread. With a less organized design, the relationship of threads to modules would have been more vague, and thus the linkage between requirements and modules that implement the requirements would have been obscured.

The thread complexity units assigned range from 1 through 4. Because the interfaces of this system are of approximately uniform difficulty, the complexity unit assignments are primarily based on volume of code involved on the individual thread. Thread 2 requires the implementation of a farily large number of new modules. Hence, it has been assigned a complexity unit rating of 4. Thread 4 also involves a considerable number of modules; it has been allocated 3 complexity units. Thread 5, 6, and 7 involve a slightly smaller amount of code; they have been allotted unit ratings of 2. The remaining threads are associated with a fairly trivial volume of code; as a result they have been assigned 1 complexity unit per thread. The rationale used here for thread complexity unit ratings is only semiquantitative. In a real project environment, it is likely that a more rigorous algorithmic mechanism would be used for enumerating the complexity units.

The threads will now be allocated to builds and specific completion dates will be assigned to each thread. The result of this exercise is recorded on a build plan. Three builds have been defined; the thread content and appropriate rationale are now described.

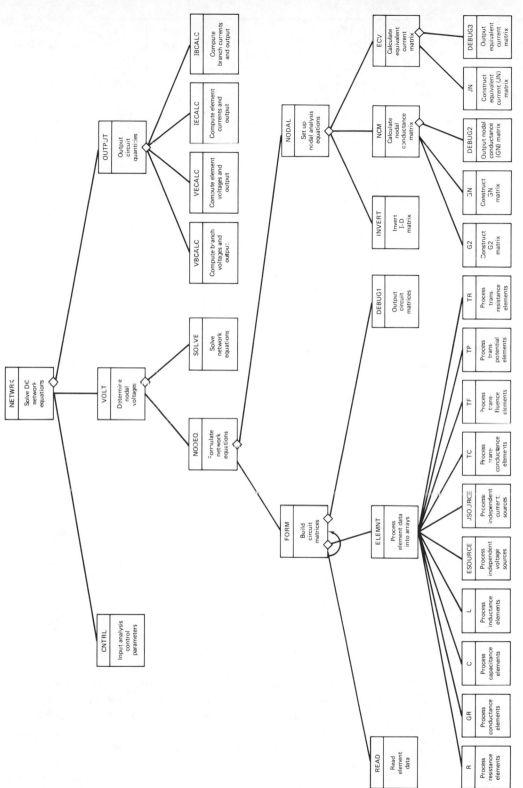

**Figure 3—3** DC network analysis system architecture.

| Requirement IDs | Thread ID | Thread Title | Com-plexity Units | Module IDs |
|---|---|---|---|---|
| C010, C020, C030, C040, C050, I010, I020, I030 I040, I050, I060, I120 | 1 | Input system para-meters | 1 | NETWRK, CNTRL |
| V010, V020, V030, V040, V050, V060, I055 | 2 | Set up matrices | 4 | NETWRK, CNTRL, VOLT, NODEQ, FORM, READ, ELEMNT, R, GR, C, L, ESOURCE, JSOURCE, TC, TF, TP, TR |
| V070, I150, I160, I170, I180, I190 | 3 | Output debug print-out set 1 | 1 | THREAD 2 MODULES + DEBUG1 |
| V080 | 4 | Nodal conductance matrix | 3 | THREAD 2 MODULES + NODAL, INVERT, NCM, G2, GN |
| V090 | 5 | Equivalent current vector | 2 | THREAD 2 MODULES + NODAL, ECV, JN |
| V100, I130, I140 | 6 | Output debug print-out set 2 | 2 | THREAD 4 MODULES, THREAD 5 MODULES + DEBUG2, DEBUG3 |
| V110 | 7 | Solution vector | 2 | THREAD 6 MODULES + SOLVE |
| P010, I070 | 8 | Printout node voltages | 1 | NETWRK, OUTPUT |
| P020, I080 | 9 | Print branch volt-ages | 1 | THREAD 2 MODULES + OUTPUT, VBCALC |
| P030, I090 | 10 | Print element volt-ages | 1 | THREAD 2 MODULES + OUTPUT, VECALC |
| P040, I100 | 11 | Print element currents | 1 | THREAD 2 MODULES + OUTPUT, IECALC |
| P050, I110 | 12 | Print branch currents | 1 | THREAD 2 MODULES + OUTPUT, IBCALC |

**Figure 3-14**   Thread functional allocation chart for network analysis system.

1. *Build 1: Basic input and output.* This build contains threads 1 and 8. This build implements the basic input interface and the basic output interface early in the development. In order to accomplish thread 8, a contrived set of nodal voltages must be provided. The availability of this output inter-face will facilitate the evaluation of the results from build 2.

2. *Build 2: Solution processing.* Threads 2, 3, 4, 5, 6, and 7 constitute this build. The basic capabilities provided by this build are the formulation of the network equations and the solution of the network equations. Also included are the capabilities to output certain debug printouts. These debug printouts will enable the evaluation of certain intermediate results.

3. *Build 3: Supplementary output parameters.* This build furnishes the capability to compute and output certain supplementary circuit quantities. Threads 9, 10, 11, and 12 are contained in this build. Each of these parameters is provided only if requested by an input control parameter.

This development approach is laid out on the build plan that is contained in Figure 3–15. We shall assign two programmers to work together as a team to construct and test this system. Experience on this size system would indicate that approximately eight schedule hours per thread complexity unit is a reasonable estimation on which to plan the scheduled duration. This rate of production is reflected on the build plan. The amount of effort required per complexity unit is dependent upon the size and complexity of the system, the number of people applied to the problem, and the overall ability of the organization to develop the system in question.

The build plan displayed in Figure 3–15 is probably a preliminary plan. The following conditions are assumed:

1. There are no intervening holidays

2. There will occur no illnesses, vacations, or other absences of a personal nature

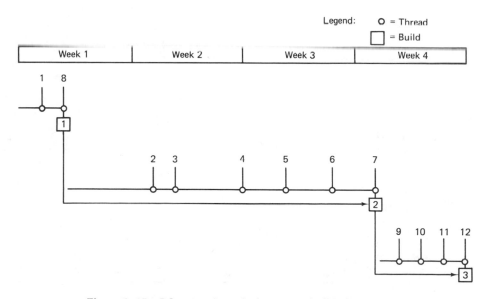

**Figure 3-15** DC network analysis system build plan.

3. The effort has been well planned and will be well managed

4. The requirements are valid and will not change

5. The necessary computer resources are available when required

With these premises, almost a perfect project environment has been assumed. In actuality, some or perhaps even all of these assumptions will be invalid to some extent. The real world is sometimes not an ideal place. Distractions, diversions, and other nonproductive phenomena must be anticipated during the planning process, and an estimate of their effects should be factored into the final plan. This system consists of a total of twenty thread complexity units, a very small system indeed. At the rate of eight schedule hours per complexity unit, the estimated duration for the construction and test of this system is four weeks.

It should be observed that because of the small size of this system, there is really no useful subset of functions that could constitute a logically complete system that would be useful to the customer or user, except, of course, the complete system itself. Build 1 does, however, consist of a system skeleton that is useful internally. It is this skeleton that is mechanized first in the build plan. The planned rate of thread production for this system is exhibited in Figure 3–16. The actual rate of progress of thread construction and test may be plotted against the planned rate to provide visibility into system development status.

The basic testing strategy of the threads approach is recounted:

- The testing consists of a succession of thread tests. Each thread test regression tests the capabilities of previous threads and culminates in a build demonstration.
- Each build demonstration is a partial dry run of the final acceptance test.
- Each build accumulates the capabilities of previous builds and, thus, the final acceptance test is a natural culminating event in a series of build demonstrations.

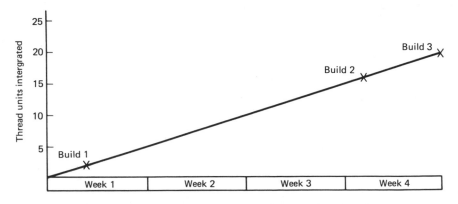

**Figure 3-16**  DC network analysis thread production plan.

The configuration for each thread test is diagrammed in Figure 3–17. Examination of the test configurations illuminates the following salient points:

1. Stubs are utilized generously to fill out the software configuration mainly as a result of the execution order nature of the threads approach.

2. Stubs are incrementally replaced by operational modules in the configuration as each thread is added.

3. The insertion of a new operational module into the configuration, in many cases, requires the creation of additional stubs subordinate to the new module.

The incremental build-up process is now narrated:

1. The thread 1 test requires the use of stubs for the modules VOLT and OUTPUT.

2. The thread 8 configuration replaces the OUTPUT stub with the actual code and necessitates the creation of stubs for the modules subordinate to OUTPUT.

3. The largest thread in the system, thread 2, inserts the operational module VOLT in place of an existing stub. A number of modules subordinate to VOLT are also added to the hierarchy, including stubs for the modules SOLVE, NODAL, and DEBUG1.

4. Thread 3 consists of the substitution of the module DEBUG1 for a stub.

5. Module NODAL and modules INVERT, NCM, G2, and GN (subordinate to NODAL) implement thread 4. Stubs for ECV and DEBUG2 complete the configuration at this point.

6. The stub for ECV is replaced by the operational modules ECV and JN in order to mechanize thread 5. A stub for module DEBUG3 is now required.

7. For thread 6, actual modules fill the place of stubs DEBUG2 and DEBUG3.

8. In thread 7, the stub for SOLVE is superseded by the operational module.

9. In threads 9, 10, 11, and 12, the stubs VBCALC, VECALC, IECALC, and IBCALC are incrementally replaced by operational modules.

The test configuration for thread 12 consists of the full system configuration and constitutes the final acceptance test.

The final planning measure entails defining the module construction sequence and making personnel assignments. The result of this process is displayed in Figure 3–18, which is the *programming assignments plan*. The personnel strategy here involves the assignment of a two-person programming team. Each team member is allotted responsibility for construction of specific modules. The emphasis is intended to be on team development. The team will function in a continuous walkthrough mode while reviewing the code collectively. The members will function in tandem while integrating and testing the threads.

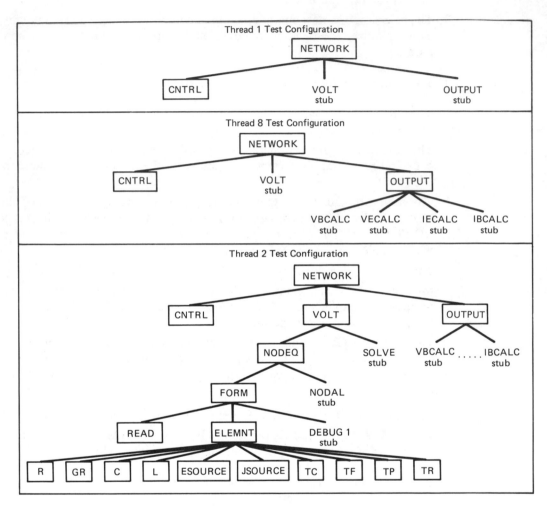

**Figure 3-17**  Thread test configurations.

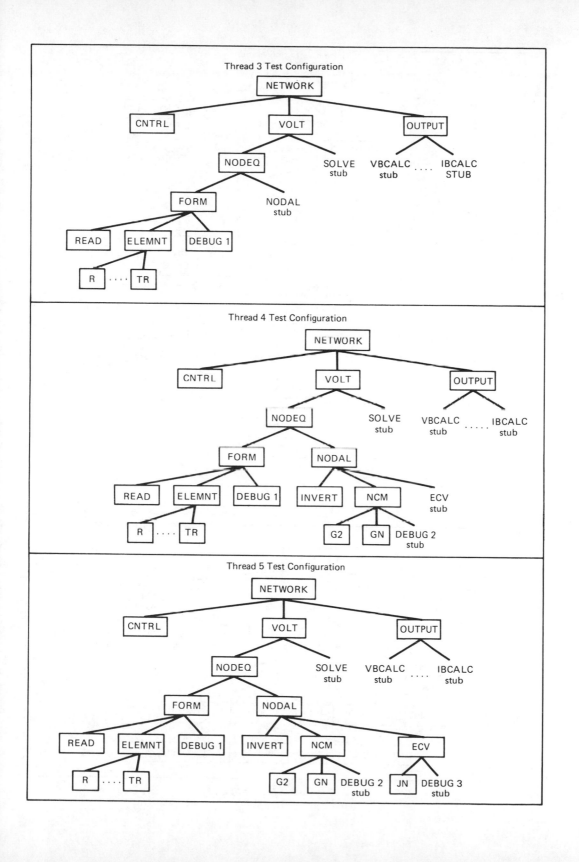

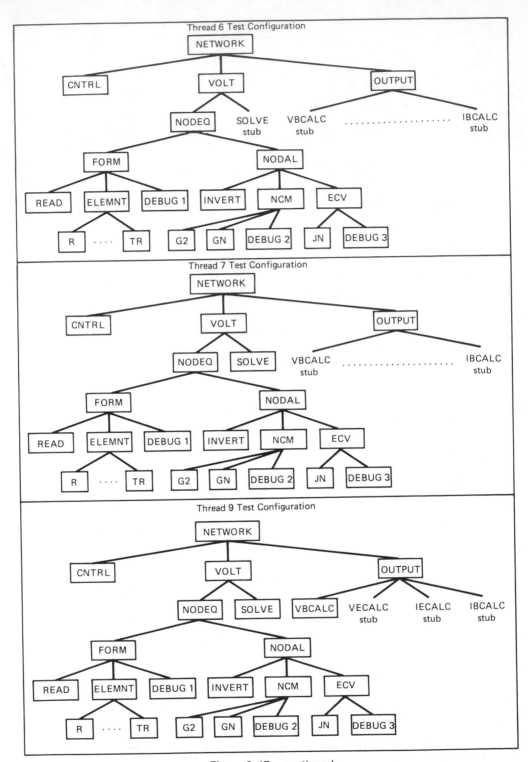

**Figure 3-17** *continued*

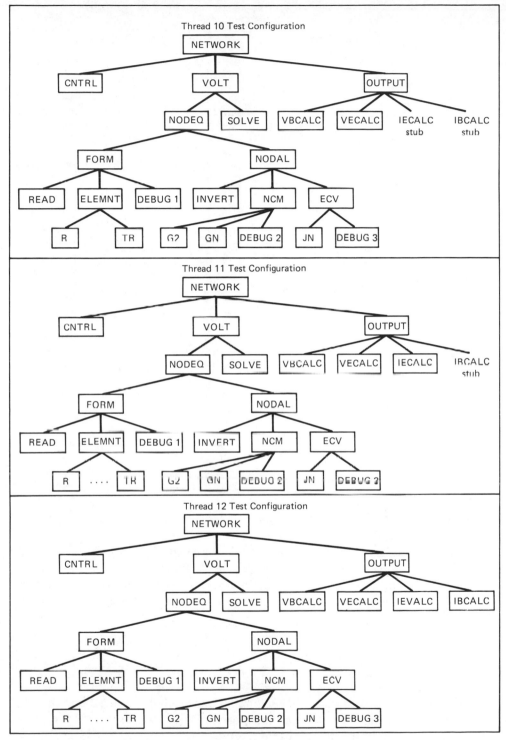

**Figure 3-17** *continued*

| Module | Thread | Due Date | Programmer |
|--------|--------|----------|------------|
| NETWRK | 1 | Day 1 | Person X |
| CNTRL | 1 | Day 1 | Person Y |
| OUTPUT | 8 | Day 2 | Person X |
| VOLT | 2 | Day 3 | Person Y |
| NODEQ | 2 | Day 3 | Person Y |
| FORM | 2 | Day 3 | Person X |
| READ | 2 | Day 3 | Person X |
| ELEMNT | 2 | Day 4 | Person Y |
| R | 2 | Day 4 | Person Y |
| GR | 2 | Day 4 | Person X |
| C | 2 | Day 5 | Person Y |
| L | 2 | Day 5 | Person Y |
| ESOURCE | 2 | Day 5 | Person X |
| JSOURCE | 2 | Day 5 | Person X |
| TC | 2 | Day 6 | Person Y |
| TF | 2 | Day 6 | Person Y |
| TP | 2 | Day 6 | Person X |
| TR | 2 | Day 6 | Person X |
| DEBUG1 | 3 | Day 7 | Person Y |
| NODAL | 4 | Day 8 | Person X |
| INVERT | 4 | Day 8 | Person X |
| NCM | 4 | Day 9 | Person Y |
| G2 | 4 | Day 9 | Person Y |
| GN | 4 | Day 10 | Person X |
| ECV | 5 | Day 11 | Person Y |
| JN | 5 | Day 12 | Person X |
| DEBUG2 | 6 | Day 13 | Person Y |
| DEBUG3 | 6 | Day 14 | Person X |
| SOLVE | 7 | Day 16 | Persons X and Y |
| OUTPUT | 9 | Day 17 | Person X |
| VBCALC | 9 | Day 17 | Person Y |
| VECALC | 10 | Day 18 | Person X |
| IECALC | 11 | Day 19 | Person Y |
| IBCALC | 12 | Day 20 | Person X |

**Figure 3-18**  Network analysis system programming assignments plan.

The dc network analysis system has been the focus of the demonstration of an end-to-end planning procedure utilizing the threads approach. Even though this is a very small system, the procedure that has been described and demonstrated entirely parallels the planning steps that would be used for a larger system.

## 3.5

## Integration and Test of Larger Systems

To some extent, the description of the threads approach has understated the complexity of modern software development projects by addressing a software system as a single development entity. Many software projects are too large and the schedule too short to manage in this fashion. The software system is decomposed into structural elements that are developed in parallel and are eventually integrated to recompose the system; on military-standard software developments, this element is referred to as the computer program configuration item (CPCI). A subset of the threads technology is an effective means of organizing the integration phase of multi-CPCI systems. Basically, the approach is similarly driven by system-level threads derived from a system-level specification. These system-level threads are correlated with CPCIs or sub-CPCIs in lieu of modules.

To further explain the application of the threads approach to integration testing, we shall use as an example an *activity planning system* for an automated production facility. The basic function of this system is to define possible production jobs, optimize a schedule of jobs, and issue commands for the equipment and instructions for the operators. The system size is approximately 150,000 higher-order-language source lines of code. The software configuration is shown in Figure 3–19.

This is an interactively controlled system running on a critical timeline but not in real time. The system consists of five loosely coupled CPCIs. Strings of CPCIs or sub-CPCIs are configured under control of predefined job control language command procedures to accomplish the required operational sequences; there is no executive program except the operating system. The *job requirements management* CPCI (JRM) accepts operator inputs from a display terminal defining requested production jobs; these job definitions are maintained in a data base. The *job opportunities* CPCI (JOP) prepares a sequence of jobs that can possibly be performed at any given time based on the equipment configuration and the assumption that the full resources of the equipment are available. The *job scheduling* CPCI (JSCH) trades off the demands of conflicting job opportunities and optimizes a job schedule based on job priorities and a model of job resource consumption. The *job commanding* CPCI (JCMD) issues machine-readable commands for the production equipment and provides hardcopy instructions for human operators based on the optimized schedule. The *job performance assessment* CPCI (JPA) receives feedback on jobs actually performed during the previous day's production and adjusts job priorities accordingly for the upcoming day's activities.

In summarizing from the system requirements specification, there are two basic operational sequences required of the system:

1. An automatic activity planning sequence to define a schedule for the next day's production
2. A quick-modification planning sequence by which operator-entered high-priority jobs can be interjected into the schedule

For the planning of this integration effort, we will assign each of these operational sequences to a build or superthread. The processing sequence for these two builds is exhibited in Figure 3–20. The component CPCIs and sub-CPCIs have previously been constructed and tested using the full procedure described in Sections 3.1 through 3.4 of this chapter.

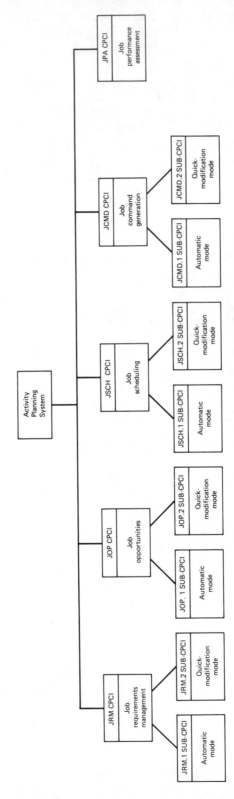

**Figure 3-19** Activity planning system software configuration.

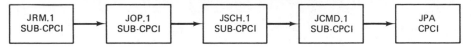

Build A — Automatic Processing Sequence

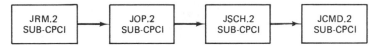

Build B — Quick-Modification Processing Sequence

**Figure 3-20** Integration build processing sequences.

Each build is now subdivided into constituent threads. This breakdown is indicated below:

1. Build A — Automatic Processing Sequence
   a. Thread A.1 — Define Jobs. This is implemented by the JRM.1 sub-CPCI.
   b. Thread A.2 — Define Job Opportunities. This is implemented by the JRM.1 and JOP.1 sub-CPCIs.
   c. Thread A.3 — Produce Job Schedule. This is implemented by the JRM.1, JOP.1, and JSCH.1 sub-CPCIs.
   d. Thread A.4 — Generate Job Commands. This is implemented by the JRM.1, JOP.1, JSCH.1, and JCMD.1 sub-CPCIs.
   e. Thread A.5 — Evaluate Job Performance. This is implemented by the JRM.1, JOP.1, JSCH.1, and JCMD.1 sub-CPCIs and the JPA CPCI.
2. Build B — Quick-Modification Processing Sequence
   a. Thread B.1 — Define Quick-Modification Job. This is implemented by the JRM.2 sub-CPCI.
   b. Thread B.2 — Define Quick-Modification Job Opportunities. This is implemented by the JRM.2 and JOP.2 sub-CPCIs.
   c. Thread B.3 — Produce Modified Schedule. This is implemented by the JRM.2, JOP.2, and JSCH.2 sub-CPCIs.
   d. Thread B.4 — Generate Modified Commands. This is implemented by the JRM.2, JOP.2, JSCH.2, and JCMD.2 sub-CPCIs.

The incremental integration build-up process is summarized on the build plan contained in Figure 3–21. Each integration thread may also be assigned points, and progress of the effort may be visualized by maintaining a production plan chart like those previously presented in Figures 3–9 and 3–16.

The threads approach for integration of larger systems can be applied on a slightly less formal basis; for example, it may be possible to forego the system

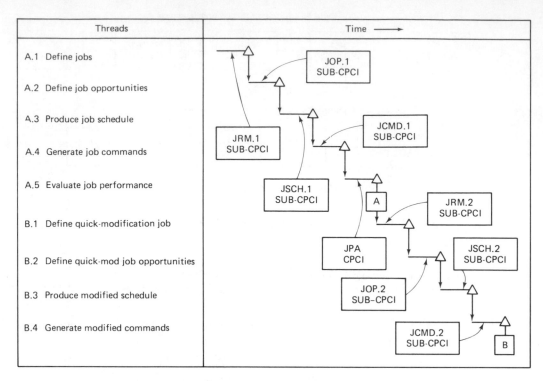

**Figure 3-21**   Integration build plan.

verification diagram and define threads on an *ad hoc* basis. The same basic benefits of the approach are realized. These merits are summarized in a concluding section.

## 3.6

## Summary and Conclusion

The benefits of the thread testing approach may be summarized as

- Allows testing and analysis in digestible quantities
- Provides early demonstration of key functional capabilities
- Forces the early availability of executable code
- Provides a meaningful measurement of project progress that is easily understood
- Defines module construction sequence and serves as a basis for allocating personnel resources
- Brings a degree of formality to software project verification and validation by validating that the end item satisfies requirements and by verifying that the end item implements the design

- Because of the analogy of thread/builds to operational functions, mission analysts can interact earlier in the testing process to scrutinize performance results

The essence of the approach may be summarized by the cliche "Build a little then test a little." This makes progress measurements feasible. Testing in small doses makes error isolation easier by requiring consideration of only a manageable small amount of program logic. This method is in contrast to "Build it all at once, throw it all together, and hope it works"; it almost always doesn't.

# Supplemental Testing Topics

---

This chapter presents a potpouri of additional software testing topics that both dovetail and, in certain instances, contrast with the methodology described in the previous chapter. In particular, much of the upcoming material focuses on software testing from a structural standpoint; to some extent this is a conflicting philosophy to the functional foundation advocated in Chapter 3. Other topics, such as the sections on size considerations and error trends, are of overall relevance and transcend this difference. The views of others are strongly relied upon to present a balanced picture in these topical discussions.

## 4.1

## Test Planning Prior to Full-Scale Development

An overall software production approach is normally established by the contractor before entering into the full-scale development phase of the system life cycle. The vehicle for establishing such an approach may be the contractor's proposal or, in the case of more complex systems, special contract definition studies performed prior to full-scale development. The factors addressed in defining the production approach include software design objectives, software test approach, software performance measures and standards, deliverable software requirements, and software documentation requirements.[1] Each of these factors will have verification and validation implications.

The early specification of software design objectives increases the overall effectiveness and efficiency of the programming function in relation to the available manpower and hardware resources.[2] It is here that design standards that produce an easily testable system should be specified, for example, the utilization of modular or structured design and programming practices. Requirements on the applications software should be identified to provide the necessary interfacing with automatic testing aids to be utilized that are available or are expected to be available for the development. Objectives and standards involving error detection, fault isolation, and data recovery that aid the testing of the software should be stated. Also, specific modes of system operation that will be used to support testing should be defined.

A software test approach should be outlined, addressing the following specific factors and goals:[3]

- Identification of multiple levels of contractor testing
- Creation of test requirements and specifications
- Preparation of test scripts and procedures oriented toward compliance with test objectives and requirements.
- Demonstrations of system integrity, serviceability, and performance in stressed situations
- Use of a test and integration group autonomous from the developers
- Testing of the overall system at both production and operational sites
- Verification of documentation
- Training of user personnel with operation and maintenance of the system as part of the testing effort
- Handling of software change proposals emanating from testing activities

A testing philosophy is recommended. The trade-offs of top-down versus bottom-up testing and phased versus incremental integration should be evaluated on a preliminary basis within the context of the system under consideration.

The responsibilities for the various levels of testing should be established. These will include informal testing conducted by the development contractor for which no formal customer consent is required; formal testing conducted by the development contractor at the contractor's plant for which customer witness and

---

[1] D. W. Kelliher, *Software Quality Assurance and Production Control Practices in the Acquisition of Large Systems* (McLean, Va.: MITRE, 1975), Technical Report MTR–6906, pp. xi–xii.

[2] Kelliher, op. cit., p. I–3.

[3] Kelliher, op. cit., p. I–6.

sign-off is required; and formal testing conducted by the integration and test contractor at the operational site.

Software performance measures and standards should be specified so as to initiate a foundation for assessing the quality of the software.[4] An early comprehensive effort directed toward defining these measures and standards will make a major contribution toward providing a direction to the verification and validation effort. As a minimum, an inclusive list of major performance metric parameters should be delineated before full-scale development goes into effect. Preferably, acceptance standards for many of the measures should also be developed; of course, some of the performance standards cannot be reasonably identified until the developer is well into the full-scale development effort, despite the magnitude of the investigation at an early time. Some examples of performance measures are: computing capacity utilization, storage utilization, response times, period between successive operations of periodic functions, and startup/startover times.[5]

The deliverable software requirements are represented by a list of computer program configuration items (CPCIs) that are to be delivered with the system to the customer. This list contains operational software items and support software items. The support software includes programs that are used as aids for developing new operational programs, for entering new data into the system, for test and analysis, and for software and hardware maintenance.[6] Not all support programs will necessarily be deliverable items (such as test tools), and these may be developed with some leniency in documentation, configuration control, and testing requirements. However, in the case of Department of Defense systems, as indicated in DOD directives, all unique support items required to develop and maintain the delivered computer resources over the system's life cycle are now specified as deliverable, in which case they should be developed under the same standards as other deliverable items. All major support programs, particularly automated testing tools, should be identified early in order to correctly scope the magnitude of the entire software development. Experiences with large software projects indicate that support software is a major source of underestimation whenever cost overruns occur.

The software documentation requirements are represented by a list of documents required to be delivered over the duration of the software development contract. Included on this list are test specifications and reports. The contents and formats of these documents should be defined before the full-scale development begins. For example, the specification document for each individual test might typically contain a statement of prerequisite conditions, test equipment, inputs, outputs, support resources, error messages, completion codes, personnel requirements, interfaces, data bases, measurement and analysis methods, tolerances, time estimates, storage and recording requirements, and clear pass/fail criteria.[7]

The resolution to many of the issues just explored will depend heavily upon

---

[4] Kelliher, op. cit., p. I–11.
[5] Kelliher, op. cit., p. I–11–13.
[6] Kelliher, op. cit., p. I–15.
[7] Kelliher, op. cit., p. I–8.

the size of the system involved. Some of the implications of system size are investigated next.

## 4.2
## Software Development Size Considerations

It is intuitively reasonable to assert that a larger software package will require a more extensive testing effort than would a smaller package (assuming, hypothetically, that all other things are equal). Independent of other factors, the size of the eventual software end product is directly related to the complexity of the development both from a technical and managerial standpoint. This is illuminated by the consideration that a larger program almost invariably produces a larger number of critical logical paths that must be checked and thus requires a larger staff of people. This increased complexity associated with the growing number of contemporary large software projects has been a motivator for the development of automated software testing tools.

The schedule requirements of customers have necessitated the development of large amounts of software over relatively short durations. Such tight schedules compel performing organizations to be more productive per unit of time. This is traditionally approached, sometimes with regret, by applying a large number of people to the problem. As more personnel become involved, the number of transactions between these people increases. The sensitivity to human fallibilities is magnified. There are more opportunities for mismatches of assumptions and logical reasoning to develop and assert a negative influence. The potential for these incompatibilities to influence the quality of the product needs to be considered when planning the testing effort.

Yourdon[8] has classified software projects into discrete categories, using source statement size. His categorization ranges from simple programs that are less than 1000 source statements to what he describes as "utterly absurd programs" that contain between 1 million and 10 million statements. For each category, he specifies the approximate number of programmers involved, the schedule length, number of software elements, and the number of subsystems. These parameters may be interpreted to identify the escalating extent and complexity of the testing that would be necessary for each category. Software systems in Yourdon's "absurd" category have been built, but these systems, with few exceptions, have not been delivered within originally planned schedules and budgets.

## 4.3
## Software Testing Strategies

A software system is typically organized in a hierarchical structure and is composed of subsystems and lower-level components. The lowest-order component is denoted here as the *unit* (alternately called a *module*). The philosophy of testing at the unit

---

[8] Yourdon, *Techniques of Program Structure and Design* (Englewood Cliffs, N. J.: Prentice-Hall, 1975), pp. 249–54.

level differs from that of integration testing in which the units are interconnected to form higher-level components. The following discussion addresses first unit testing and then integration testing philosophies.

## UNIT TESTING PHILOSOPHIES

For all but the most simple software project, it is usual and prudent to approach testing in a progressive hierarchical manner, beginning at the software unit level. This is because the software, when viewed at the system level, can be understood only in terms of its higher-level components. The intricacies of the actual code cannot be intellectually grasped at that level. Deferring testing until the entire software system can be assembled would be a disastrous experience. Error detection, description, isolation, and rectification would be extremely difficult, if not impossible, and would, at the least, be economically infeasible. A large data base of experience has verified that it is less costly to discover and rectify errors early in the development cycle. For these reasons, testing is begun at the unit level. It is at this level that the code can be most easily comprehended and viewed.

It is easier to test software exhaustively in small units. It is here that structurally oriented testing goals, such as number of logical paths traversed, percentage of statements executed, number of possible inputs to be tested, and so on, are applied. The expectation is that a very large percentage of errors will be discovered and corrected at this level, where the cost of doing so will be minimal. It is less feasible, both technically and economically, to attain these objectives after software units are interconnected. The testing on this level emphasizes the verification of logic, computations, data handling, time, and sizing.

The goals of logic testing involve the exhaustive exercise of the program code and its component logic structures. The coverage is usually measured according to the amount of source code exercised by the test or by the number of logical paths traversed out of the possible number that exist. Computational testing verifies the quantitative accuracy of the results of operation of the software. Data handling testing ensures that input data is properly ingested, output data is stored in the proper location and format, data conversions have been properly performed, bad data is properly handled, data is not improperly discarded, and timing is within specified limits.

## INTEGRATION TESTING PHILOSOPHIES

After successful unit-level testing, the units are connected to determine whether they function together in tandem. This integration will assemble the software into larger components. The assembly process will progress to the integration of the software into subsystems and then finally culminate at the system level where the subsystems are connected together. Integration testing treats the software at the component level rather than at the detailed level of the code that was the subject of unit testing. Thus, the main testing emphasis is on the interaction between software components and their interfaces. As the software is built up into higher-level components, it becomes possible to demonstrate complete processing functions. This, then, allows the validation of performance requirements. Thus, testing assumes a functional theme at this point.

At the system level, subtle errors resulting from the complex interaction between pieces of software never before interconnected will be exposed. The deterrent to surprises in this phase of the testing is thorough and comprehensive testing at lower levels. Despite the best efforts of all involved, some errors will still remain undetected until the system-level test. A high-quality testing effort at earlier levels will, nonetheless, limit the severity and number of these errors.

Up to this point, the testing has likely occurred within the contractor's facility. This has been in a controlled environment, using artificially contrived test case data. On the basis of this testing, it cannot be firmly demonstrated that the software system will perform ably in its actual operating environment. Thus, additional testing is required in the field where the software will eventually operate. At least one and perhaps several additional tests will be necessary at the operational site. It is here that the software system is tested in the actual computers and hardware environment where it is intended to reside. These tests will be run under live conditions and in conjunction with other software that may be competing for the resources of the system. It is customary that the actual users eventually run the system in an operational manner. This testing is usually referred to as *acceptance testing* or *field testing*.

## 4.4
## Methods for Combining Software Components

The assembly and testing of software organized in a hierarchical structure may be approached in several ways. The options of choice occur in two categories—phased versus incremental and top-down versus bottom-up. In practice, it is often the case that the selection in each category is not monolithic, and hybrid approaches are applied. A reference software component structure is diagrammed in Figure 4–1.

The distinction between phased and incremental integration is best explained by example. The phased approach would typically consist of first testing components (2,2,0), (2,2,1), (2,2,2), (2,2,3), and (2,2,4) from Figure 4–1 individually. The next step would be to interconnect these four components and test them as the next higher-level component CPCI G (Figure 4–1). A colorful commentary on the phased approach is provided by Yourdon and Constantine:

> The phased approach to implementation could be described in the following (slightly tongue-in-cheek) manner:
>
> 1. Design, code, and test each module by itself. (Commonly known as "unit test.")
> 2. Throw all the modules into a large bag.
> 3. Shake the bag very hard. (Commonly known as "system integration and test.")

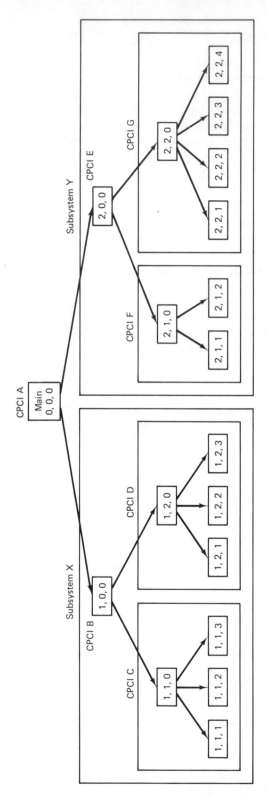

**Figure 4-1**  Representative software component structure.

4. Cross your fingers and hope that it all works. (Commonly known as "field test.")[9]

The major liability associated with this approach is that, in simultaneously combining all four components (previous example), the next incident of failure or error cannot be easily associated with the malfunctioning component(s). Thus, fault isolation is difficult.

An analogous description of the incremental approach is offered by Yourdon and Constantine:

> In contrast, some programmers follow an incremental approach to testing. This approach can be paraphrased in the following manner:
>
> 1. Design, code, and test one module by itself.
> 2. Add another module.
> 3. Test and debug the combination.
> 4. Repeat steps 2 and 3.
>
> The essential characteristic of this approach, then, is that we are adding only one new (and potentially "buggy") module to the system at a time.[10]

The obvious advantage of the incremental approach over the phased approach is that the process is self-focusing on the source of new errors. Any new malfunction is caused either by a defect in the most recently added component or by some new interaction between the new component and the rest of the system. A regression back to the previous state of the system before the new component was added is easily accomplished. This is a valuable attribute, not present with the phased approach, that facilitates a systematic investigation into the causes and sources of errors.

Any permutation of phased/incremental with top-down/bottom-up is potentially viable, depending on the specific circumstances. An approach in the first category is not married to an approach in the second category; the choice is independent.

For large, complex systems, it is most common that integration of the large software components is carried forward in a bottom-up manner. This might typically consist of the sequence of CPCI tests, subsystem tests, and the system test. This chronological progression starts at the lower level of the hierarchy (CPCI) and culminates at the highest level (system). In Figure 4–1, CPCI's B,C,D,E,F, and G would be assembled and tested individually. The modules would then be assembled to form subsystems X and Y. These subsystems would then be integrated to construct the entire system.

The top-down approach begins at the top of the structure and then proceeds to test components at progressively lower levels in the hierarchy. For example,

---

[9] Edward Yourdon and Larry L. Constantine, *Structured Design: Fundamentals of a Discipline of Computer Program and Systems Design,* © 1979, pp. 377–89. Reprinted by permission of Prentice-Hall, Inc., Englewood Cliffs, New Jersey.

[10] Yourdon and Constantine, op. cit., pp. 377–89.

referring to CPCI C in Figure 4–1, component (1,1,0) would be tested first, with testing of components (1,1,1), (1,1,2), and (1,1,3) to be achieved later.

Bottom-up integration requires *drivers*. A driver exercises the software component that is the present testing target by simulating the activity of the next higher-level component. Top-down integration requires *stubs*. A stub is a dummy component that simulates the functioning of the next component(s) subordinate to the component that is the present testing target. Yourdon and Constantine may be referred to for detailed information on the attributes of drivers and stubs.

In reality, a combined top-down/bottom-up approach to testing and integration is most frequently the case. In Figure 4–1, components (0,0,0), (1,0,0), and (2,0,0) are actually CPCIs. Although not shown, such CPCIs probably will have an infrastructure similar to C, D, F, and G. CPCIs (0,0,0), (1,0,0), and (2,0,0) typically might be developed in parallel with C, D, F, and G. The testing of the elements internal to each CPCI may be accomplished with either approach, depending upon the circumstances. The test configurations for each CPCI are charted in Figure 4–2. Usage of both drivers and stubs is indicated. It can be seen that testing at the CPCI level proceeds from both the bottom and top of the hierarchy. The subsystem test configurations are shown in Figure 4–3. CPCI A, if it is available at the

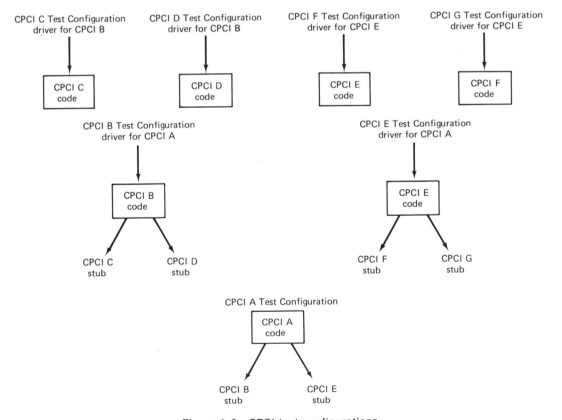

**Figure 4-2** CPCI test configurations.

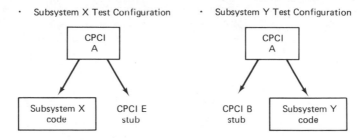

**Figure 4-3** Subsystem test configurations.

time, would be coupled to subsystems X and Y for individual testing of these subsystems. A driver would be substituted for CPCI A if it were not available in time for subsystem testing. The stubs for CPCIs B and E are incrementally replaced by the actual subsystems. For the system-level test, all drivers and stubs would be replaced by the actual modules.

The structure shown in Figure 4–1 is representative for a system contained in a single computer. In more complicated multiprocessor systems, particularly for realtime applications, the system is contained in several (or more) digital hardware units, both programmable computers and special purpose processors. These systems cannot be represented by a tree-like structure with centralized control at the top. The invocation structure will likely involve data-driven or interrupt-driven interfaces between computers.

Yourdon and Constantine have provided an extensive discussion on the virtues of both the top-down and bottom-up approaches. They first examined each of the supposed benefits of top-down testing. Excerpts from this discussion are:

*Top-Down Testing Eliminates System Testing and Integration*

This is generally true, but it is a characteristic of incremental testing, not top-down testing per se . . . top-down testing tends to be done in an incremental fashion, while most bottom-up testing has traditionally been done in a phased manner.

There is nothing to prevent the disciplined programmer from following a bottom-up incremental testing approach. Similarly, there is nothing to prevent the undisciplined programmer from following a phased top-down testing approach!

*Top-Down Testing Tests the Most Important Things First*

. . . In some systems, the modules at the bottom of the hierarchy are critically important, and it could be advantageous to test them first.

For example, in a real-time system with stringent processing requirements, the most critical problems may be at the bottom of the hierarchy. . .

If interface problems . . . are anticipated—and it is reasonable to expect them in any project involving more than one team of programmers—then the top-down testing does have some distinct benefits.

... The situation of a large, real-time system developed by multiple teams in geographically remote areas of the country: We may anticipate serious problems at both the bottom and the top of the hierarchy. We have no simple answers here: there may in fact be an argument for implementing from the top down and from the bottom up, at the same time.

### Top-Down Testing Allows Users to See a Preliminary Version of the System

A skeleton version of a system can be demonstrated to the users to ensure that the programmers are implementing the system that the users requested ...

It is important to realize that if a complete structural design has been accomplished, the programmer can choose to implement any sub-system first; some lower-level sub-systems may be valuable and productive to the user on a "stand-alone" basis.

### Top-Down Testing Allows One to Deal with Problems More Gracefully

... If the circumstances (which may be beyond our control) are such that the entire system is not finished when the deadline arrives, which parts of the system would we prefer to have finished and demonstrable?

With a *traditional* or phased bottom-up approach, there is a good chance that the programmer will have finished all of the coding and possibly all of the "unit testing." However, there is an equally good chance that the "brown bag" test will have failed—that is, none of the pieces work together because of a bug in one or more modules. From the user's point of view, there is nothing *tangible* that works ...

The top-down approach, on the other hand, is more likely to result in a skeleton that will show some tangible evidence of working. ...

### Debugging Is Easier with Top-Down Testing

This is not really a characteristic of top-down implementation, but rather of incremental implementation ... debugging is considerably easier if we add only one new (and potentially "buggy") module at a time to an existing combination of debugged modules.

### Requirements for Machine Time are Distributed More Evenly throughout a Top-Down Project

If we analyze the situation closely, though, we find that the phenomenon is caused by incremental testing—not by top-down testing per se. That is, every day we add one new module to the existing system and run through all the test data again--hence we use about the same amount of computer test time each day.

### Programmer Morale Is Improved

This point deserves to be emphasized! It is not just the users and the... managers who are pleased by the tangible evidence of progress in a typical top-down project—the programmers also derive a great sense of satisfaction from seeing something that actually runs to end-of-job at an early stage in the implementation process.

*Top-Down Coding and Testing Substitutes for Complete Design*

In the absence of a complete, prior structural design, coding and testing must proceed entirely or essentially in a top-down manner because the bottom-level modules are not known![11]

Yourdon and Constantine note that the best justification for bottom-up testing concerns the situation in which a large portion of system "criticality mass" is located in low-level modules. If the system has only a few critical low-level modules, they add, the project could return to the top-down approach after testing the critical low-level modules.

They also amplify on other considerations that might favor bottom-up implementation: As most systems would typically contain large numbers of modules at the bottom of the structural hierarchy, a favorite management technique has been to assign large numbers of programmers to work on these modules in parallel. Experiences have shown that, with this approach, serious interface problems develop between the low-level modules. However, this seems to be more associated with the ill-advised usage of the phased approach rather than bottom-up. Another problem occasionally encountered is the one in which an adequate volume of test case data can be generated only via a driver. In this situation, a bottom-up testing approach is appropriate for these modules.

## 4.5

## Error Trends throughout Testing

Examination of error report statistics gathered from the testing associated with a large-scale, complex, real-time development reveals some significant and interesting trends over the testing duration and the initial period of operations. Figure 4–4[12] exhibits the profile over time of the rate of errors reported for each successive phase of testing.

Within each testing category, the error report rate rises sharply (as the test team intensifies its efforts), reaches a peak, and then declines as the causes of the errors are isolated and then corrected. The error report rate again escalates as the testing progresses to the next phase. The peak rate of errors does show a steady decline with each progressive stage of testing. The explanation for the repetition of the error-rate ascent/descent profile appears to be twofold: (1) Each test is conducted by a different test team; the complacent disposition unconsciously developed by a test team concluding their testing effort is replaced by a fresh, unbiased outlook of a new test team initiating the next phase of testing; the fresh approach directly finds new sources of errors. (2) Each successive phase of testing will exer-

[11] Yourdon and Constantine, op. cit., pp. 377–89.
[12] This data was compiled and analyzed by Mr. J. L. McElrath of Hughes Aircraft Company.

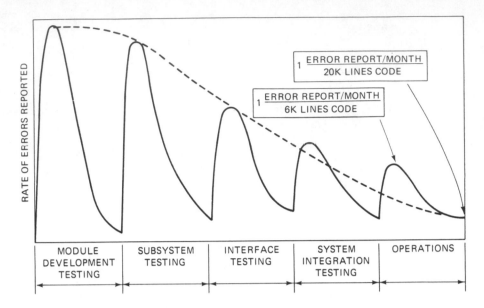

**Figure 4-4** Error trends over the testing cycle. (Michael S. Deutsch, "Verification and Validation," *Software Engineering,* ed. Jensen & Tonies, © 1979, p. 402, fig. 5-30. Reprinted by permission of Prentice-Hall, Inc., Englewood Cliffs, N.J.)

cise more extensive and complex interactions between software elements that were not previously tested, thus discovering more errors. Nelson[13] documents a very similar error trend from statistics reported from the Site Defense Program; he notes that logical errors tend to be discovered early in the testing while inaccuracies are detected later.

Some residual errors are usually accepted at the end of each phase, provided that they are not critical in nature. The testing phase is concluded as a practical matter, and the liens are carried into the next test phase. There is a tendency at the higher levels of integration to reach closure of the test phase with a higher rate of residual errors. This situation exists because the more complex processing interactions not previously tested produce deficiencies that require more time to rectify than might be available within the scheduled duration of the test. This practice of early closure is not necessarily advocated on a technical basis as it may, if not cautiously handled, produce an unstable baseline for the next phase. What is evident is the exercise of management's prerogative (both buyer and seller collectively) to show compliance with intermediate schedule milestones.

At the onset of operations, Figure 4-4 shows the incidence of errors declining from one error report per month for each 6000 lines of code to one error report per month for each 20,000 lines of code at a steady-state level. This error profile might be predicted to recur each time a new software version is introduced to the system.

[13] Eldred C. Nelson, "Software Reliability, Verification and Validation," in *Proceedings of the TRW Symposium on Reliable, Cost-Effective, Secure Software* (Redondo Beach, Ca.: TRW, 1974), pp. 5-16-17.

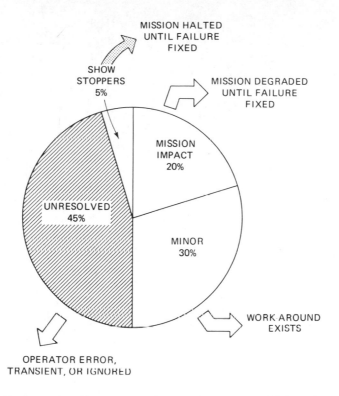

**Figure 4-5** Operational error reports by severity category. (Michael S. Deutsch, "Verification and Validation," *Software Engineering*, ed. Jensen & Tonies, ©1979, p. 404, fig. 5-31. Reprinted by permission of Prentice-Hall, Inc., Englewood Cliffs, N.J.)

Two possible explanations have been advanced for constant steady-state error detection rate after software is operational: (1) Correction of an error may produce the ripple effect by implanting other errors into the system. (2) Because in most software systems a small portion of the code is exercised most of the time, large sections of the code are minimally exercised with the result that errors in those sections are not discovered until much later.[14] Figure 4-5[15] shows the incidence of the steady-state errors by severity category. The collection of these statistics can aid in planning the level of effort required to maintain the software. However, such figures should be employed with some caution because the experiences on one project are not necessarily transferable to other projects.

The methodologies described in this chapter have addressed testing mainly from a structural view; that is, the test strategy is primarily influenced by the structure of the modules. Top-down and bottom-up testing are structural concepts. The

[14] C. V. Ramoorthy and Siu-Bun F. Ho, "Testing Large Software with Automated Software Evaluation Systems," in *IEEE Transactions on Software Engineering*, SE-1 (1975), pp. 48–49.

[15] This data was compiled and analyzed by Mr. J. L. McElrath of Hughes Aircraft Company.

weakness of these testing methodologies is their vague association with operational functions. The threads approach enumerated in Chapter 3 is strongly advocated by this author as a superior methodology because of the rigorous affiliation of modules under test with functional requirements. The threads methodology manifests itself in structural terms as an execution order construction and test scheme, neither top-down nor bottom-up.

# Special Testing Problems

Each particular system application requires individual consideration and tailoring of basic testing concepts to suit the particular system's needs. Every type of software application requires an analysis of system attributes in order to develop the most effective testing approach. Although there are an almost endless number of special data processing problems which could be addressed as to their peculiar testing needs, a few specialized areas of widespread interest have been selected for discussion in this chapter. These specialized subjects are

- Testing of real-time systems
- Testing of data dominated systems
- Testing during maintenance phase
- Testing of microprocessor firmware

The particular considerations, characteristics, and points of emphasis associated with these distinctive subject areas are explored in the following sections.

## 5.1
## Testing Real-Time Systems

Because real-time systems possess additional attributes that must be accorded special consideration in the testing process, special mention is provided here.

*Real-time* can be defined as:

Pertaining to the performance of computation during the actual time that the related physical process, event, or phenomenon transpires. . . . Thus, for computations to be considered as taking place in real time, they must proceed fast enough so as to permit the results to influence the related process that is under way.[1]

The ever-increasing volume and complexity of problems presented to industry and government (including the military) have led to more extensive application of data processing technology. Responding to this motivation, the development of technology has kept pace to some extent and has made itself more cost-effective hardwarewise. Thus, more and more critical functions that require quick responses to developing situations have been entrusted to data processing, such as air traffic control, control of industrial manufacturing processes, and control of guidance of satellites. In concert with the more prolific application of real-time data processing to critical functions are the potentially disastrous consequences that could result from software errors that cause malfunction or disablement of a system. The launch failure of the Mariner I spacecraft and the destruction of a French meteorological satellite occurred as a result of software errors.[2] Thus, the nature of real-time functions and the associated complex time-dependent interactions present additional problems not encountered by batch-oriented systems.

The criticality of the functions (more stringent timing and storage constraints) and the more competitive environment demand higher testing standards. Head[3] describes the testing problem in real-time systems as two fold:

1. More intensive testing is needed to achieve a reliable operational status.

2. It is more difficult to satisfy the higher testing standards.

Head[4] further identifies the attributes of real-time systems that complicate the testing effort. These are paraphrased as

1. Magnitude of programming effort—Many real-time systems have a very large number of programs that have to be interconnected and tested.

[1] Martin H. Weik, *Standard Dictionary of Computers and Information Processing* (New York: Hayden, 1969), p. 295.

[2] H. Hecht, "Fault-Tolerant Software for Real-Time Applications," *ACM Computing Surveys,* 8 (1976), p. 392.

[3] Robert V. Head, "Testing Real-Time Systems. Part 1: Development and Management," *Datamation,* July 1964, p. 42.

[4] Head, op. cit., pp. 42–48.

2. Repeatability—Because of slight differences in timing, the same sequence of test case inputs, phased slightly differently each time, may result in different outputs. This will be particulary evident on interactive systems that involve operator inputs from display consoles or remote terminals.

3. Equipment interaction: Multiprocessing—Many real-time systems involve multiple processors that must exchange information. Development of software typically is performed by machine-oriented groups of personnel who work in semi-isolation to produce their machine-peculiar subsystem. As two or more subsystems are tested and integrated, the impact of the lack of communication is felt.

4. Program interaction: Multiprogramming—Several programs will typically share the computer at the same time. Without strict control of interfaces, significant errors will result because of unplanned or erroneous program interaction.

5. Inherent logical complexity—Real-time systems will usually contain many more decision points or branches than batch-oriented, scientific computation problems.

6. Random access storage—Real-time systems typically access storage much more often in a random manner than sequentially. As a consequence, it is more difficult to discover and isolate problems.

Another consideration in the testing of real-time systems involves the credibility of testing in an environment other than the one in which the system will eventually operate. Testing is normally first performed at the developer's facility before moving on to the operational site. An extra effort is necessary to simulate with reasonable exactness the operating environment and live inputs. Such an effort improves the confidence of the customer or user that the system will operate properly in the operational environment.

The sometimes severe execution time constraints of real-time systems are attributes that require special consideration. Usually, most of the execution mass (and hence, the time consumption) is concentrated in two or three critical functions. Because of stringent timing requirements on the system, it may well be that the overall success of the development pivots on an early secureness of these few critical functions. Therefore, when formulating the build plan for the system, it would be in the best interests of the project to schedule implementation of the threads associated with these critical functions early in the development.

Most real-time systems involve communication exchanges that are initiated or driven by the availability of data that requires processing. This availability may be signalled by an *interrupt* sent from one processing element to another. These exchanges may be between programs operating in the same computer, between programs operating in separate computers, or between a program and an external digital hardware device. Included in this latter category might be a radar signal processor that provides position and range information, or a digitizer from a temperature sensor associated with a chemical manufacturing process. These communication exchanges may also be regarded as critical aspects of the system, and they should also be scheduled early in the project build plan.

Desmonde[5] has outlined a seven-phase testing procedure for a typical real-time system (which appears to be an interactive reservations system). The approach is oriented around the validation of threads. In this system, a thread is initiated by an entry from a remote terminal console. The testing begins with the exercise of single threads and then progresses to testing of multithreads. The testing phases are paraphrased here:

- *Phase I.* This consists of testing individual elements, testing of threads one at a time, and tracking of paths through each thread by using different inputs. A simulated control program is used in this phase. This provides the flexibility to use debugging aids, such as tracers and memory prints, that would most likely not be available with the actual control program.

- *Phase II.* This again tests threads one at a time and traces paths through the threads. However, in this phase the actual control program is utilized. Testing occurs by using only one entry at a time per thread.

- *Phase III.* The procedures from Phase II are repeated here while using more than one entry at a time for the same thread.

- *Phase IV.* This is the first time the entire configuration is tested. Simulated inputs are used to test more than one thread at a time in order to detect interference among threads. A major objective in this phase is to stress the system and determine its throughput capacity. This is accomplished by loading the queues to capacity and observing whether the system takes the proper emergency measures. Also, invalid messages are input in order to observe if they are appropriately rejected.

- *Phase V.* In this phase the on-line terminals are incrementally connected. The testing begins with a single-terminal, one-thread test and builds into a multiterminal test.

- *Phase VI.* The transition from artificial to real entries is made in this phase. Again, the number of terminals participating in the testing is gradually increased.

- *Phase VII.* This phase consists of a trial operation period. The period concludes when the incidence of bugs is reduced to an acceptable level, and the system performs smoothly.

A word of caution needs to be introduced here on the use of program measurement tools that instrument the code. The instrumentation introduces side effects. Significant changes in time and space (storage) may be incurred. As time and storage are key factors in real-time systems, automated test tools should be utilized with great caution.

The amount of difficulty encountered at each level of testing depends in-

[5] William H. Desmonde, *Real-Time Data Processing Systems: Introductory Concepts* (Englewood Cliffs, N.J.: Prentice-Hall, 1964), pp. 153–56.

versely on the thoroughness of testing at the previous level. This is applicable to all types of systems, but its importance is magnified with real-time systems. After a real-time system is operational, it becomes especially difficult to isolate and correct errors; thus, the importance of adequate preinstallation testing is amplified.

The problems encountered in the development of conventional data processing systems are magnified by the added complexity of real-time systems. It is, therefore, important that the system concept be validated before the start of implementation. This is often accomplished by modeling the system in an analytical simulation to verify timing, capacity, and throughput. Such simulations have also been used to determine allocation of storage and to determine which programs should be kept in other storage devices.[6]

During the design of the real-time system, equal attention must be directed toward the preparation of program test facilities. These include all the utility programs, test evaluation programs, and simulations necessary to execute the testing effort. The development of these programs must be planned in concert with the master project schedule so as to be available to support development and testing of the operational programs.

For real-time systems, it has frequently become necessary to use simulation to generate a sufficient volume of test input data to stress the system. For some systems, this has entailed simulating the output of various sensing devices such as radars. On interactive systems, simulators have been used to prepare scripts of input requests that normally would have been generated by operators at display consoles. Remote terminal simulators have been used to present input messages to the main computer before the terminals are in place. These simulation scripts provide a chronology of inputs that is identical from test run to test run; hence, repeatability of inputs is attained that would not be possible by using real operators, consoles, and terminals.

It is not uncommon in real-time system developments to expend at least as much labor to develop test tools as is used to develop the operational software.

## 5.2
## Testing Data-Dominated Systems

Data-dominated systems are characterized by large volumes of data residing in time-delayed storage and by the complexity of the data structures. The amount of effort required to design and build the data base is at least comparable to that of the programs. In data-dominated systems, the data-base structure, content, accessing methods, and integrity of the data are as important as the programs. Because of the criticality of the data base resource, testing of data-dominated systems takes on a perspective oriented toward demonstrating correctness of both programs and data.

A data base may contain certain information whose protection is vital to the owning organization. Data loss or unauthorized disclosure could compromise

---

[6] M. G. Ginzberg, "Notes on Testing Real-Time System Programs," *IBM Systems Journal,* 4 (1965), p. 58.

the organization's position or neutralize some of its assets. In general, because of the complexity and volume of data structures and security requirements, data-dominated systems are somewhat more difficult to test than program dominated systems. Several special considerations associated with testing of data-base-oriented systems are listed below:

- A long lead effort is required to build a test data base that is available for early use in program checkout and testing.
- Data base and program development/testing must be coordinated to ensure that security features such as passwords, privacy locks, and so forth are comprehensively tested.
- Planning must ensure the availability of utility programs which can edit or modify the basic data base to easily contrive additional test cases.
- Testing should demonstrate data base recovery and restoration techniques when system *crashes* occur.

Development planning should emphasize the early availability of a data base, even if it is a primitive version, to support program testing. The availability of more sophisticated simulation tools and portions of the operational software will refine the data base as the project proceeds.

Testing goals for data-dominated systems should derive from the requirements specification, as is true in the general case. The requirements spec would be expected to contain specific requirements pertaining to the data base that will serve as the basis for acceptance testing. For very large and complex data bases, a separate data-base requirements specification is sometimes generated. A comprehensive test of the data base would entail full exercise of all data base elements with successful processing results from the programs. However, unlike programs, tools for measurement of data base testing coverage are unfortunately very limited. Some data base management systems (DBMS) have transaction journals that can be used advantageously to support testing. The transaction journal provides a history of types of accesses, data accessed, and modifications to the data base. For file-based systems, practically no useful coverage measurement tools exist.

The term *data base* has been used generically to connote a time-delayed body of data. The implementation mechanism for the data base may be either a data base management system or a physical file system. A DBMS provides the advantages of

- Minimal dependency between programs and data
- Standard methods of accessing data
- Ease in modifying
- Ease in testing

Improved testability associated with a DBMS-based system comes about because of the basically more simple, standardized, and visible methods of accessing the data base on a logical basis rather than the more involved mechanisms associated with accessing physical files directly. The disadvantages of using a DBMS include longer access times and a larger development investment to implement the data base. In any trade-off of a DBMS versus a physical file system, the true life cycle costs of the decision should be factored in. The improved testability and maintainability of a DBMS may well turn out to offer a lower life cycle cost even though development costs may appear higher.

Data bases are used to provide common accessibility to data items by computer programs. They serve as one of the communication links connecting individual programs into an integrated software system. Because of their importance to computer program interfaces and their influence on a system's operational effectiveness, data bases implemented through a DBMS are designated as configuration items (DBCI). They are designed, tested, and documented in a manner similar to computer program configuration items (CPCI).

A DBCI is defined by a data dictionary. As shown in Figure 5-1, compilation and loading of a data dictionary results in a system-useable data base. DBCI's evolve through a similar life cycle as a CPCI. A data-requirements document is prepared for each DBCI. Based on the requirements document, a data dictionary design document is generated for each data base. DBCIs, like CPCIs, are formally evaluated by design reviews. After successful completion of a critical design review, the data dictionary is coded and checked out. Testing is governed by a formal test plan and procedure. After a data base is formally tested, it can be used to support testing of the CPCIs.

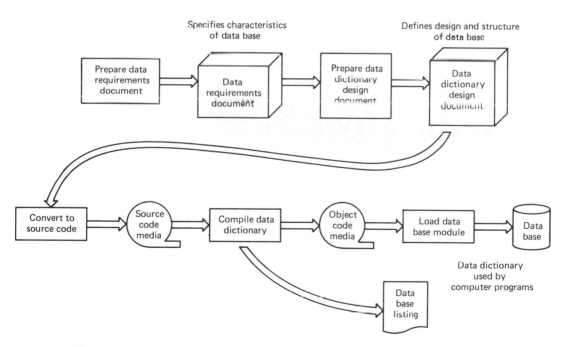

**Figure 5-1**  Activities and products included in a DBCI's life cycle. (Courtesy of Hughes Aircraft Company.)

## 5.3
## Testing during Maintenance Phase

Continuous modification of software after initial delivery occurs as a result of accrued experience with the use of the software and changing requirements. The magnitude of efforts involved in maintaining software is not intuitively obvious. For defense systems, it is not uncommon for 80% of the total software life cycle costs to be expended on maintenance. Commercial users of software frequently allocate 50% of their data processing budgets on maintaining existing programs. Based on these figures, it is a reasonable supposition that software maintenance is a subject area deserving individual emphasis and has historically not been given appropriate attention.

Changes required during maintenance may be due to

- Errors not discovered during original testing
- Failures outside the data processing system, which can be corrected by software changes
- Changing requirements for use of system
- Modifications to make people in system more efficient
- Modifications to make hardware and software more efficient
- Modifications to algorithms to take account of experience with real data

From consideration of these factors that cause changes during maintenance, it can be inferred that maintenance changes are partitionable into three categories—correction of errors, enhancements, and compensations for deficiencies in other parts of the system (including personnel). Modified operational software must be submitted to a series of tests that are similar to the testing of development software, as shown in Figure 5-2[7]. The extent of these tests will vary depending upon the magnitude of the changes. In many cases, particularly when the requirements specifications are unaffected by the changes, the original development test plans and procedures (or their subsets) can be used to design the retests.

In evaluating the extent of retesting required for a change or series of changes, one of the key analyses that must be performed is to identify the modules that have to be retested. The list of modules will include not only those modules in which changes were made but also the other modules possibly affected by repercussions of the changes. Automated tools such as the one described in Chapters 6 and 7 can assist this determination. By means of static analysis, this tool can easily identify the set of modules that invoke the changed module and the set of modules that the changed module invokes. The dynamic analysis capabilities, through instrumentation, can identify the path segments and single modules that remain untested on reexecution of the old test case set with the changed software. These untested path segments and modules then become the targets for additional retesting.

[7] *Hughes Software Engineering Manual* (Culver City, Ca.: Hughes Aircraft Co., 1980), Part VII, p. 1–2.

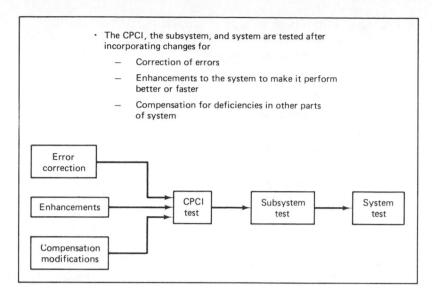

**Figure 5-2** Operational software thoroughly tested after changes.

Maintenance action is usually initiated by operations personnel. When the operation of the system appears to deviate from that which is expected and necessary to support mission operations, the experienced problem is documented along with all possible supporting data in a trouble report. Trouble reports are referred to the system engineering organization for an investigation of cause and recommendation of corrective action.

When the cause and source of errors is not self-evident, a troubleshooting team may be assigned to investigate. The team will isolate the cause of the problem using a procedure that includes:

- Review of the problem report and documentation to determine if a system or procedural problem exists

- Analysis of memory dumps, printouts, and recorded output and input

- Attempt to recreate the problem in a test environment by trying to establish the data and operational conditions which created the problem

- Careful review of the code and logic in the suspected area of the system. This includes application of a "what if?" type of mental exercise to identify bad logic and thus pinpoint the problem.

- Installation of traps and special diagnostic output that will provide more data on the problem when and if it recurs

- Careful collection of information regarding the conditions that existed during multiple occurrences of the problem until a condition is defined common to all occurrences[8]

[8] *Hughes Software Engineering Manual,* op. cit., 5-4.

A number of dispositions of a given trouble report are possible:

- Error in code or data base
- User procedures require correction
- User error
- User problem requires system improvement that exceeds requirements specifications
- Insufficient data to properly diagnose

Any recommended change arising from the disposition of a trouble report must be submitted as a formal change request to a change board. A change request to rectify an error can usually be unilaterally approved by the maintenance contractor. A system improvement would almost always require customer approval.

Approved change requests are referred to the responsible software organization for implementation. If the changes are significant enough to necessitate formal testing, the test program would be conducted by a test organization independent of the implementors.

Depending on the particular maintenance environment, changes may be installed continuously or in block changes. The continuous method involves installing small changes as they are developed and tested in response to approved change requests. This method of managing change incorporation has the following advantages:

- Responsiveness in that individual changes can be installed on the basis of priority
- Fault isolation such that new problems appearing after change incorporation can often be traced quickly to their source if a limited number of changes are installed at one time
- Planning in that it is easier to plan the installation of a small set of changes into an operational system as compared to the block change method, and operations would not be seriously impacted
- Minimized testing in that testing of the software system after change incorporation can be tailored around the specific changes being implemented[9]

The block change method entails grouping several or more changes for simultaneous incorporation. This method is more appropriate for changes of a substantial nature which require formal testing. The advantages of this installation approach are

- Efficiency in that multiple changes to the software in the same area of the system can be designed, tested, and installed together
- Continuous operation such that the operational system is not impacted between successive block changes

[9] *Hughes Software Engineering Manual,* op. cit., p. 5–0.

- Reduction in personnel on field assignment in that it is not necessary to retain large numbers of personnel at field locations on a permanent basis. The support for the block changes can be provided on a *temporary duty* (TDY) basis as a function of the size and nature of the changes[10]

The block change technique is almost essential for a facility that operates on a twenty-four hour per day basis.

A regression test philosophy can assure that software changes do not inadvertently propagate errors into other previously operable functions. During development, the testing program normally starts with small, simple test cases and then builds up to large, complex ones. With regression testing as applied to maintenance changes, the chronology is reversed. The complex test cases are run first. If these are unsuccessful, the simpler, localized cases are run to isolate the problem.

The use of a system may progress to a position that was not originally envisioned when the system was developed. If it is to play a more critical or crucial role, the customer may wish to revalidate the system with higher standards in mind. As part of such an effort, portions of the software may be upgraded to make it more fault-tolerant so that the system would continue to perform at some minimum level when faced with unexpected demands. In this situation, a retesting program would be undertaken during maintenance. The objective of the revalidation effort is to obtain a more reliable system. This would occur as a result of: (1) the fault-tolerance software upgrades, and (2) the retesting that forecloses on more of the opportunities for errors to occur. This sequence has occurred when a system that was originally developed as a backup to another system now assumes the primary role.

## 5.4
## Testing of Microprocessor Firmware

Special testing considerations of microprocessor firmware are intimately associated with the basic contrasts between firmware and software development. Firmware and software are markedly different. This is mainly because of major dissimilarities in the development support and operating environments of software and firmware. These differences are examined and certain implications of testing firmware are inferred in the following text.

Figure 5–3 provides a comparison of software and firmware development environments. The key development methodologies and tools normally associated with a modern software development are listed, and their applicability or utility to firmware are denoted. Key points of this comparison are

- Frequently, it is not possible to equip the operational microprocessor system with the I/0 devices and man/machine interfaces necessary for program development and testing. In such cases a development/test environ-

---

[10] *Hughes Software Engineering Manual,* op. cit., pp. 5-0, 5-1.

| Factor, Tool, Methodology | Software | Firmware |
|---|---|---|
| • Target computer | Frequently same as development computer | Development frequently not on target computer |
| • Structured analysis | Applicable | Applicable |
| • Structured design | Applicable | Applicable |
| • Higher order programming language | Almost universally used | Sometimes used |
| • Structured programming methodology | Relatively easy to implement | Very difficult to implement but possible |
| • Structured languages | Structured preprocessors and languages widely available | Not available |
| • Interactive programming | Commonly available | Sometimes available |
| • Debug aids | Sophisticated on-line debuggers available | Primitive debug tools |
| • Automated test assistance tools | Widely available | Not available |
| • Thread and build testing methodology | Applicable | Applicable |
| • Automated configuration management tools | Commonly available | Sometimes available |

**Figure 5-3** Comparison of software and firmware development environments.

ment is simulated in a general purpose computer, in which all the necessary services are available.

- Structured analysis (see Chapter 9), a means of constructing a readable and understandable requirements specification, is a valuable methodology for firmware and software.

- Structured design is applicable to both firmware and software.

- Higher-order languages (HOL) are available on some microprocessor systems. At present, the inefficiencies of HOLs on microprocessors neutralize many of their advantages.

- Structured programming is very difficult to implement on microprocessor when coding is done in assembly language.

- Structured programming languages, with occasional exceptions, are not available on microprocessor systems.

- Interactive editors for source code construction are available, but editors are of limited capabilities.

- Debugging is more difficult with microprocessors because of a lack of sophisticated debugging aids.

- Automated test assistance tools utilize resources not available with microprocessor systems.

- The thread and build testing methodology described in Chapter 3 is also an effective approach to firmware testing.

- Configuration management tools developed for general purpose computer environments usually require resources that exceed most microprocessor systems' capacity.

When a simulated development environment on a general purpose computer is used, a dual-faceted testing program must be carefully planned to ensure that conditions in the development/test environment reasonably represent operational conditions. This situation is not new or unique to microprocessors. Many systems with embedded computers such as fire control systems or on-board satellite processors have historically used a simulated development environment.

Debugging is very difficult with microprocessors. This is because of the absence of effective debug aids to locate errors and also because of the close interaction between the firmware and hardware. Basically, the typical contemporary microprocessor firmware development environment closely resembles the software development environments of the late 1950's.

Although microprocessors offer many advantages to the applications involved, the operating environment and characteristics of microprocessors present a number of difficulties. These include a minimum of standard input/output interfaces, a limited instruction set, and slow instruction execution times. A heavy testing emphasis is required to verify the tailored external hardware interfaces. Because of these constraints and limitations, there is a tendency to use clever tricks and coding techniques. This, of course, compounds the difficulties by making it harder to locate and correct errors.

In a recent spaceborne microprocessor application, a number of problems in planning the test effort were observed.[11] On this project, error isolation was extremely difficult; it was never clear whether the error source was in the firmware, read-only-memory, microprocessor, simulator, test procedure, or some external source. The actual test planning had to take place during conduct of the testing; it was also necessary to maintain the test procedures on a daily basis and to continually focus the test procedures on fault isolation.

Microprocessor firmware development generally takes place in a more primitive and less standard environment than software. Many of the tools and methodologies that have become standard in software developments have limited availability and application to firmware. In microprocessor systems, testing and error isolation are more difficult tasks because of the close interaction of firmware and hardware.

[11] Winston W. Royce, "A Look Forward—Microprocessor Software Development," in *Software Management Conference 1980,* p. 110.

# Automated Verification

# Automated Testing

## 6.1
### Motivation for Automation

The basic approach to software construction and testing presented in Chapter 3 prescribed that testing of each thread include the exercise of all path segments in the associated modules. This is an ambitious goal and perhaps costly to attain. In this chapter, the motivation for this objective is explored and tools which will help achieve this end are described.

As software systems have grown to immense proportions in both size and complexity, the effort required to test these systems has grown more than proportionately. The need for a mass application of human resources has arisen. This has been both costly and not particularly effective in terms of the reliability produced. Despite expenditures of up to one half of software development budgets for testing, significant numbers of errors remain in delivered software that often severely deter normal system operations. This situation has inspired the development of automatic test tools that assist in the production of effective tests and analyze the test results. In essence, much of the time-consuming, mechanical aspects of testing are taken out of human hands.

Automatic test tools provide the following attributes that are not as easily attained by manual testing approaches:

- Improved organization of testing through automation
- Measurement of testing coverage
- Improved reliability

Automatic tools furnish machine amplification of human capability and relieve test personnel of routine time-consuming chores. Even though routine, tasks such as manual error-checking are preferably removed from human hands. This is because manual error checking itself is an error-prone process performed more reliably through automation. Budget and schedule considerations foreclose on the slow, tedious process of manual testing with the result that volume of testing is often insufficient. Relief is available through utilization of automated tools.

The complex content of large software systems requires the application of many test cases to thoroughly exercise the code. The generation of the test cases and analysis of the paths exercised in order to determine the extent of the resulting testing coverage would quickly exceed human capacity. Testing aids can instrument the code, measure the coverage provided by a test case, and furnish a report that shows the number of times each statement and sequence of statements was executed.

Improved reliability results when potential sources and avenues of errors are more closely investigated; this occurs as more experience in the use of the software is accumulated through carefully directed testing. Automatic tools enable a higher volume of testing than would be attainable manually for the same cost. In addition to cost and time savings, other ancillary benefits are accrued through automation of testing:

- Automation brings rigor and engineering discipline to the testing process
- Use of an automated tool makes possible the enforcement and acceptance of exhaustive testing goals.

In this chapter, the subject of automated test assistance tools is explored through discussion of the following topics:

- Spectrum of applications of automated tools over the software life cycle
- Generic attributes of automated verification systems
- A commercial automated verification system
- An on-line debugging system

## 6.2
## Scope of Automated Tools

Practically the entire software development process can be assisted by some form of automated tool. An example breakdown of automated tools according to functional classification is provided below:

1. **Requirements analysis tools,** which provide facilities for statement of requirements in a formal language and perform automated consistency checks on the language syntax

2. **Computer-aided design**

   (a) *On-line design tools,* which interact with the designer from a display terminal and record the design in a machine-readable data base.

   (b) *Design quality measurements,* which quantitatively provide a measure of design goodness.

   (c) *Automated simulation tools,* which model a definition of the system architecture to determine its performance characteristics.

3. **Source program static analysis**[1]

   (a) *Tools for code analysis,* which perform syntax analysis on the source code and look for error-prone constructions.

   (b) *Tools for program structure checks,* which generate graphs and look for structural flaws.

   (c) *Tools for proper module interface checks,* which detect inconsistencies in the declaration of data structures and improper linkages among modules.

   (d) *Tools for event-sequence checking,* which compare event sequences in the program with conventions of event sequences (e.g., I/O sequences).

4. **Source program dynamic analysis**

   (a) *Tools for monitoring program run-time behavior,* which collect program execution statistics

   (b) *Tools for automated test case generation,* which aid testers to construct test cases that will comprehensively exercise the code

   (c) *Tools for checking assertions,* which detect violations of assertions embedded into the code by testers

   (d) *Tools for inserting software defenses,* which provide security measures to protect a program against unexpected or unauthorized modifications

[1] C. V. Ramoorthy and Sui-Bun F. Ho, "Testing Large Software with Automated Software Evaluation Systems," in IEEE Transactions on Software Engineering, SE–1 (1975), pp. 50–54.

5. **Maintenance**

   (a) *Tools for documentation generation,* which record information extracted during code analysis and program structure analysis for documentation

   (b) *Tools for validating modifications,* which aim at predicting the effect of proposed changes

6. **Performance**

   (a) *Tools for program restructuring,* which assist in reorganizing programs for optimization

   (b) *Tools to extract and validate parallel operations,* which identify parallel tasks to aid parallel processing scheduling

7. **Software quality validation tools,** which strive to assign a figure-of-merit to a program on the basis of comparison to desirable characteristic attributes

The previous characterization is specified to illuminate the spectrum of applications for which automated tools have been constructed. The interest in this chapter focuses on a restricted subset—those tools that assist in the preparation of test cases and provide facilities for measuring the performance of the software and effectiveness of test cases. Specific tools in other categories are discussed later in this book, including

- Problem statement language/problem statement analyzer—a computer aided requirements analysis tool (Chapter 9)

- Structure chart graphics—a display interactive tool for the construction of structure charts (Chapter 10)

- Design quality metrics—a tool that measures the goodness of a design based on a complexity algorithm (Chapter 10)

- Operational function diagram analyzer—an interactive/graphical capability to define system operational flow and model operational scenarios (Chapter 9)

- Distributed data processing model—a tool to predict performance characteristics such as equipment utilization, queuing statistics, and timing from a formal definition of the system architecture (Chapter 9)

## 6.3
## The Automated Verification System

The set of tools that measures the coverage of test cases and assists in the preparation of test cases have been popularly termed *automated verification systems* (AVS). There are five basic functions performed by the AVS:

1. Analysis of source code and creation of a data base
2. Generation of reports based on static analysis of the source code that reveal existing or potential problems in the code and identify the software control and data structures.
3. Insertion of software probes into the source code that permit data collection on code segments executed and values computed and set in storage.
4. Analysis of test results and generation of reports.
5. Generation of test assistance reports to aid in organizing testing and deriving input sets for particular tests.

The AVS derives its information from the source code of the program being analyzed. The principles of the Automated Verification System are explained by first identifying generically the components of the AVS and then exploring the test objectives that are achieved by the use of an AVS.

## GENERIC ELEMENTS OF THE AUTOMATED VERIFICATION SYSTEM

The elements of a typical AVS which perform the functions stated previously are diagrammed in Figure 6–1.

The static analysis module analyzes the static structure of the code without actually executing the program. Typically, such a module partitions each routine into sequences of statements between branching nodes (statements to or from which program control is transferred). The thoroughness of testing is often judged by measuring the number of these sequences exercised by test cases. This partition provides a data base (AVS function 1) that supports a later evaluation of test thoroughness by the analyzer module. The static analysis module also analyzes the static invocation structure of the program; the routines invoking and invoked by a particular routine are characterized in a tree structure. This information is captured in a data base file and also formated for output as a printed report (AVS function 2).

The instrumentation module acts as a preprocessor by inserting additional statements within the original source code. During execution, these additional statements or *probes* intercept the flow of execution at key points and record program performance statistics and signals in an intermediate file (AVS function 3). Typically, the instrumentation permits tallies to be kept on which statements are executed and how many times, which statement sequences are traversed and how many times, and which subroutines are called from each routine. The probes facilitate recording of minimum/maximum data ranges and intermediate values of specified variables. The instrumentation module might also provide the capability to inject assertions into the source code. Assertions are statements made by the test investigator regarding the expected ranges of variables or the instantaneous relationship between several variables. If an assertion is violated during execution, it

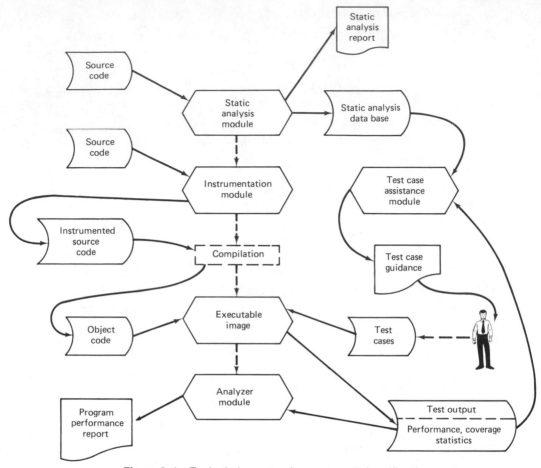

**Figure 6-1** Typical elements of an automated verification system.

is flagged and recorded. The instrumented source code is compiled, an executable image is built, and the image is executed.

The analyzer module functions as a postprocessor after the program execution. It formats and edits data recorded in an intermediate file during program execution and provides a printed report (AVS function 4). The report furnishes information on testing coverage, including

- Statements executed and frequency; percentage of statements executed
- Statement sequences traversed; percentage of sequences traversed; listing of sequences not traversed
- Data ranges of variables
- Assertion violations

The analyzer module may also compare anticipated test-case output augmented by any user-supplied evaluation criteria (prestored in a file) with actual output and list resulting discrepancies. This module may be located in a separate test computer wherever immediate evaluation of test data is necessary.

The test case assistance module aids testing personnel in the selection of test inputs that will economically attain comprehensive testing goals (AVS function 5). The module uses the static analysis data base and the coverage data recorded during executions to guide the testers in the preparation of additional test cases. These then exercise paths in the program not executed by previous test cases. An algorithm detects statements and branches not exercised and indicates conditions necessary to traverse that path.


## TEST GOALS AND MEASURES

The end objective of all verification and validation activities is to ensure that the delivered software product satisfies all specified functional and performance requirements. If test cases are selected strictly with these high-level objectives in mind, then the set of test cases is probably not representative of the anticipated operational usage. Thus, the reliability of the software is not necessarily demonstrated nor guaranteed. It is a frequent occurrence to find software errors during operational use that were not discovered during testing because no test case ever exercised certain sections of code. Delivery of reliable systems necessitates a testing activity that thoroughly exercises every routine and function of every program in the system. This will involve the construction, execution, and evaluation of a huge number of test cases that, in all likelihood, will be economically beyond human capacity. Thus, automated tools are relied upon to evaluate test results, to measure the extent of the software exercised, and to assist in generating test cases that will exercise those portions of the software not previously covered.

The following statement appeared in the statement-of-work included in a recent *request for proposal* from a governmental agency:

The testing shall fully exercise the program code and data base.

This requirement is typical of customers' contemporary awareness of the software reliability problem and their unwillingness to accept partially tested systems. It is to be expected that similar full exercise requirements will more frequently appear as provisions in future software procurements.

Clearly, the means of compliance to this full exercise requirement is not specified in the previous statement. In particular, the term "fully exercise" is not at all defined. Thorough testing to fully exercise the program code is susceptible to a spectrum of interpretation. It could entail exercise of

- All permutations of control paths through the program
- All control paths
- All paths from outcomes of decision statements
- All statements in the program

These full exercise conditions are listed in descending order of difficulty.

The testing of all possible combinations of paths through a program will probably require thousands of years or more of computer time even for common structures that appear deceptively simple. A discussion in Chapter 1 centering on Figure 1-2 showed that there are about $10^{20}$ different paths through a flow chart of a frequently encountered structure. This test goal is clearly not practical.

The testing of all individual control paths is an objective of questionable attainability. Programs with looping structures have at least as many control paths as there are possible iterations through the loops. All sizeable programs will have significant looping content. Thus, this test goal is likely to be prohibitive in most situations.

The testing of all path segments derived from outcomes of decision statements has been demonstrated to be achievable in practical software development environments. The difference between this goal and the testing of all individual control paths concerns the looping structure. In defining decision paths, the loop structure would normally consist of two paths—the loop execution and loop escape.

The testing of all program statements at least once can usually be attained without particular difficulty but is not considered to be sufficient. This objective does not test all outcomes of decision elements. Many errors involve erroneous transfer of control. This type of error is not necessarily detected with this goal. As an incidental observation, the testing of all decision elements will also exercise each program statement at least once.

Before developing the full exercise matter further, let us digress momentarily to explore the conceptual basis for full exercise testing. We have been made aware from many sources that testing will never fully validate program correctness. We have been told that testing confirms the presence of errors but not their absence. The line of reasoning is that an economically feasible number of test cases is an insufficient statistical base from which to conclude program correctness and, hence, the absence of errors. On a theoretical basis, it is hard to contest this argument. As a realistic matter, however, testing is the only practical device available to ascertain the likely correctness of the physical software product for any but the most trivial of software systems. The only pragmatic approach is to use testing efficiently to increase the *probability* of program correctness. This is done by carefully directing the selection of test inputs to fully traverse as many path segments of the program control structure as possible.

From the prior discussion of full exercise options, the testing of all decision paths has emerged as a goal that is achievable, beneficial, and economically practical. We shall specifically define this path as consisting of the sequence of statements lying between the outcome of a decision up to and including the next decision. This sequence is immediately executable, once the initial decision outcome has been evaluated, and is the basic logical segment of the control structure. The sequence shall be formally identified as a *decision-to-decision path* and abbreviated for convenient future reference as DD-path. Illustrated in Figure 6-2 is a typical flow sequence and the partitioning of this sequence into DD-paths. The structure of this module consists of, in sequence:

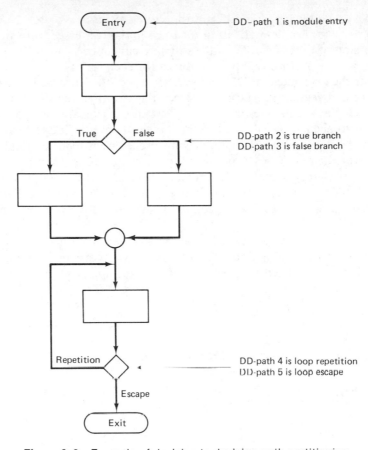

**Figure 6-2** Example of decision-to-decision path partitioning.

- Module entry and a simple sequential function
- A decision construct
- An iteration construct

This control structure is partitioned into five DD-paths:

- DD-path 1 is module entry to first decision element
- DD-path 2 is true branch from decision element
- DD-path 3 is false branch from decision element
- DD-path 4 is a loop iteration
- DD-path 5 is loop escape to module exit

By defining a set of inputs that exercise all five DD-paths with successful results, there is a high probability that this module is correct.

Such testing would begin using a set of *natural* or functionally oriented test cases. The specific motivation for these initial test cases will vary according to the mission of the system. With the software having been previously instrumented with probes, a coverage report is produced for each series of test cases. This report will note the percentage of DD-paths traversed and the specific DD-paths not exercised. Untested regions are identified from the coverage report. Specific DD-paths are selected as the next testing targets. Test case inputs are devised to force the desired flow to occur that will exercise the target DD-paths. The test cases are run and the next coverage report is analyzed. This procedure is repeated until the path coverage is brought to 100% or, perhaps, above some lower testing goal. It has been observed in practice that a substantial number of paths other than the immediate DD-path test targets are incidentally exercised. Because of this collateral coverage, the actual number of test cases required is substantially lower than the number of DD-paths.

The generic elements of an automated verification system have been discussed along with the testing goals that an AVS will assist in attaining. A commercially available automated verification system that implements many of these capabilities is now described.

## 6.4

## A Commercial Automated Verification System

In this section, a commercially available automated verification system is described. This system is composed of two tools:

- V-IFTRAN™—a structured FORTRAN preprocessor with an executable assertion capability.
- RXVP80™—a tool for automated test assistance and source program analysis.

These tools are built and marketed by General Research Corporation of Santa Barbara, California. RXVP80™ and V-IFTRAN™ have been utilized at Hughes Aircraft Company in a production environment with generally successful results. However, no assertion is made here regarding the merits of these tools relative to other tools which may offer comparable capabilities. These tools have been chosen as subjects of discussion in this text because they are the choice of the marketplace; that is, these tools and their variations appear to have the most extensive user-base of any of the automated verification tools.

In the following paragraphs, the capabilities of V-IFTRAN™ and RXVP80™ are described and the use of these tools in the software development and testing process is explained. An illustrative application of RXVP80™ to a sample problem will be included in Chapter 7, as well as an analysis of the cost benefits of this tool to a recent software project at Hughes Aircraft Company.

V-IFTRAN™ provides the capability of using structured programming concepts in FORTRAN and the capability to debug and verify the resulting software through the use of executable assertions. Executable assertions are statements that are included in FORTRAN programs to define conditions that should exist at various points. The V-IFTRAN™ preprocessor translates them into equivalent FORTRAN statements for compilation by the FORTRAN compiler. During execution, if conditions defined by the executable assertions are violated, informative messages are provided that report exactly where the violation occurred.

V-IFTRAN™ does not replace the FORTRAN compilation process. Instead, it preprocesses the combined FORTRAN statements, program control structures, and V-IFTRAN™ executable assertions as shown in Figure 6–3. The combined source file is used as the input to the V-IFTRAN™ preprocessor. V-IFTRAN™ then translates the program control structures and executable assertions into standard FORTRAN while passing normally coded FORTRAN statements into a file, which is then used as input to the FORTRAN compiler.

Most installations set up a single run procedure which incorporates the preprocessing and compilation steps into what appears to the user as a single process. It is usually only necessary to maintain the V-IFTRAN™ source listing. The FORTRAN listing is used by programmers for debugging under infrequent circumstances when

1. The error must be traced through a program dump, or
2. Error trace information refers to FORTRAN source statement numbers

Other debugging is more effectively assisted by the more readable V-IFTRAN™ listing. See Figure 6–4 for an example V-IFTRAN™ source listing.

The structured programming concepts supported by V-IFTRAN™ allow FORTRAN programs to be written in a top-down, block-structured manner, mak-

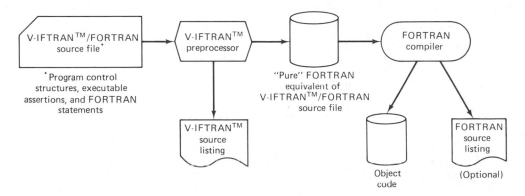

**Figure 6–3**  V-IFTRAN™ preprocessor configuration.

```
SEQ NEST SOURCE              SUBROUTINE IECALC (G,VE,BRNCHS,IE,IEOUT)

 1            SUBROUTINE IECALC (G,VE,BRNCHS,IE,IEOUT)
 2        C   ROUTINE TO CALCULATE NETWORK ELEMENT CURRENTS AND OUTPUT
 3        C   RESULTS IF REQUESTED
 4        C
 5        C   DESCRIPTION OF VARIABLES
 6        C      G       - BRANCH CONDUCTANCE MATRIX
 7        C      VE      - ELEMENT VOLTAGE VECTOR
 8        C      BRNCHS  - NUMBER OF CIRCUIT BRANCHES
 9        C      IE      - ELEMENT CURRENT VECTOR
10        C      IEOUT   - ELEMENT CURRENT OUTPUT FLAG
11        C      LUNIN   - LOGICAL INPUT UNIT
12        C      LUNOUT  - LOGICAL OUTPUT UNIT
13        C      MISC    - DEBUG OUTPUT FLAG
14        C
15        C------------------------------------------------------------
16        C
17            INTEGER BRNCHS
18            REAL IE
19            LOGICAL IEOUT
20            COMMON /UNITS/ LUNIN,LUNOUT
21            COMMON /DEBUG/ MISC
22        C
23            DIMENSION G(50,50), VE(50), IE(50)
24        C
25            IF (MISC.EQ.3)
26   1        .     WRITE (LUNOUT,900) IEOUT
27            END IF
28        C
29        C------------------------------------------------------------
30        C   CALCULATE ELEMENT CURRENTS     IE(J) = G(J,J)*VE(J)
31        C------------------------------------------------------------
32        C
33            DO (I=1,BRNCHS)
34   1        .     IE(I) = G(I,I)*VE(I)
35            END DO
36        C
37        C------------------------------------------------------------
38        C   OUTPUT ELEMENT CURRENTS
39        C------------------------------------------------------------
40        C
41            IF (IEOUT)
42   1        .     WRITE (LUNOUT,910)
43   1        .     DO (I=1,BRNCHS)
44   2        .  .        WRITE (LUNOUT,920) I,IE(I)
45   1        .     END DO
46            END IF
47        C
48            IF (MISC.EQ.3)
49   1        .     WRITE (LUNOUT,930)
50            END IF
51            RETURN
52        C------------------------------------------------------------
53        900 FORMAT (5X,22HENTER IECALC. IEOUT = ,L1)
54        910 FORMAT (5X,16HELEMENT CURRENTS ,//
             1        5X,16HELEMENT    VALUE ,/
             1        5X,16H-------    ----- )
55        920 FORMAT (8X,I2,2X,1PE12.5)
56        930 FORMAT (5X,11HEXIT IECALC )
57            END
```

**Figure 6-4** Example V-IFTRAN™ listing.

ing them more readable, more uniform, more reliable, and easier to maintain. These concepts are made available through the use of the following program control structures:

- IF . . . OR IF . . . ELSE . . . END IF
- CASE OF . . . CASE . . . CASE ELSE . . . END CASE

- WHILE . . . END WHILE
- REPEAT . . . UNTIL
- DO . . . END DO
- LOOP . . . EXIT IF . . . EXIT . . . END LOOP
- FOR . . . END FOR
- INVOKE-BLOCK . . . END BLOCK

Program control structures that have been included in the source file cause V-IFTRAN™ to generate the FORTRAN source code equivalents of the structures; executable assertion statements also cause V-IFTRAN™ to generate the FORTRAN source code equivalent of these statements during its translation process. This generated code is then compiled with the rest of the program and run in a normal manner. If the assertion statements are violated during execution, messages describing the violations are automatically printed, thereby pinpointing where problems exist in the program. The diagram on Figure 6–5 graphically depicts the executable assertion implementation process.

There are two types of V-IFTRAN™ executable assertion statements available to the programmer:

1. Debug printing
2. Dynamic integrity

Debug printing statements provide the capability of automatically printing variables by name and value. Dynamic integrity statements allow the programmer to assert conditions that should exist at various points in the program.

The programmer can implant debug printing statements within the source code of a V-IFTRAN™ or FORTRAN program that will cause specific information to be printed while the program is running. These statements are the

- INPUT statement, which is used to print the names and values of input variables.
- DEBUG statement, which is used to print the names and values of intermediate variables.
- OUTPUT statement, which is used to print the names and values of output variables.

The debug print statements can be activated or deactivated by control commands which are included in the source file as comment statements.

In order to illustrate the usage of the debug print statements, consider the example bubble sort routine shown in Figure 6–6a. Assume that another programmer now wishes to check out this routine using the capabilities of V-IFTRAN™. The

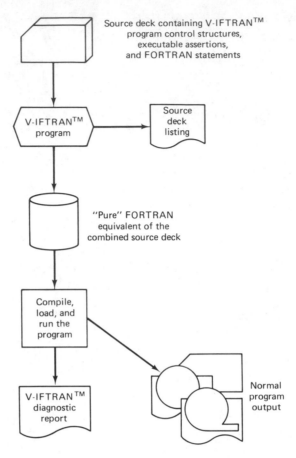

Source deck containing V-IFTRAN™
program control structures,
executable assertions,
and FORTRAN statements

V-IFTRAN™
program

Source
deck
listing

"Pure" FORTRAN
equivalent of the
combined source deck

Compile,
load, and
run the
program

V-IFTRAN™
diagnostic
report

Normal
program
output

**Figure 6-5**  Executable assertions implementation.

three debug print statements (INPUT, DEBUG, and OUTPUT) could be used in the manner shown in Figure 6–6b.

Now, when the program is run, the names and values of the input calling sequence parameters ARRAY and NUMBER (at line 5) would be printed as they were received by SUBROUTINE BUBBLS in the following manner:

```
INPUT FOR MODULE BUBBLS AT STATEMENT 5
     NUMBER              =        10
     (ARRAY(I),I = 1,NUMBER)  =   10.0    9.0    8.0    7.0    . . . etc.
```

Then (at line 15), every time an exchange was made during the sorting process, the contents of **ARRAY** would be printed by name and value in the following manner thereby showing the percolation effect of this type of sort:

```
DEBUG FOR MODULE BUBBLS AT STATEMENT 15
     (ARRAY(I),I = 1,NUMBER) =  9.0     10.0    8.0    7.0    . . . etc.
```

```
 1              SUBROUTINE  BUBBLS  (ARRAY,NUMBER)
 2              DIMENSION  ARRAY(NUMBER)
 3              IF  (NUMBER.NE.1)
 4              •         DO (LOW = 2,NUMBER)
 5              •         •         DO (JUMP = 2,LOW)
 6              •         •         •         LOOK = LOW—JUMP + 1
 7              •         •         •         NEXT = LOOK + 1
 8              •         •         •         IF  (ARRAY(LOOK).GT.ARRAY(NEXT) )
 9              •         •         •         •   TEMP = ARRAY(LOOK)
10              •         •         •         •   ARRAY(LOOK) = ARRAY(NEXT)
11              •         •         •         •   ARRAY(NEXT) = TEMP
12              •         •         •         END IF
13              •         •         END DO
14              •         END DO
15              END IF
16              RETURN
17              END                          (a)
```

```
 1              SUBROUTINE  BUBBLS  (ARRAY,NUMBER)
 2    C.TRACE = ON
 3    C.DEBUG = ON
 4              DIMENSION  ARRAY(NUMBER)
 5              INPUT  (INTEGER/NUMBER/REAL/(ARRAY(I), I = 1,NUMBER))
 6              IF  (NUMBER.NE.1)
 7              •         DO (LOW _ 2,NUMBER)
 8              •         •         DO (JUMP = 2,LOW)
 9              •         •         •         LOOK = LOW-JUMP + 1
10              •         •         •         NEXT = LOOK + 1
11              •         •         •         IF   (ARRAY(LOOK).GT.ARRAY(NEXT))
12              •         •         •         •   TEMP = ARRAY(LOOK)
13              •         •         •         •   ARRAY(LOOK) = ARRAY(NEXT)
14              •         •         •         •   ARRAY(NEXT) = TEMP
15              •         •         •         •   DEBUG  (/REAL/(ARRAY(I),I = 1,NUMBER))
16              •         •         •         END IF
17              •         •         END DO
18              •         END DO
19              END IF
20              OUTPUT  (/REAL/(ARRAY(I),I = 1,NUMBER))
21              RETURN
22              END                              (b)
```

**Figure 6-6**   (a) Example bubble sort routine. (b) Bubble sort routine with debug print statements embedded.

Just prior to RETURNing to the calling routine (at line 20), the contents of ARRAY would again be printed by name and value in the following manner, thus showing that, indeed, the sort was successful:

```
OUTPUT  FOR MODULE BUBBLS AT  STATEMENT  20
    (ARRAY(I),I = 1,NUMBER)  =  1.0    2.0    3.0    4.0    . . . etc.
```

So far, so good . . . but there still could be more imbedded problems in this routine. For example, what if the calling routine CALLed BUBBLS with NUMBER less than or equal to 0? Also, what if, during a production run, the sort should fail? These types of questions are answered by the V-IFTRAN™ dynamic integrity statements.

The dynamic integrity statements allow the programmer to define conditions that should exist within the program. These statements are the

- INITIAL statement, which is used to define the initial conditions that should exist when entering a program unit
- ASSERT statement, which is used to define conditions that should exist at different points within a program unit
- FINAL statement, which is used to define the final conditions that should exist just before leaving a program unit.

Using the bubble sort routine as an example again, these statements could be implanted as shown in Figure 6–7.

Now, when the program is running, information will be printed only if the specifications in the INITIAL, ASSERT, or FINAL statements are violated.

If NUMBER was received by SUBROUTINE BUBBLS containing a value less than or equal to 0, the following message would be automatically provided:

FOR MODULE BUBBLS INITIAL FALSE AT STATEMENT 7

```
1          SUBROUTINE BUBBLS (ARRAY,NUMBER)
2    C.TRACE = OFF
3    C.DEBUG = OFF
4    C.ASSERT = ON
5          DIMENSION ARRAY(NUMBER)
6          INPUT (/INTEGER/NUMBER/REAL/(ARRAY(I),I = 1,NUMBER))
7          INITIAL (NUMBER.GT.0)
8          IF (NUMBER.NE.1)
9          •          DO (LOW = 2,NUMBER)
10         •          •          DO (JUMP = 2,LOW)
11         •          •          •          LOOK = LOW—JUMP + 1
12         •          •          •          NEXT = LOOK + 1
13         •          •          •          IF (ARRAY(LOOK).GT.ARRAY(NEXT))
14         •          •          •          •     TEMP = ARRAY(LOOK)
15         •          •          •          •     ARRAY(LOOK) = ARRAY(NEXT)
16         •          •          •          •     ARRAY(NEXT) = TEMP
17         •          •          •          •     ASSERT (ARRAY(NEXT).GT.ARRAY(LOOK))
18         •          •          •          •     DEBUG (/REAL/(ARRAY(I),I = 1,NUMBER))
19         •          •          •          END IF
20         •          •          END DO
21         •          END DO
22   END IF
23   OUTPUT (/REAL/(ARRAY(I),I = 1,NUMBER))
24   FINAL (.ALL.I.IN.(1,NUMBER—1) (ARRAY(I + 1).GT.ARRAY(I)))
25   RETURN
26   END
```

Figure 6-7   Example bubble sort routine with assertions embedded.

When an exchange was made during the sorting process and it didn't result in the next value being greater than the previous value, the following message would be automatically provided:

FOR MODULE BUBBLS ASSERT FALSE AT STATEMENT 17

Then, prior to RETURNing to the calling program, if ARRAY was not in ascending order [the FINAL statement reads: "For all I from 1 to NUMBER–1, ARRAY(I + 1) must be greater than ARRAY(I)."], the following message would be automatically provided:

FOR MODULE BUBBLS FINAL FALSE AT STATEMENT 24

Applying this to our example, suppose the calling routine sent SUBROUTINE BUBBLS a –10 value for NUMBER; the following would be automatically printed:

FOR MODULE BUBBLS INITIAL FALSE AT STATEMENT 7

After printing this message, processing would continue normally. If, however, the programmer would like to perform some type of recovery or print a more informative message should the previous condition occur, a FAIL block can be used with the INITIAL statement (as it also can be used with the ASSERT and FINAL statements).

Suppose that if NUMBER is received less than or equal to 0, you want to print an informative message and then stop processing altogether. This can be done by changing the INITIAL statement as follows:

```
5              DIMENSION  ARRAY(NUMBER)
6              INPUT (/INTEGER/NUMBER/REAL/(ARRAY(I),I = 1,NUMBER))
7              INITIAL (NUMBER.GT.0), FAIL (KILL RUN)
8              IF (NUMBER.NE.1)
9           •  DO (LOW = 2,NUMBER)
```

Then just before the END card, the more informative message would be defined as shown below:

```
23             OUTPUT(/REAL/(ARRAY(I),I = 1,NUMBER))
24             FINAL: (.ALL.I.IN.(1,NUMBER—1) (ARRAY(I + 1).GT.ARRAY(I)))
25             RETURN
26             BLOCK (KILL RUN)
27          •  WRITE (6,100) NUMBER
28      100 •  FORMAT (30H NUMBER WAS RECEIVED EQUAL TO ,I10,/,
29          2•         24HORUN WILL BE TERMINATED.)
30          •  CALL WALKBK
31          •  CALL ABORT
32             END BLOCK
33             END
```

Then, after the automatic message was printed, this more informative message would print and the job would be ABORTed.

The executable assertions may be activated ( = ON) or deactivated ( = OFF) by command statements, which are inserted into the source text as comments. The overall control flow for assertion expressions is depicted on Figure 6–8.

For the most effective utilization of these capabilities, programmers should use dynamic integrity statements (INITIAL, ASSERT, and FINAL) with FAIL blocks when they are developing their programs while specifications are still fresh in mind. The dynamic integrity statements should be set = ON. Also during code development, the debug printing statements INPUT and OUTPUT should be implanted in each program unit but should be set = OFF until needed for debugging. Having INPUT and OUTPUT statements in program units, even while not activated, provides a valuable 'statement of intent' for the interface variables. During debugging, the already-implanted INPUT and OUTPUT statements may be activated and additional information gathered through the use of DEBUG statements.

## RXVP80™

RXVP80™ is a tool for analyzing source programs written in V-IFTRAN™ or FORTRAN. It is a software system to be used as an aid in improving, documenting, and validating the quality of software and software testing by providing for

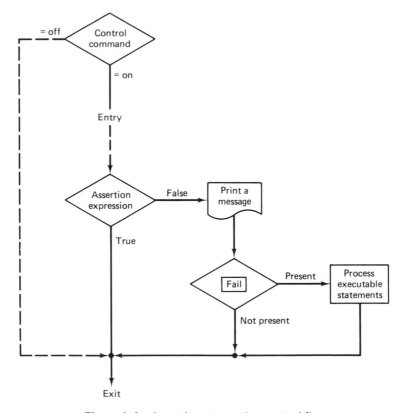

**Figure 6-8**  Assertion expression control flow.

- Syntax and structural analysis of source programs
- Static analysis to detect inconsistencies in program structure or in the use of variables
- Automated documentation
- Instrumentation of the source code
- Analysis of testing coverage
- Retesting guidance

Figure 6–9 shows how RXVP80™ fits into the software development cycle to augment software analysis and testing. The user's source code is analyzed by RXVP80™ and the results will be output in reports which help the user decide if the acceptance criteria are being met. RXVP80™ can also instrument the source code prior to test execution and provide an analysis of the behavior of the program during testing.

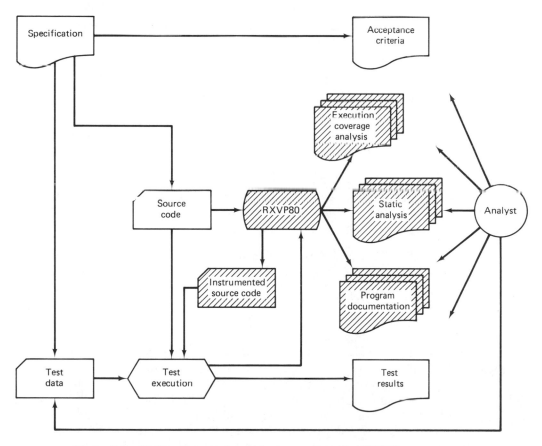

**Figure 6-9** Software analysis and test augmented by RXVP80.

The type of processing to be performed by RXVP80™ is specified through one or more option selection commands. RXVP80™ processing is segmented into two parts:

- Preexecution processing and reporting
- Postexecution analysis

The options associated with each of these processing areas are now described.

DESCRIPTION OF PREEXECUTION OPTIONS  The possible set of options are listed here:

- LIST—produces an enhanced indented source listing of each module
- SUMMARY—provides an analysis of statements, common blocks, and module dependencies
- DOCUMENT—produces descriptive reports on characteristics of each module and also multimodule reports characterizing module relationships
- STATIC—produces a report of static errors for each module
- INSTRUMENT—instruments the source code for test coverage and writes the instrumented code to a file
- SELF-METRIC—instruments the source code for collection of performance statistics and writes the instrumented code to a file
- INPUT/OUTPUT—same as INSTRUMENT, but also translates V-IFTRAN™ INPUT/OUTPUT statements into FORTRAN.
- REACHING SET—provides assistance in identifying paths to designated code segments within specified modules

These options are not mutually exclusive, and more than one may be specified at a time in any combination. Figure 6-10 shows the RXVP80™ options cross-correlated with their possible uses. A brief description of each option is provided in the following paragraphs.

LIST  The LIST option produces a source listing which shows the number of each statement and the levels of indentation. With an automatically indented listing, the programmer is relieved of having to calculate and keypunch each indentation manually; this is especially useful when changes are made to the code which would require changes in the nesting level.

An indented listing clearly indicates the control structures and makes the program much more readable, not only to the original programmer but especially to someone unfamiliar with the code who is trying to understand it. The indented statement listing on the output file is the sole report from the LIST option. Figure 6-4 has shown an example of this listing. When the LIST option is used with the INSTRUMENT option (OPTION=INSTRUMENT,LIST.), the module listing normally produced by the LIST option alone is further enhanced with annotations indicating the number and type of all generated DD-paths.

| Options Usage | List | Summary | Document | Static | Instrument | Self-Metric | Input/Output | Reaching Set |
|---|---|---|---|---|---|---|---|---|
| Software documentation | ✓ | ✓ | ✓ | | | | | |
| Maintenance | ✓ | ✓ | ✓ | ✓ | | ✓ | | |
| Implementation | ✓ | ✓ | ✓ | ✓ | ✓ | ✓ | ✓ | |
| Obtain interface data | | ✓ | ✓ | ✓ | | | | |
| Trace ranges of variables | | | | | | ✓ | ✓ | |
| Execution test | | | | | ✓ | ✓ | ✓ | ✓ |
| Incomplete test coverage | | | | | ✓ | ✓ | ✓ | ✓ |
| System test information | ✓ | ✓ | ✓ | | | | | |
| Single module information | ✓ | ✓ | | ✓ | | | | |
| Code changes | ✓ | ✓ | ✓ | ✓ | | ✓ | | |
| Unknown behavior | | | | ✓ | ✓ | ✓ | ✓ | |

**Figure 6-10** Uses of RXVP80 options.

SUMMARY   The SUMMARY option is intended to be used when a brief introduction to a set of modules is desired. It provides an analysis of statements, common blocks, and module dependencies. The statements of individual modules are classified separately as either declaration, executable, decision, or documentation. Under each classification, a tabulated account of the various subtypes is listed. A separate *statement profile* report with this information is generated for each module.

An overall view of the modules is given by the *invocations summary* and the *common matrix* reports. The invocations summary report shows the invokee and invoker modules and shows "who calls whom." The common matrix report correlates all the common blocks encountered with their usage in each of the modules. When program changes are made, the invocations summary and commons matrix reports can be used to identify modules which may be affected.

DOCUMENT   The DOCUMENT option generates a set of eight different reports. Four are individual module reports and are produced for each module in the library that is submitted to RXVP80™.

- Symbols report indicating the type of usage (set, used, set and used, etc.) of each symbol
- Cross-reference report for all symbols
- Invocation space report, which shows all invocations, along with the statement numbers, to and from the specified module
- Invocation bands report shows the selected module within the invocation heirarchy. At the center is the specified module. Each successive band of modules from the center to the left shows the calling modules; each successive band to the right shows the called modules. A sample of this report is displayed in Figure 6–11.

The other four are multimodule reports.

- INPUT/OUTPUT statements report provides a list of all the modules in which INPUT/OUTPUT statements appear. The syntax of these statements is reproduced along with their associated formats. This report may be used to locate all the points where variables are being input to the system and output from the system.

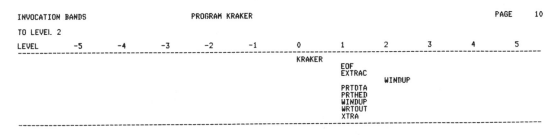

**Figure 6-11**   Example invocation bands report.

LEGEND (C=FIRST USED IN A CALL,E=EQUIVALENCED,S=SET,U=USED,X=SET AND USED)

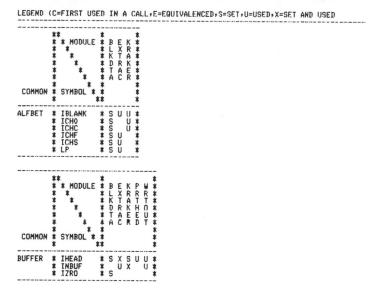

**Figure 6-12**  Example common matrices report.

- A global cross-reference report that provides a symbol cross reference for all modules on the library. The symbol types are variables, file names, and common block names. Adjacent to the statement numbers where each symbol appears in the source text are flags which indicate the use of each symbol (used, set, or equivalenced).

- A cross-reference report that provides an external name (subroutine, function, etc.) cross reference to the statement numbers where each external is referred to in the source text.

- Commons matrix report, which correlates each common block and constituent symbols with modules which use, set, or equate the symbols in the common block. An example commons matrix is contained on Figure 6-12.

This set of reports can be used throughout the testing process. Together with the execution coverage reports produced as a result of instrumentation, they help to identify which modules may require retesting when changes are made in the code. The global cross-reference report is particularly useful in finding where variables are set in order to alter test cases, and also where a variable is being used that is affected by a change in a module.

STATIC   The STATIC analysis techniques available in RXVP80™ include

- *Mode and type checking,* which identifies possible misuse of constants and variables in expressions, assignments, and invocations

- *Invocational checking,* which validates actual invocations against formal declarations while checking for consistency in number of parameters and type
- *Set and use checking,* which uncovers possible use before set conditions and similar program abnormalities within a module
- *Graph checking,* which identifies possible errors in program control structure, such as unreachable code

A rigorous analysis of program variables, including interprocedural checking, provides RXVP80™ with the capability to uncover subtle inconsistencies which lead to errors, such as

- The number of parameters listed does not agree with those of the routine called.
- The mode of an actual parameter does not match that of the corresponding formal parameter.
- A parameter is listed in the calling argument list as a single, nonsubscripted variable but is used in the routine as an array.
- Uninitialized variables or arrays are used.

Another consistency check is performed on the structure of the program. The graph for each module is checked to see that all statements are reachable from the module's entry and that the module's exit is reachable from each statement. Unreachable statements represent extra overhead in terms of memory space required for a module, while statements from which the exit cannot be reached represent potentially catastrophic system failures.

INSTRUMENT   The INSTRUMENT option inserts a set of probe statements into each module. The probe statements are inserted into the source text at each entry and each exit of the modules and at each statement which begins a DD-path. Each probe includes a call to a data collection routine, which records information concerning the flow of control in the executing module(s). A special probe is inserted at the end of the main program to signal the end of test execution. The user can also have this special probe inserted at other points in his code, which has the effect of breaking one test execution into multiple test cases. A source listing with the DD-paths defined is generated for each instrumented module if the LIST option is included (OPTION = INSTRUMENT,LIST.).

The instrumented source text is written to a file, either in V-IFTRAN™ or FORTRAN, depending on the language being processed. The file can be input to the FORTRAN compiler (after first being processed by the V-IFTRAN™ preprocessor, if that was the source language). The instrumented object code is then ready for loading and test execution along with an automatically supplied data collection routine.

SELF-METRIC Statistical performance data may be gathered during execution by inserting more detailed instrumentation into each module. Probes are inserted into the source text after each executable statement. These probes provide calls to data collection routines, which record execution counts of each statement, initial and final values of variables or logical expressions, and maximum/minimum values of variables.

As with the INSTRUMENTATION option, the instrumented source text is written to a file and is available for compilation. After compilation, the instrumented object code is available for linkage and execution.

The resulting report generated after execution of the instrumented code is valuable for tracing ranges and status of variables, evaluating program performance, and investigating anomalous behavior.

INPUT/OUTPUT Additional information may be gathered during the execution test by inserting V-IFTRAN™ INPUT and OUTPUT statements into each source module. The INPUT statements are used to list the global variables (either calling sequence parameters or in COMMON) that should have a value whenever the routine is invoked; the OUTPUT statements are used to list variables that will be assigned a value in the routine. An INPUT variable may also be an OUTPUT variable. The INPUT/OUTPUT option provides a dynamic tracing of the values of the program variables by translating the INPUT and OUTPUT statements into FORTRAN code.

The INPUT/OUTPUT option also performs the same functions as the INSTRUMENT option. A DD-path definitions report identical to the one from the INSTRUMENT option will be generated, provided that the LIST option is included.

REACHING SET The analysis specified by the REACHING SET option executes the module retesting assistance of RXVP80™. Presuming that a set of untested DD paths has been isolated, the user can identify a section of code he desires to exercise. He inputs the desired DD-path number to be "reached," and RXVP80™ generates the reaching set of paths from module entry or from a designated DD-path up to the second DD-path number that has been specified. RXVP80™ prints a list of DD-paths on the reaching set. Coordination of this output with the DD-path definitions report allows the user to identify which parts of the program need to be executed (and therefore which program values need to be modified) for the selected DD-path to be executed. Once this determination is made, test cases can be constructed, and the user may rerun the instrumented code to ascertain the additional program coverage provided by the new set of test cases.

POSTEXECUTION ANALYSIS OPTIONS A variety of coverage analysis reports can be generated from data collected during execution of a program containing one or more modules that have been instrumented by RXVP80™.

In order to proceed with verification of the software testing, the source text (which has been instrumented by RXVP80™) is compiled and executed. At program linkage time, any user externals necessary for execution of the instrumented code must be supplied. During test execution, the program operates normally, reading its own data and writing its own outputs. The instrumented modules call the data collection routine, which records, on a file, the accumulated data on module DD-path traversals and/or module performance.

Postexecution analysis reports are generated in response to the selection of one or more options. If the preexecution INSTRUMENT option was specified, the user may elect one or more of the following options:

- SUMMARY
- NOTHIT
- DETAILED

If the preexecution SELF–METRIC option was selected, the user may generate a performance report by specifying the STATEMENT PROBE ANALYSIS option. Each of the postexecution analysis options is described below.

SUMMARY  The SUMMARY option produces a report that summarizes testing coverage for all instrumented and invoked modules. The SUMMARY report lists the following information:

- Test case number
- Module names and numbers of DD-paths
- Number of module invocations, number of DD-paths traversed, and percentage coverage for this test case
- Cumulative number of module invocations, number of DD-paths traversed, and percent coverage for all test cases

When multiple test cases are involved, the SUMMARY report shows data from the current test case and the immediately preceding test case. When the end of the trace data is encountered, a cumulative summary of all test cases is produced.

NOTHIT  The NOTHIT option requests a report that identifies DD-paths not executed for all instrumented and invoked modules. The NOTHIT report lists the following information:

- Module names
- Test case number
- Number of DD-paths not traversed for this test case and for all test cases
- DD-path numbers not traversed for this test case and for all test cases

From this report, untested DD-paths can be selected as the next testing target in order to improve testing coverage. A representative NOTHIT Report is shown in Figure 6–13.

```
===================================================================================================
  MODULE   I  TEST   I PATHS  I
   NAME    I NUMBER  I NOT HIT I              LIST OF DECISION TO DECISION PATHS NOT EXECUTED
===================================================================================================
<MAIN   > I    1   I    0   I
          I CUMUL  I    0   I
---------------------------------------------------------------------------------------------------
<SUBA   > I    1   I    6   I   3   5   7   9  10  11
          I CUMUL  I    6   I   3   5   7   9  10  11
---------------------------------------------------------------------------------------------------
<SUBC   > I    1   I    1   I   8
          I CUMUL  I    1   I   8
---------------------------------------------------------------------------------------------------
<SUBB   > I    1   I    0   I
          I CUMUL  I    0   I
---------------------------------------------------------------------------------------------------
```

**Figure 6-13** Example NOT HIT report.

DETAILED    The DETAILED option command selects a report which shows a breakdown of individual DD-path coverage. A single test case report is generated for each specified module which was instrumented and invoked, and contains the following information:

- Module name
- Test case number
- List of DD-path numbers, with an indication of those which were not executed, a graphical representation of the number of executions, and an itemized listing of the number of executions

STATEMENT PROBE ANALYSIS    The STATEMENT PROBE ANALYSIS option produces a report which specifies performance data for each executable statement in modules that have been instrumented by the SELF-METRIC option. The STATEMENT PROBE ANALYSIS report lists the following information for each executable statement:

- Statements for which no value is computed (WRITE, READ, CALL, etc.)—execution count
- Logical expressions—execution count, times true, times false, final value of expression
- Statements that compute a numeric value—execution count, initial value, final value, maximum value, minimum value

The example report included in Figure 6-14 illustrates these features.

## USE OF AN AVS IN SOFTWARE DEVELOPMENT AND TEST

The V-IFTRAN™ and RXVP80™ products which comprise an automated verification system have been described. Without an AVS, testing will suffer from lack of formalized, systematic, and enforceable techniques. Testing with an AVS not only offers an accurate means of determining exactly what portions of the software have been exercised but also assists in the preparation of test data. These capabilities

```
STATEMENT PROBE ANALYSIS FOR TEST SET  1
TEST SET TERMINATED AT COMPLETION OF TEST EXECUTION


STATEMENT PROBE ANALYSIS REPORT
                                                                    EXECUTION
NO.   LABEL   SOURCE TEXT                                           COUNT

  1           PROGRAM TESTDO                                          1
  2           DOUBLE PRECISION DX,DY,DZ
  3           COMPLEX C


  4           COMPLEX*8 C8                                            4
  5           CHARACTER*10 STR1(4),STR2
  6           DATA STR1 /'ABCDEFGHIJ','KLMNOPQRST','LOCATION 3','LOCATION 4' /
  7           DO 100 I = 1 , 4                                             INIT =        1    FINAL =        4
                                                                          MIN  =        1    MAX   =        4

  8           DX = I                                                 4    INIT  =      0.100000000000000D+01
                                                                          FINAL =      0.400000000000000D+01
                                                                          MIN   =      0.100000000000000D+01
                                                                          MAX   =      0.400000000000000D+01

  9           DZ = 1.0 / DX                                          4    INIT  =      0.100000000000000D+01
                                                                          FINAL =      0.250000000000000D+00
                                                                          MIN   =      0.250000000000000D+00
                                                                          MAX   =      0.100000000000000D+01

 10           X = I                                                  4    INIT =        1.000000    FINAL =        4.000000
                                                                          MIN  =        1.000000    MAX   =        4.000000

 11           C = CMPLX ( X , X / 2 )                                4    ONLY VALUE= (   1.000000    ,   0.0000000E+00)

 12           C8 = 2 * I                                             4    ONLY VALUE= (   2.000000    ,   0.0000000E+00)

 13           STR2 = STR1 ( I )                                      4
 14           PRINT * , DX , DZ                                      4
 15           PRINT * , C                                            4
 16           PRINT * , C8                                           4
 17           PRINT * , STR2                                         4
 18    100    CONTINUE                                               4
 19           STOP                                                   1
 20           END
```

**Figure 6-14**  Example statement probe analysis report.

greatly improve the effectiveness of testing toward a much higher probability that the tested software is correct. Side benefits of an AVS are automated, high-quality, accurate documentation; reports that are useful for code optimization; and dynamic testing capability with embedded assertion statements for expected software behavior. The objective of this section is to synthesize the AVS capabilities into a coherent software development and test methodology and to explain that methodology. This overall methodology is delineated in Figure 6–15.

The modern approach to software construction and testing is oriented toward incremental build-up of capabilities. Small software packages of tractable size are incrementally added to an evolving baseline. A methodology for this approach was presented in Chapter 3. This incremental technique dovetails perfectly with the characteristics and limitations of an AVS. The resources required to test each package or thread must be considered. For example, once it is instrumented, the software requires more memory (because of the code expansion due to the instrumentation) and more computer time (because of the overhead of executing the probes). These side effects usually have minimal impact to the normal development procedures when instrumentation is applied to only a few new modules at a time that are being added to the configuration. When RXVP80™-supported testing has been applied to large volumes of software, however, the additional resource utilization may become detrimental to the overall effort and perhaps frustrating to the test personnel. Thus, testing with RXVP80™ can be more effective when applied to a few modules at a time using an incremental test philosophy. It should also be noted that when software is being tested to validate performance requirements such as execution time, it should be performed without the instrumentation.

In Figure 6–15, the methodology begins with the coding of the modules in V-IFTRAN™. Executable assertions identifying expected program behavior are included. Also inserted are debug print statements at potential problem sites. The assertions and debug statements can be activated or deactivated on any given compilation as demanded by the need for error isolation assistance. The V-IFTRAN™ code is precompiled into FORTRAN, and the FORTRAN is compiled into object modules. This step is iterated until all compilation errors are removed. Most installations merge the two-step precompile/compilation process into a single procedure.

The source modules are then submitted to RXVP80™ for static analysis in order to detect additional problem areas. The V-IFTRAN™ source is modified and recompiled until no further static errors remain. At this point, the RXVP80™ documentation reports may be generated for later reference if necessary during testing and debugging.

The object modules are linked to form an executable image. The software is now ready to execute with a set of functional test cases. Before processing with RXVP80™, each of the initial functional tests should be used to exercise the software and the output should be evaluated against the test criteria. This is important for two reasons:

- It provides a baseline set of output from the uninstrumented software for later comparison to that from instrumented software.

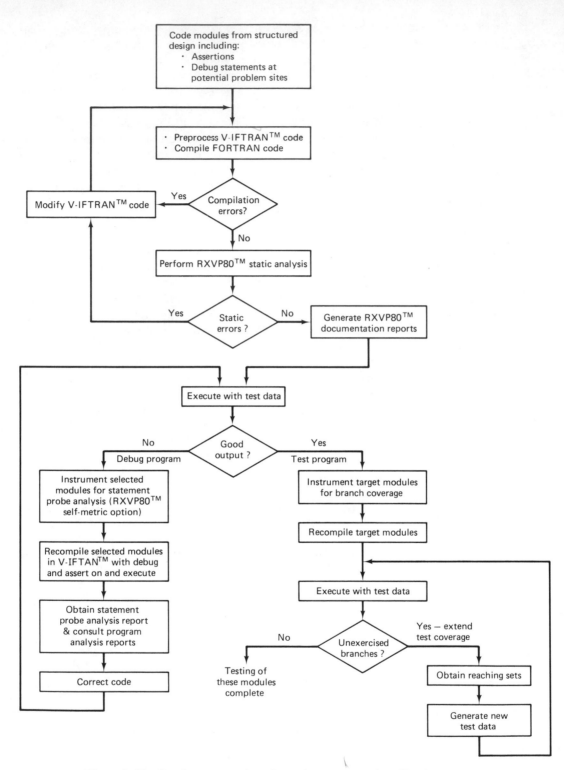

**Figure 6-15** Development and testing using automated verification system.

- It demonstrates the ability of the test team to prepare test data, execute the program, and interpret results.

This step requires that test data result in acceptable execution (though not necessarily expected behavior).

If good test results are not achieved with this initial execution of functional test cases, it becomes necessary to locate and correct the sources of the errors, that is to debug the software. RSVP80™ provides tools for systematic debugging. For each of the modules that are suspected error-contributors, the following steps are taken:

- Instrument the modules for a statement probe analysis report using the RXVP80™ SELF–METRIC component
- Activate the V-IFTRAN™ assertion and debug print statements
- Recompile the selected modules, link, and reexecute the test cases

One additional approach may be available—an on-line debugging system. An on-line debugging system is not part of the AVS but is provided by some computer vendors as part of their system software. The capabilities of on-line debugging systems are addressed in Section 6.5.

Reexecution of the test cases will provide V-IFTRAN™ debug printouts and assertion violation outputs, while the statement probe analysis report will provide performance data on each executable source statement. Using this data and the documentation reports previously produced, the errors are located and corrected. The software is then recompiled and reexecuted until good output is obtained for the set of functional test cases.

Once the test team is convinced that satisfactory results are being achieved with the test data, each of the functional tests is then executed with instrumented software to determine program coverage. It is very important that the normal program output generated from an instrumented test execution is checked against the previously prepared baseline (uninstrumented) output. If discrepancies exist between the two, this is direct evidence that the addition of instrumentation, in some way, has exposed a software malfunction. Some of the reasons for this type of error are

- The software test object is sensitive to time or space perturbations (i.e., it is not suitable for AVS testing).
- The probe routines were improperly added (e.g., placed in a wrong overlay link).
- The test data or test environment of the instrumented code is different from that of the baseline (uninstrumented) test.
- The computation process has caused the malfunction (e.g., inconsistent code generated by the compiler).
- Computer resources are inadequate to process instrumented code (e.g., compiler or loader limitations regarding number of external symbols, or memory capacity for expanded code).

Outputs from the instrumentation process and the instrumented execution include module source text listings with DD-path definitions, a coverage report for each instrumented module, summary of test coverage obtained with the run, and identification of DD-paths that have not been "hit."

Once the test team is confident of the quality achieved in obtaining initial functional test results, testing proceeds with RXVP80™ assistance as follows:

- Select a testing target from information in the RXVP80™ coverage reports for previous tests.
- Construct new test cases to improve coverage using the RXVP80™ retesting assistance capability.
- Perform test execution with new test cases and save, or stockpile, software behavior data (probe file).
- Analyze test coverage results from the RXVP80™ execution coverage reports.

These steps are repeated until the test coverage objectives have been met.

If the test coverage objectives are still not met, before constructing new test cases information about the control structure of the module and its input domain must be used. The relationship of individual modules to the system must be determined in order to test the module in its normal environment (i.e., its position in the invocation structure of the software system). This may prove difficult, or not even possible, because communication paths to the module may be blocked (e.g., by protective code or by lack of knowledge). If this is the case, a special test environment may be needed to thoroughly exercise the module.

The testing process for extending the coverage has a single objective—to construct test cases which cause execution of as yet unexecuted DD-paths within the program. Testing is over when all DD-paths have been exercised or when those which have not been exercised are shown by the program tester to be logically unexecutable.

Two questions arise in addressing the task of extended coverage retesting:

1. What are the targets for retesting?
2. Once the targets are selected, what assistance is available to exercise the targets?

The DD-path selection criteria should attempt to maximize collateral testing, that is, to exercise more than one unexercised DD-path with each new test case. Several guidelines can be used to aid the selection:

1. In a cluster of unexercised paths, choose an untested DD-path that is on the highest possible control nesting level. (RXVP80™ source listings print the nesting level.) This selection assures a high degree of collateral testing,

because some of the DD-paths leading to and from the target must be executed.

2. A reaching set is a sequence of DD-paths which lead to a specified DD-path. At user request, RXVP80™ determines reaching sets. Choose a DD-path which is at the end of a long reaching set as the target.

3. If a prior test case carries the program near one of the untested DD-paths, it may be more economical to determine how that test case can be modified to execute the unexercised path.

4. Analyze the untested DD-path predicate (conditional formula) in the reaching set for key variable names which may lead directly to the input.

5. Choose DD-paths whose predicates evaluate functional boundaries or extreme conditions; exercising these paths frequently uncovers program errors.

The process of relating paths which are targets for retesting to the input required for generating new test cases is highly dependent upon the design of the program under test. The tester must analyze the predicates in the testing targets for important variables, which may be described in program comments or documentation. These variables can be traced throughout the program by using the RXVP80™ cross reference, library interdependence, and invocation parameter reports.

When the new set of test cases is generated, the software test configuration is executed again. The results of this execution are then processed by RXVP80™ to see if the coverage is satisfactory. At this time, the programmers may see problems in the software which require code changes. The RXVP80™ documentation reports are then used to determine the effects that the code modification may have on other modules in the system.

It is difficult to assess the exact impact of widespread use of AVS testing technology because of only a limited experience base from which estimates of effect on software life cycle costs can be made. Intuitively, the AVS testing technology can be expected to

- Decrease the overall cost of comprehensively tested software, or increase the level of testing coverage achieved for the same cost
- Identify programming constructs that are difficult to test and eventually eliminate their use in critical software systems
- Assure that software systems subjected to the AVS-based testing methodology will have a significantly decreased likelihood of failure in actual use, particularly if the software failures could result from lack of comprehensive testing

An analysis of life cycle cost impact resulting from the use of RXVP80™ on a recent software project is presented in Chapter 7.

# 6.5

## An On-Line Debugging System

Testing and debugging are two distinct but closely related activities. Testing identifies the presence of errors or anomalous behavior in the software. Debugging is the practice of locating and correcting the errors revealed by the testing activity. Debugging is a tedious and difficult task. Until recently, debugging was a primitive "black magic" craft practically unsupported by tools and methodologies. The activity was governed by the programmer's intuition and artistic placement of print statements within the operational code to capture the status of key variables at strategic points in the execution flow.

More modern approaches to debugging still heavily rely on the programmer's accumulated experience and common sense but are assisted by the availability of automated tools. These tools bring more rigor and discipline to the debugging process. Tool-assisted debugging is still oriented toward revealing the status of variables and tracing the execution flow. The automated tools offer the advantages of making the process more efficient, dynamic, and systematic in order to accomplish the result in a shorter period of time. The programmer is no longer obligated to rely totally on his own *ad hoc* methodologies for debugging. Paramount among debugging aids is the category of tools known as the *on-line debugging system*. The on-line debugging system allows the programmer to go about the traditional debugging process on-line during the program execution using symbology from the source program. Several computer hardware vendors now offer on-line debugging systems as a standard product.

We shall explore the representative set of on-line debugging capabilities provided by Digital Equipment Corporation's Symbolic Debugger for that company's VAX computer. The symbolic debugger permits the programmer to monitor and control the execution of a program while being able to examine and change the values of variables at intermediate points during execution. The user converses with the debugger interactively from the terminal. All references to locations in the program are in terms of labels and identifiers of the source program. The symbolic debugger supports several different languages, including FORTRAN. The debugger furnishes the following services:

- Setting of breakpoints where program execution is suspended and status of the program may be examined
- Setting of tracepoints where the debugger displays a message indicating that the tracepoint was traversed
- Watches of specific program symbols that are activated each time the location is modified. The old and new values of the location are displayed each time it is modified.
- When execution is suspended, the contents of variables can be examined and changed.

- User-directed expressions can be evaluated at suspension points.
- Initiation and suspension of program execution[2]

Conversation between user and debugger is accomplished through a command language on-line from the terminal. Prior to activation of the debugger during execution, certain options must be enabled at compile and link time.

The capabilities of the symbolic debugger are now demonstrated. Our user is trying to implement a program named NETWRK. In particular, irregular behavior of this program points to the subroutine IBCALC as the probable trouble spot. The NETWRK program, and subroutine IBCALC, have been coded in IFTRAN, a structured FORTRAN preprocesser. Because the symbolic debugger can reference only the standard FORTRAN, we are compelled to use the precompiled FORTRAN text for debugging in this case in lieu of the more readable IFTRAN source. The FORTRAN source text for subroutine IBCALC is displayed in Figure 6–16. Note that the original IFTRAN source statements appear as comments in the precompiled FORTRAN listing.

The user would like to accomplish the following goals by investigating the behavior of subroutine IBCALC using the symbolic debugger:

- Verify that IBCALC was entered.
- Examine the contents of locations ERROR (1) through ERROR (5) each time through the loop that begins with statement 27.
- Examine the value of location ERRTOT each time it is modified.

We now show how the capabilities of the symbolic debugger support these objectives on-line during program execution.

Contained in Figure 6–17 is a hardcopy record of a symbolic debugger session that addresses the debugging needs previously stated. The transactions with the debugger are displayed in chronological order of their occurrence. Line numbers have been superimposed on the figure for easy reference to this narration. The user has entered a run command for the program NETWRK on line 1. Lines 2 and 3 are the system reaction to this command, indicating that the symbolic debugger has been entered and is awaiting instruction from the user. The debugger provides the prompt DBG> to denote that a command is expected from the user.

On line 4, a command has been entered to instruct the debugger that the immediate scope of interest is the module IBCALC. This is necessary in case identical symbols have been used in two or more modules. Line 5 shows that a tracepoint has been set at line 9 of IBCALC. This will result in display of an informative message when line 9 is reached during the execution. The user has set this tracepoint at the beginning of the subroutine to verify that IBCALC was entered. The user now asks on line 6 for a breakpoint to be set at line 29 of IBCALC. This will enable examina-

---

[2] *VAX-11 Symbolic Debugger Reference Manual* (Maynard, Ma.: Digital Equipment Corp., 1978) pp. 1-2-3.

```
0001              SUBROUTINE IBCALC (G,VE,JS,NODES,BRNCHS,IB,A,IBOUT)    FO    1
          C       ROUTINE TO CALCULATE NETWORK BRANCH CURRENTS AND OUTPUT FO    2
          C       RESULTS IF REQUESTED.                                   FO    3
          C       ROUTINE ALSO CALCULATES NODAL CURRENT UNBALANCES TO VALIDATE FO 4
          C       SOLUTION ACCURACY.                                      FO    5
          C                                                               FO    6
          C       DESCRIPTION OF VARIABLES                                FO    7
          C          G        - BRANCH CONDUCTANCE MATRIX                 FO    8
          C          VE       - ELEMENT VOLTAGE VECTOR                    FO    9
          C          JS       - INDEPENDENT CURRENT SOURCE VECTOR         FO   10
          C          BRNCHS   - NUMBER OF CIRCUIT BRANCHES                FO   11
          C          IB       - BRANCH CURRENT VECTOR                     FO   12
          C          IBOUT    - BRANCH CURRENT OUTPUT FLAG                FO   13
          C          A        - NODAL INCIDENCE MATRIX                    FO   14
          C          MISC     - DEBUG OUTPUT FLAG                         FO   15
          C          LUNIN    - LOGICAL INPUT UNIT                        FO   16
          C          LUNOUT   - LOGICAL OUTPUT UNIT                       FO   17
          C          ERROR    - CURRENT UNBALANCE VECTOR                  FO   18
          C          ERRTOT   - TOTAL CURRENT UNBALANCE                   FO   19
          C                                                               FO   20
          C-----------------------------------------------------------FO   21
          C                                                               FO   22
0002              INTEGER A,BRNCHS                                        FO   23
0003              REAL JS,IB                                              FO   24
0004              LOGICAL IBOUT                                           FO   25
0005              COMMON /UNITS/ LUNIN,LUNOUT                             FO   26
0006              COMMON /DEBUG/ MISC                                     FO   27
          C                                                               FO   28
0007              DIMENSION A(20,50), G(50,50), VE(50), JS(50), IB(50)    FO   29
0008              DIMENSION ERROR (20)                                    FO   30
          C                                                               FO   31
          C       IF (MISC.EQ.3)                                          IF   32
0009              IF(MISC.EQ.3) GO TO 19997                                    32
0010              GO TO 19998                                                  32
0011        19997 CONTINUE                                                     32
0012              WRITE (LUNOUT,900) IBOUT                                FO 1 33
          C       END IF                                                  IF   34
0013        19998 CONTINUE                                                     34
0014        19999 CONTINUE                                                     34
          C                                                               FO   35
          C-----------------------------------------------------------FO   36
          C       CALCULATE BRANCH CURRENTS    IB = G*VE-JS              FO   37
          C-----------------------------------------------------------FO   38
          C                                                               FO   39
          C       DO (I=1,BRNCHS)                                         IF   40
0015              DO 19996 I=1,BRNCHS                                          40
0016              IB(I) = 0.0                                             FO 1 41
          C       DO (J=1,BRNCHS)                                         IF 1 42
0017              DO 19994 J=1,BRNCHS                                          42
0018                  IB(I) = IB(I)+G(I,J)*VE(J)                          FO 2 43
          C       END DO                                                  IF 1 44
0019        19994 CONTINUE                                                     44
0020        19993 CONTINUE                                                     44
0021              IB(I) = IB(I)-JS(I)                                     FO 1 45
          C       END DO                                                  IF   46
0022        19996 CONTINUE                                                     46
```

**Figure 6-16**  Subroutine IBCALC FORTRAN source listing.

tion of the ERROR array and other locations if necessary at each iteration through the loop. Next, on line 7, a watchpoint has been set on the variable ERRTOT. Each time this location is modified, execution is suspended and the old and new values of the location are displayed. Now, with the preliminaries concluded, the GO command is entered on line 8 to start execution. Line 9 is the system response to the GO command.

As the execution traverses source line 9 of IBCALC, a tracepoint message is

```
0023  19995 CONTINUE                                                        46
      C                                                               FO    47
      C--------------------------------------------------------------FO    48
      C         CALCULATE NODAL CURRENT UNBALANCE      ER = A*IB      FO    49
      C--------------------------------------------------------------FO    50
      C                                                               FO    51
0024              ERRTOT = 0.0                                        FO    52
      C         DO (I=1,NODES)                                        IF    53
0025          DO 19992 I=1,NODES                                            53
0026              ERROR(I) = 0.0                                      FO 1  54
      C             DO (J=1,BRNCHS)                                   IF 1  55
0027              DO 19990 J=1,BRNCHS                                       55
0028                  ERROR(I) = ERROR(I)+A(I,J)*IB(J)               FO 2  56
      C             END DO                                            IF 1  57
0029  19990 CONTINUE                                                       57
0030  19989 CONTINUE                                                       57
0031              ERRTOT = ERRTOT+ABS(ERROR(I))                      FO 1  58
      C         END DO                                                IF    59
0032  19992 CONTINUE                                                       59
0033  19991 CONTINUE                                                       59
      C                                                               FO    60
      C--------------------------------------------------------------FO    61
      C         OUTPUT BRANCH CURRENTS                                FO    62
      C--------------------------------------------------------------FO    63
      C                                                               FO    64
      C         IF (IBOUT)                                            IF    65
0034          IF(IBOUT) GO TO 19986                                        65
0035          GO TO 19987                                                  65
0036  19986 CONTINUE                                                       65
0037              WRITE (LUNOUT,910)                                 FO 1  66
      C         DO (I=1,BRNCHS)                                       IF 1  67
0038          DO 19985 I=1,BRNCHS                                          67
0039              WRITE (LUNOUT,920) I,IB(I)                         FO 2  68
      C         END DO                                                IF 1  69
0040  19985 CONTINUE                                                       69
0041  19984 CONTINUE                                                       69
      C         END IF                                                IF    70
0042  19987 CONTINUE                                                       70
0043  19988 CONTINUE                                                       70
      C                                                               FO    71
      C--------------------------------------------------------------FO    72
      C         OUTPUT NODAL CURRENT UNBALANCE                        FO    73
      C--------------------------------------------------------------FO    74
      C                                                               FO    75
0044          WRITE (LUNOUT,930) ERRTOT                              FO    76
      C         IF (ERRTOT.GT.0.001)                                 IF    77
0045          IF(ERRTOT.GT.0.001) GO TO 19981                             77
0046          GO TO 19982                                                  77
0047  19981 CONTINUE                                                       77
0048              WRITE (LUNOUT,950)                                 FO 1  78
0049              WRITE (LUNOUT,960) (I,ERROR(I),I=1,NODES )         FO 1  79
      C         END IF                                                IF    80
0050  19982 CONTINUE                                                       80
0051  19983 CONTINUE                                                       80
      C                                                               FO    81
      C         IF (MISC.EQ.3)                                        IF    82
```

**Figure 6-16**  *continued*

displayed (line 10 of Figure 6–17). At line 24 of IBCALC, location ERRTOT has been reset; this is indicated on line 11 of the figure. Lines 12 and 13 show the old and new value of ERRTOT (which happens to have been reset to its original value). Execution is now in a suspended state awaiting further instruction from the user. The user reinitiates execution on line 14 with a GO command. Line 15 is the system response.

On line 16 the system announces that it has suspended execution at source line

```
$ RUN NETWRK

2          VAX/VMS DEBUG V1.5   04 January 1979

3  %DEBUG-I-INITIAL, language is FORTRAN, scope and module set to 'NETWRK'
4  DBG>SET SCOPE IBCALC
5  DBG>SET TRACE %LINE 9
6  DBG>SET BREAK %LINE 29
7  DBG>SET WATCH ERRTOT
8  DBG>GO
9  routine start at NETWRK\NETWRK
10 trace at IBCALC\IBCALC %line 9
11 write to IBCALC\ERRTOT at PC IBCALC\IBCALC %line 24
12         old value =    0.0000000E+00
13         new value =    0.0000000E+00
14 DBG>GO
15 start at IBCALC\IBCALC %line 25
16 break at IBCALC\IBCALC %line 29
17 DBG>EXAMINE ERROR(1):ERROR(5)
18 IBCALC\ERROR(1):    -0.3612320
19 IBCALC\ERROR(2):     0.0000000E+00
20 IBCALC\ERROR(3):     0.0000000E+00
21 IBCALC\ERROR(4):     0.0000000E+00
22 IBCALC\ERROR(5):     0.0000000E+00
23 DBG>GO
24 start at IBCALC\IBCALC %line 29
25 break at IBCALC\IBCALC %line 29
26 DBG>EXAMINE ERROR(1):ERROR(5)
27 IBCALC\ERROR(1):    -0.4106490
28 IBCALC\ERROR(2):     0.0000000E+00
29 IBCALC\ERROR(3):     0.0000000E+00
30 IBCALC\ERROR(4):     0.0000000E+00
31 IBCALC\ERROR(5):     0.0000000E+00
32 DBG>CANCEL BREAK %LINE 29
33 DBG>GO
34 start at IBCALC\IBCALC %line 29
35 write to IBCALC\ERRTOT at PC IBCALC\IBCALC %line 31 +13
36         old value =    0.0000000E+00
37         new value =    5.9604645E-08
38 DBG>GO
39 start at IBCALC\IBCALC %line 32
40 write to IBCALC\ERRTOT at PC IBCALC\IBCALC %line 31 +13
41         old value =    5.9604645E-08
42         new value =    5.9604645E-08
43 DBG>GO
44 start at IBCALC\IBCALC %line 32
45 FORTRAN STOP
46 %DEBUG-I-EXITSTATUS, is '%SYSTEM-S-NORMAL, normal successful completion'
47 DBG>EXIT
   $
```

**Figure 6-17**  Symbolic debugger session.

29 of IBCALC as instructed by the breakpoint command previously entered on line 6. The user on line 17 asks to examine locations ERROR(1) through ERROR(5). The debugger reacts by displaying the contents of these locations on lines 18 through 22. Execution is reactivated by entry of the GO instruction on line 23. This entire transaction sequence is repeated on lines 24 through 31 as a result of iterating through the loop a second time. At this point, the user is satisfied with the information obtained on the status of the ERROR array and the breakpoint is cancelled on line 32. Execution is again resumed (lines 33 and 34).

The debugger suspends execution at line 31 of IBCALC where the variable ERRTOT has again been modified. This information is displayed on lines 35 to 37 of Figure 6-17. The user again reinstates execution (lines 38 and 39). As shown on lines 39 through 44, the location ERRTOT is again reset, and the user orders a resumption of the execution. Finally, execution of the NETWRK program is automatically terminated in a normal manner (lines 45 and 46). The user elects no further interaction with the debugger and enters an EXIT command on line 47 to conclude the session.

Through this sample session we have seen the capabilities of an on-line debugging system as represented by the VAX Symbolic Debugger. Debugging performed in a conversational mode permits the user the flexibility to examine program status on-line and respond to displayed information with additional debug inquiries if necessary all in a single run. Such a series of information requests would require several individual runs when debugging is performed in the traditional batch environment. An on-line debugging system offers a uniform and flexible mechanism to support the difficult debugging task in a manner more efficient than earlier *ad hoc* procedures.

# Application of an Automated Verification System

In this chapter, an example software package is submitted for analysis to RXVP80™ to demonstrate the software development and testing methodology outlined on Figure 6–15 of the previous chapter. Beginning at the point where a static analysis is performed, the outputs of RXVP80™ are illustrated and their significance to the development and test process is explained. Also included in this chapter is a recount of the use of RXVP80™ on a recent software project at Hughes Aircraft Company to enforce an exhaustive test discipline; of particular interest is an analysis of the life cycle cost advantages accrued as a result of employing RXVP80™ to support testing on this project.

## 7.1
**Application of RXVP80™**

The dc network analysis system, originally introduced in Chapter 3, will again be the subject of analysis. The application of RXVP80™ to part of this system will more fully demonstrate the RXVP80™ capabilities and products. The following subject areas are addressed:

- Test configuration
- Static analysis
- Statement probe analysis
- Test instrumentation and analysis
- Test coverage extension and test data selection
- Retest analysis

The order of presentation of these topics closely follows the flow of the development and test methodology previously depicted in Figure 6-15.

## TEST CONFIGURATION

The overall configuration of the dc network analysis system is shown in Figure 7-1 in abbreviated form. A single thread, thread 12, has been selected from Figure 3-14 in Chapter 3 as the demonstration item for analysis and testing using RXVP80™. The function of this thread is to print the branch currents. The thread consists of two modules:

1. OUTPUT—This module outputs the circuit quantities and controls the computation of certain optional output data sets.
2. IBCALC—This module computes and outputs the branch currents, one of the optional output data sets.

This is the final thread of the dc network analysis system and, thus, completes the system. Hence, the test configuration for this thread is the entire dc network analysis system architecture. No stubs or drivers are required.

## STATIC ANALYSIS

It is assumed that the two modules of this thread, OUTPUT and IBCALC, have been compiled and all compilation errors have been removed. The modules are now submitted to a static analysis by RXVP80™. The purpose of this analysis is to perform consistency checks on certain types of possible error conditions not examined by compilers and to produce a set of documentation reports which aid test personnel to understand the organization of the code. RXVP80™ is run with the STATIC, LIST, SUMMARY, and DOCUMENT options turned on to perform this analysis and obtain the documentation outputs.

The results of a static analysis of module OUTPUT are contained in Figure 7-2. This static analysis report consists of an indented IFTRAN™ source listing of

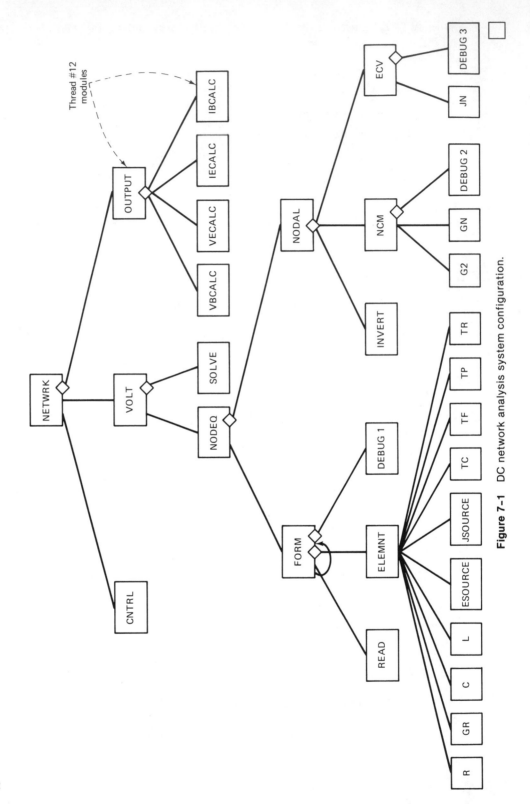

**Figure 7-1**  DC network analysis system configuration.

the OUTPUT module with error/warning messages intermixed at the statements where the irregularities are detected. A number of semantic inconsistencies have been discovered by RXVP80™ in this module:

- Statement 74—The BRNCHS and A parameters of this call sequence are used as *real* parameters in OUTPUT but are declared as *integers* elsewhere. Also, the routine VBCALC is called with only five arguments but actually requires six arguments.
- Statements 79, 84, and 90 have mode mismatches similar to statement 74's.

We shall assume that the programmer will rectify these potential errors before proceeding further.

A number of documentation reports based on an analysis of the source text are produced by RXVP80™. Both multimodule reports and reports on individual modules are generated. The multimodule reports provide summary analyses based on all the modules in the library. Because we are focusing on the testing of the final thread of the dc network analysis system, the library now consists of all the modules of that system. Two of the multimodule reports (Figures 7–3 and 7–4) are described in the following paragraphs.

LIBRARY DEPENDENCE (FIGURE 7–3)   This report provides an overall view of the module interconnections. For each module, the caller module and the modules invoked by this module are specified. This report is useful, when a bug is detected, in delimiting possible source areas. When program changes are made, the report is also useful in identifying modules which may be affected.

COMMON MATRICES (FIGURE 7–4)   This report provides an overview of the usage of each common block and each symbol within the common block. These data items are cross-referenced to the modules with type of usage annotated (set, used, equivalenced). The common matrices are also useful in identifying potentially affected data and modules when changes are made.

The single module reports (Figures 7–5 through 7–8) reveal detailed data about the organization and interfaces of each individual module. These reports are described in the following text. The module IBCALC is the subject of these reports.

INVOCATION BANDS (FIGURE 7–5a)   The bands report shows all levels of invocation (upward and downward) for the module IBCALC. IBCALC is listed at level 0; its invocation chains downward are listed under positive levels, and invocation chains that lead to the module from higher levels are listed under negative levels. This report completely describes the module's position in the invocation hierarchy and shows the other modules in the system that will need to be retested if the referenced module is changed.

INVOCATION SPACE (FIGURE 7–5b)   This is the most detailed report of module invocations for a single module. First, it lists all first-level invocations from the

...SOURCE TAB

| STMT | NEST | LINE | SOURCE... |
|------|------|------|-----------|
| 1 | | 1 | SUBROUTINE OUTPUT (NODES,BRNCHS,OUT,VN,A,DI,ES,JS,G,NOED) |
| | | 2 | C   ROUTINE TO OUTPUT COMPUTED CIRCUIT QUANTITIES. |
| | | 3 | C   DRIVING ROUTINE TO CONTROL INDIVIDUAL OUTPUT CALCULATIONS |
| | | 4 | C |
| | | 5 | C   DESCRIPTION OF VARIABLES |
| | | 6 | C     MISC   - DEBUG OUTPUT FLAG |
| | | 7 | C     OUT    - VECTOR OF OUTPUT REQUEST FLAGS |
| | | 8 | C     VN     - NODE VOLTAGE VECTOR |
| | | 9 | C     A      - NODAL INCIDENCE MATRIX |
| | | 10 | C     DI     - INVERSE OF (I-D) MATRIX |
| | | 11 | C     ES     - INDEPENDENT VOLTAGE SOURCE VECTOR |
| | | 12 | C     JS     - INDEPENDENT CURRENT SOURCE VECTOR |
| | | 13 | C     G      - BRANCH CONDUCTANCE MATRIX |
| | | 14 | C     NOED   - NO DEPENDENT VOLTAGE SOURCES FLAG |
| | | 15 | C     LUNIN  - LOGICAL INPUT UNIT |
| | | 16 | C     LUNOUT - LOGICAL OUTPUT UNIT |
| | | 17 | C     NODES  - NUMBER OF CIRCUIT NODES |
| | | 18 | C     BRNCHS - NUMBER OF CIRCUIT BRANCHES |
| | | 19 | C     VB     - BRANCH VOLTAGE VECTOR |
| | | 20 | C     VE     - ELEMENT VOLTAGE VECTOR |
| | | 21 | C     IE     - ELEMENT CURRENT VECTOR |
| | | 22 | C |
| | | 23 | C |
| | | 24 | C |
| 2 | | 25 | REAL JS,IE |
| 3 | | 26 | LOGICAL OUT,NOED,VNOUT,VBOUT,VEOUT,IEOUT,IBOUT |
| 4 | | 27 | COMMON /UNITS/ LUNIN,LUNOUT |
| 5 | | 28 | COMMON /DEBUG/ MISC |
| | | 29 | C |
| 6 | | 30 | DIMENSION OUT(5), VN(20), A(20,50), DI(50,50), G(50,50) |
| 7 | | 31 | DIMENSION ES(50), JS(50) |
| 8 | | 32 | DIMENSION VB(50), VE(50), IE(50) |
| | | 33 | C |
| 9 | | 34 | IF (MISC.EQ.3) |
| 10 | 1 | 35 | .   WRITE (LUNOUT,900) OUT |
| 11 | | 36 | END IF |
| 12 | | 37 | VNOUT = OUT(1) |
| 13 | | 38 | VBOUT = OUT(2) |
| 14 | | 39 | VEOUT = OUT(3) |
| 15 | | 40 | IEOUT = OUT(4) |
| 16 | | 41 | IBOUT = OUT(5) |
| | | 42 | C |
| | | 43 | C |
| | | 44 | C |
| | | 45 | C   SET UP REQUIRED CIRCUIT QUANTITY VECTORS FOR OUTPUT |
| | | 46 | C |
| | | 47 | C |
| | | 48 | C |
| | | 49 | C   INITIALIZE OUTPUT REPORT |

**Figure 7-2**   Static analysis report for OUTPUT module.

```
                SUBROUTINE OUTPUT (NODES,BRNCHS,OUT,VN,A,DI,ES,JS,G,NOED)

                                                                 ...SOURCE TAB

STMT NEST LINE  SOURCE...

           50  C
           51  C
 17        52        WRITE (LUNOUT,910)
           53  C
           54  C     OUTPUT NODE VOLTAGES
           55  C
           56  C
           57  C
 18        58        IF (VNOUT)
 19     1  59    .      WRITE (LUNOUT,920)
 20     1  60    .      DO (I=1,NODES)
 21     2  61    .   .      WRITE (LUNOUT,930) I,VN(I)
 22     1  62    .   .    END DO
 23        63        END IF
           64  C
           65  C     SET UP CIRCUIT QUANTITY VECTORS AND OUTPUT REMAINING
           66  C     QUANTITIES AS REQUESTED
           67  C
           68  C
           69  C
 24        70        IF (VBOUT.OR.VEOUT.OR.IEOUT.OR.IBOUT)
           71  C
           72  C     COMPUTE VB AND OUTPUT IF REQUESTED
           73  C
 25     1  74    .      CALL VBCALC (NODES,BRNCHS,A,VN,VB)

                              MODE WARNING
                  -PARAMETER  2 OF VBCALC    ACTUAL PARAMETER HAS MODE REAL
                                            FORMAL PARAMETER HAS MODE INTEGER

                              MODE WARNING
                  -PARAMETER  3 OF VBCALC    ACTUAL PARAMETER HAS MODE REAL
                                            FORMAL PARAMETER HAS MODE INTEGER

                              CALL ERROR
                      VBCALC    CALLED WITH  5 ACTUALLY HAS   6 ARGUMENTS

 26     1  75    .      IF (VEOUT.OR.IEOUT.OR.IBOUT)
           76  C
           77  C     COMPUTE VE AND OUTPUT IF REQUESTED
           78  C
 27     2  79    .   .      CALL VECALC (DI,VB,ES,BRNCHS,NOED,VE,VEOUT)

                              MODE WARNING
                  -PARAMETER  4 OF VECALC    ACTUAL PARAMETER HAS MODE REAL
                                            FORMAL PARAMETER HAS MODE INTEGER
```

**Figure 7-2** *continued*

165

STATIC ANALYSIS\     SUBROUTINE OUTPUT (NODES,BRNCHS,OUT,VN,A,DI,ES,JS,G,NOED)

...SOURCE TAB

```
STMT  NEST  LINE   SOURCE...

 28    2     80          IF (IEOUT.OR.IBOUT)
             81     C
             82     C         COMPUTE IE AND OUTPUT IF REQUESTED
             83     C
 29    3     84                CALL IECALC (G,VE,BRNCHS,IE,IEOUT)
                                       MODE WARNING
                               -PARAMETER  3 OF IECALC    ACTUAL PARAMETER HAS MODE REAL
                                                          FORMAL PARAMETER HAS MODE INTEGER

 30    3     85                IF (IBOUT)
             86     C
             87     C         COMPUTE IB AND NODAL CURRENT UNBALANCES
             88     C         OUTPUT IF REQUESTED
             89     C
 31    4     90                   CALL IBCALC (G,VE,JS,NODES,BRNCHS,IB,A,IBOUT)
                                       MODE WARNING
                               -PARAMETER  5 OF IBCALC    ACTUAL PARAMETER HAS MODE REAL
                                                          FORMAL PARAMETER HAS MODE INTEGER
                                       MODE WARNING
                               -PARAMETER  6 OF IBCALC    ACTUAL PARAMETER HAS MODE INTEGER
                                                          FORMAL PARAMETER HAS MODE REAL
                                       MODE WARNING
                               -PARAMETER  7 OF IBCALC    ACTUAL PARAMETER HAS MODE REAL
                                                          FORMAL PARAMETER HAS MODE INTEGER

 32    3     91                   END IF
 33    2     92                END IF
 34    1     93             END IF
 35          94          END IF
             95     C
 36          96          IF (MISC.EQ.3)
 37    1     97             WRITE (LUNOUT,940)
 38          98          END IF
 39          99          RETURN
            100     C
 40         101     900 FORMAT (5X,20HENTER OUTPUT, OUT = ,5L1)
 41         102     910 FORMAT (1H1///20X,19HDC CIRCUIT RESPONSE , /
 41         103          1        20X,19H----------------------  /// )
```

**Figure 7-2**  *continued*

STATIC ANALYSIS\

SUBROUTINE OUTPUT (NODES,BRNCHS,OUT,VN,A,DI,ES,JS,G,NOED)

STMT NEST LINE SOURCE...                                                    ...SOURCE TAB

```
42      104   920 FORMAT (5X,13HNODE VOLTAGE , //
42      105     1          5X,13HNODE     VALUE  , /
42      106     2          5X,13H---        -----     )
43      107   930 FORMAT (6X,12,2X,1PE12.5)
44      108   940 FORMAT (5X,11HEXIT OUTPUT  )
45      109       END
```

```
        STATIC  ANALYSIS  SUMMARY        ERRORS  WARNINGS
        ------------------------------   ------  --------
        GRAPH CHECKING                      0        0
        CALL CHECKING                       1        0
        MODE CHECKING                       0        7
        SET/USE CHECKING                    0        0
```

**Figure 7-2** *continued*

```
INVOCATION SUMMARY

ENTRY      ---------------------------------------------------------------

C        IS CALLED BY - FORM
         AND CALLS    - -NONE-

CNTRL    IS CALLED BY - NETWRK
         AND CALLS    - -NONE-

ECV      IS CALLED BY - NODAL
         AND CALLS    - -NONE-

ESORCE   IS CALLED BY - FORM
         AND CALLS    - LUDOUT

FORM     IS CALLED BY - NODEQ
         AND CALLS    - C       ESORCE  GR      JSORCE  L      R      TC
                      - TF      TP      TR

GR       IS CALLED BY - FORM
         AND CALLS    - -NONE-

IBCALC   IS CALLED BY - OUTPUT
         AND CALLS    - ABS

IECALC   IS CALLED BY - OUTPUT
         AND CALLS    - -NONE-

INVERT   IS CALLED BY - NODAL
         AND CALLS    - ABS

JSORCE   IS CALLED BY - FORM
         AND CALLS    - -NONE-

L        IS CALLED BY - FORM
         AND CALLS    - -NONE-

NCM      IS CALLED BY - NODAL
         AND CALLS    - -NONE-

NETWRK   IS CALLED BY - -NONE-
         AND CALLS    - CNTRL   NODEQ   OUTPUT  SOLVE

NODAL    IS CALLED BY - NODEQ
         AND CALLS    - ECV     INVERT  NCM

NODEQ    IS CALLED BY - NETWRK
         AND CALLS    - FORM    NODAL

OUTPUT   IS CALLED BY - NETWRK
         AND CALLS    - IBCALC  IECALC  VBCALC  VECALC

R        IS CALLED BY - FORM
         AND CALLS    - -NONE-
```

**Figure 7-3**  Library dependence report.

```
INVOCATION SUMMARY
ENTRY                     ------------------------------------------------------------------

SOLVE     IS CALLED BY - NETWRK
          AND CALLS    - ABS
TC        IS CALLED BY - FORM
          AND CALLS    - -NONE-
TF        IS CALLED BY - FORM
          AND CALLS    - -NONE-
TP -      IS CALLED BY - FORM
          AND CALLS    - -NONE-
TR        IS CALLED BY - FORM
          AND CALLS    - -NONE-
VBCALC    IS CALLED BY - OUTPUT
          AND CALLS    - -NONE-
VECALC    IS CALLED BY - OUTPUT
          AND CALLS    - -NONE-
```

**Figure 7-3** *continued*

module, giving invoked modules names in alphabetical order, each one followed by a list of the numbered statements that contain that invocation. Then the report shows an alphabetical list of all modules with invocations to the referenced module that give statement number and text of the invocation. There is only one invocation to IBCALC and one invocation from IBCALC. This report enables the tester to easily identify the actual arguments used in all invocations to and from the module.

STATEMENT PROFILE (FIGURE 7-6)   The statements of the module IBCALC are classified as either declaration, executable, decision, or documentation. Under each classification, a tabulated account of the various subtypes is listed.

CROSS REFERENCE (FIGURE 7-7)   This report is a symbol cross reference listing for the specified module. The symbol types cover variables, file names, block names, and subprogram names. The statement numbers where each symbol appears within the module are indicated. Each occurrence of the symbol is flagged as to its use (used, set, or equivalenced). This report is mainly utilized to find where variables are set in order to alter test cases.

I/O STATEMENTS (FIGURE 7-8)   This report delineates all the INPUT/OUTPUT statements and formats contained in each module of the library. The report pinpoints all the locations where data are being input to the system and output from the system.

```
LEGEND (C=FIRST USED IN A CALL,E=EQUIVALENCED,S=SET,U=USED,X=SET AND USED
--------------------------------------------------------------------------
  --------------------------------------------------------------------
      **           *           .            .              .         *
    * * MODULE   * C C E E F.G I I I J.L N N N N.O R S T T.T T V V *
    *  *         *   N C S O.R B E N S.  C E U O.U   O C F.P R B E *
    *   *        *   I V O R. C C V U. M I D D.T   L       .   C C *
    *    *       *   R R M. A A E R.   W A E.P   V       .     A A *
    *     *      *   L   C. . L L R C.   R L Q.U   E       .     L L *
    *      *   * *       E . C C T E.   K   .T             .     C C *
    *       * * *           .            .              .         *
COMMON * SYMBOL * *         .            .              .         *
    *         **            .            .              .         *
  --------------------------------------------------------------------
DEBUG   * MISC    * U X U U U.U U U U U U.U U   U U.U U U U U.U U U U *
  --------------------------------------------------------------------

  -------------------------------------------.------
      **           *           .         *
    * * MODULE   * C C F G L.N R *
    *  *         *   N O R .E   *
    *   *        *   I R   .T   *
    *    *       *   R M   .W   *
    *     *      *   L     .R   *
    *      *   * *         .K   *
    *       * * *          .    *
COMMON * SYMBOL * *         .    *
    *         **            .    *
  -------------------------------------------.------
LIMITS  * OPEN    * U S   U  . U *
    * SHORT   *   S   U U. U *
  -------------------------------------------.------

  --------------------------------------------------------------------
      **           *           .            .              .         *
    * * MODULE   * C C E E F.G I I I J.L N N N N.O R S T T.T T V V *
    *  *         *   N C S O.R B E N S.  C E U O.U   O C F.P R B E *
    *   *        *   I V O R. C C V U. M I D D.T   L       .   C C *
    *    *       *   R R M. A A E R.   W A E.P   V       .     A A *
    *     *      *   L   C. . L L R C.   R L Q.U   E       .     L L *
    *      *   * *       E . C C T E.   K   .T             .     C C *
    *       * * *           .            .              .         *
COMMON * SYMBOL * *         .            .              .         *
    *         **            .            .              .         *
  --------------------------------------------------------------------
UNITS   * LUNIN   * U     U.            .     S     .              *
    * LUNOUT  * U U U   U.U U U U U U.U U S U U.U U U U U.U U U U *
  --------------------------------------------------------------------
```

**Figure 7-4**  Common matrices report.

## STATEMENT PROBE ANALYSIS

At this point, all of the compilation and static errors have been removed. The thread test configuration is now ready for dynamic execution. For the initial run, a set of natural or functionally oriented test cases is utilized. In the unlikely event that good output is achieved from this first try, the following discussion is no longer pertinent. However, in the more probable situation that the system developers are in fact mortal and something has gone awry, there are several options available to the testers. In order to locate the cause of the trouble, they may

- Turn on DEBUG and/or ASSERT statements if the software was coded in V-IFTRAN™

INVOCATION BANDS

TO LEVEL 2

SUBROUTINE IBCALC (G,VE,JS,NODES,BRNCHS,IB,A,IBOUT)

LEVEL    -5   -4   -3   -2   -1    0    1    2    3    4    5

                                  OUTPUT   IBCALC
                                           ABS

PAGE    36

(a)

INVOCATION SPACE

SUBROUTINE IBCALC (G,VE,JS,NODES,BRNCHS,IB,A,IBOUT)

INVOCATIONS FROM WITHIN THIS MODULE

MODULE ABS
STMT =  25        ABS ( ERROR ( I ) )

INVOCATIONS TO THIS MODULE FROM WITHIN LIBRARY

MODULE OUTPUT
STMT =  32        CALL IBCALC ( G , VE , JS , NODES , BRNCHS , IB , A , IBOUT )

(b)

**Figure 7-5** (a) Invocation bands report. (b) Invocation space report.

171

INTERFACE CHARACTERISTICS
-------------------------

| | | |
|---|---|---|
| ARGUMENTS | 8 | |
| COMMON | 2 | |
| ENTRY | 1 | |
| EXIT | 1 | |
| WRITE | 7 | |

| STATEMENT CLASSIFICATION | STATEMENT TYPE | NUMBER | PERCENT |
|---|---|---|---|
| DECLARATION... | | | |
| | COMMON | 2 | 2.1 |
| | DIMENSION | 2 | 2.1 |
| | FORMAT | 7 | 7.4 |
| | INTEGER | 1 | 1.1 |
| | LOGICAL | 1 | 1.1 |
| | REAL | 1 | 1.1 |
| | TOTAL | 14 | 14.9 |
| EXECUTABLE... | | | |
| | ASSIGNMENT | 7 | 7.4 |
| | END | 1 | 1.1 |
| | ENDIF | 4 | 4.3 |
| | IFTRAN-DO | 5 | 5.3 |
| | RETURN | 1 | 1.1 |
| | WRITE | 7 | 7.4 |
| | TOTAL | 25 | 26.6 |
| DECISION... | | | |
| | ENDDO | 5 | 5.3 |
| | IFTRAN-IF | 4 | 4.3 |
| | SUBROUTINE | 1 | 1.1 |
| | TOTAL | 10 | 10.6 |
| DOCUMENTATION... | | | |
| | COMMENT | 45 | 47.9 |
| | TOTAL | 45 | 47.9 |

\* TOTAL PERCENTAGE MAY BE MORE THAN 100 BECAUSE OF OVERLAPPING CLASSIFICATIONS

**Figure 7-6** Statement profile report.

- Use an on-line debugging system if one is available
- Instrument the code for a statement probe analysis, using the SELF-METRIC option of RXVP80™

Of course, all these devices may be applied to the problem if necessary and appropriate. In this section, the statement probe analysis capability is discussed.

Instrumentation using the SELF-METRIC option provides data collection calls for each executable statement, permitting a complete record of the values stored during execution. This level of instrumentation would normally only be ap-

CROSS REFERENCE                 SUBROUTINE IBCALC  (G,VE,JS,NODES,BRNCHS,IB,A,IBOUT)

NAME     SCOPE      MODULE    USED/SET/EQUIVALENCED   ( * INDICATES SET )

| NAME | SCOPE | MODULE | USED/SET/EQUIVALENCED |
|------|-------|--------|-----------------------|
| A | PARAMETER | IBCALC | 23 |
| ABS | EXTERNAL | IBCALC | 25 |
| BRNCHS | PARAMETER | IBCALC | 12  14  22  25 |
| ERROR | LOCAL | IBCALC | 21*  23*  25  36 |
| ERRTOT | LOCAL | IBCALC | 19*  25*  35  34 |
| G | PARAMETER | IBCALC | 15 |
| I | LOCAL | IBCALC | 12  13  15  15  17  17  17  20  21  23  23  23  25  29  30  36  36  36 |
| IB | PARAMETER | IBCALC | 13*  15*  17*  17  23  30 |
| IBOUT | PARAMETER | IBCALC | 10  27 |
| J | LOCAL | IBCALC | 14  15  15  25  23  23 |
| JS | PARAMETER | IBCALC | 17 |
| LUNOUT | UNITS | IBCALC | 10  28  30  35  36  39 |
| MISC | DEBUG | IBCALC | 9  38 |
| NODES | PARAMETER | IBCALC | 20  36 |
| VE | PARAMETER | IBCALC | 15 |

**Figure 7-7**  Cross reference report.

I/O STATEMENTS\

THE FOLLOWING MODULES CONTAIN I/O STATEMENTS

```
CNTRL
NODEQ
SOLVE
VBCALC
VECALC
IECALC
OUTPUT
IBCALC
FORM
R
GR
C
L
ESORCE
JSORCE
TC
TF
TP
TR
NODAL
INVERT
NCM
FCV
```

I/O STATEMENTS AND ASSOCIATED FORMATS

--- CNTRL ---

```
STMT NEST LINE  SOURCE...                                              ...SOURCE TAB

  8        47        READ (IUNIN,900) NODES,BRNCHS,MISC,SHORT,OPEN
           48    C
           49    C   DETERMINE ANALYSIS OUTPUTS REQUIRED
           50    C
           51    C
  9        52        READ (LUNIN,910) OUT
 11        54            WRITE (LUNOUT,920) NODES,BRNCHS,OUT
 14        58    900 FORMAT (3I5,2F10.0)
 15        59    910 FORMAT (5L10)
 16        60    920 FORMAT (5X,11HEXIT CNTRL.,5X,I3,I3,2X,5L1)
```

**Figure 7-8**  I/O statements report.

I/O STATEMENTS          SUBROUTINE VBCALC (NODES,BRNCHS,A,VN,VB,VBOUT)

```
STMT NEST LINE  SOURCE...                                          ...SOURCE TAB
-------------------------------------------------------------------------------
27        57             1          5X,15HBRANCH       VALUE ,/
27        58                        5X,15H-----         ----- )
28        59    920 FORMAT (7X,I2,2X,1PE12.5)
29        60    930 FORMAT (5X,11HEXIT VBCALC  )


--- VBCALC ---

STMT NEST LINE  SOURCE...                                          ...SOURCE TAB
-------------------------------------------------------------------------------
 8        27             WRITE (LUNOUT,900) VBOUT
25        57             WRITE (LUNOUT,910)
27        59             WRITE (LUNOUT,920) I,VB(I)
31        64             WRITE (LUNOUT,930)
34        68    900 FORMAT (5X,22HENTER VBCALC. VBOUT = ,L1)
35        69    910 FORMAT (5X,16HELEMENT VOLTAGES ,//
35        70             1          5X,16HELEMENT       VALUE ,/
35        71                        5X,16H-----         ----- )
36        72    920 FORMAT (8X,I2,2X,1PE12.5)
37        73    930 FORMAT (5X,11HEXIT VBCALC )


--- IBCALC ---

STMT NEST LINE  SOURCE...                                          ...SOURCE TAB
-------------------------------------------------------------------------------
 9        26             WRITE (LUNOUT,900) IBOUT
15        42             WRITE (LUNOUT,910)
17        44             WRITE (LUNOUT,920) I,IB(I)
21        49             WRITE (LUNOUT,930)
24        53    900 FORMAT (5X,22HENTER IBCALC. IBOUT = ,L1)
25        54    910 FORMAT (5X,16HELEMENT CURRENTS ,//
25        55             1          5X,16HELEMENT       VALUE ,/
25        56                        5X,16H-----         ----- )
26        57    920 FORMAT (8X,I2,2X,1PE12.5)
27        58    930 FORMAT (5X,11HEXIT IBCALC )


--- IBCALC ---

STMT NEST LINE  SOURCE...                                          ...SOURCE TAB
-------------------------------------------------------------------------------
10        33             WRITE (LUNOUT,900) IBOUT
28        66             WRITE (LUNOUT,910)
30        68             WRITE (LUNOUT,920) I,IB(I)
33        76             WRITE (LUNOUT,930) ERRTOT
35        78             WRITE (LUNOUT,950)
36        79             WRITE (LUNOUT,960) (I,ERROR(I),I=1,NODES )
39        83             WRITE (LUNOUT,940)
```

**Figure 7-8** *continued*

175

plied to selected modules for which more detailed information is needed to isolate an anomaly or to ensure that testing covers a proper range of computational results.

The executed code containing the SELF-METRIC instrumentation produces the statement probe analysis report shown in Figure 7-9 for the module OUTPUT and Figure 7-10 for the module IBCALC. OUTPUT contains mainly logical operations, while IBCALC is dominated by mathematical computations. Three types of reports are provided for the source statements. If the statement has no value computed (e.g., a CONTINUE, WRITE, READ, CALL, or assignment of a constant), then only the execution count is printed. Statements that test logical expressions report times true, times false, and final value of the logical expression. Statements that compute a numeric value report initial, final, maximum, and minimum values. This information is often helpful in highlighting suspicious results and ranges of computational values. Once likely trouble spots are identified, more intensive debugging operations may proceed using other tools, such as an on-line debugger.

## TEST INSTRUMENTATION AND ANALYSIS

By this time, the test configuration has been debugged and corrected such that proper results have been obtained with the set of functional test cases. The next objective is to instrument the test target modules (OUTPUT and IBCALC) in order to determine the DD-path coverage that has been achieved with the functional test case set.

The modules OUTPUT and IBCALC are instrumented with test coverage data collection calls by running RXVP80™ with the instrumentation option. RX-VP80™ performs a structural analysis of the subject modules and produces a module source text listing with the DD-paths identified. This module text for IBCALC is included as Figure 7-11. The left-most column is the statement number, and adjacent to that is a nesting level number that identifies nesting depth. Also provided is an ordinal numbering of each line. Each statement is printed, indented consistent with nesting level, and then, for each statement that starts a DD-path, the path numbers are annotated. This module text printout identifies the DD-paths that are referred to in test coverage analysis reports.

Collection of program flow statistics is facilitated by the instrumentation of the program control structure. RXVP80™ examines the code and automatically inserts a call to a data collection routine that is invoked each time a control branch is taken. When the instrumented code is executed, the collection routine notes the module and code section executed and builds up a data file from which the test analyzer generates its reports. The function of the posttest analyzer is to supply the reports that can be evaluated against testing goals. For the thread that consists of the modules OUTPUT and IBCALC, these test analysis reports are described in the following paragraphs.

COVERAGE SUMMARY (FIGURE 7-12)   The top-level view of testing progress is shown by this report. For each test case and for the cumulative of all tests, the table lists

- TEST CASE—Sequential test number
- MODULE NAME—Name of all instrumented and invoked modules in the test
- NUMBER OF DD-PATHS—Total number of DD-paths in the module

Under SUMMARY–THIS TEST:

- NUMBER OF INVOCATIONS—Total times module was invoked in the single test
- DD-PATHS TRAVERSED—Number of distinct DD-paths executed by this test case
- PER CENT COVERAGE—Distinct DD-paths executed by this test case as a percent of the total DD-paths in the module

Under CUMULATE SUMMARY:

- NUMBER OF TESTS—Total number of tests accumulated
- INVOCATIONS—Cumulative number of module invocations over all tests
- TRAVERSED—Cumulative number of DD-paths executed over all tests
- COVERAGE—Cumulative DD-paths executed over all tests as a percent of the total DD-paths in the module

At this point, only one test case has been run, yielding a coverage percentage of 69.44. Thus, the cumulative provides no additional information.

DD–PATHS NOT HIT (FIGURE 7–13)   This report indicates which DD-paths were not executed by each test case and which remain untested after all tests are accumulated.

DETAILED DD–PATH EXECUTION COUNTS (FIGURE 7–14)   This report gives the finest detail on DD-path execution for each test case. For each DD-path for which the execution count is 0, an entry is made under NOT EXECUTED. For execution counts greater than 0, the bar represents the count as a percent of the maximum number of executions for a single path. This report shows where the most execution mass is being spent in a module. The report also shows more graphically where there are large segments of code that are not being tested.

## TEST COVERAGE EXTENSION AND TEST DATA SELECTION

The decision point has been reached where it is determined whether to continue testing or terminate. The coverage summary report (Figure 7–12) immediately discloses the testing status; only 69.44% of the DD-paths have been traversed by the

STATEMENT PROBE ANALYSIS REPORT

| NU. | LABEL | SOURCE TEXT | EXECUTION COUNT |
|---|---|---|---|

```
  1          SUBROUTINE OUTPUT (NODES,BRNCHS,OUT,VN,A,DI,ES,JS,G,NOED)       1
            *ROUTINE TO OUTPUT COMPUTED CIRCUIT QUANTITIES.
            *DRIVING ROUTINE TO CONTROL INDIVIDUAL OUTPUT CALCULATIONS
            *
            *DESCRIPTION OF VARIABLES
            *   MISC    - DEBUG OUTPUT FLAG
            *   OUT     - VECTOR OF OUTPUT REQUEST FLAGS
            *   VN      - NODE VOLTAGE VECTOR
            *   A       - NODAL INCIDENCE MATRIX
            *   DI      - INVERSE OF (I-D) MATRIX
            *   ES      - INDEPENDENT VOLTAGE SOURCE VECTOR
            *   JS      - INDEPENDENT CURRENT SOURCE VECTOR
            *   G       - BRANCH CONDUCTANCE MATRIX
            *   NOED    - NO DEPENDENT VOLTAGE SOURCES FLAG
            *   LUNIN   - LOGICAL INPUT UNIT
            *   LUNOUT  - LOGICAL OUTPUT UNIT
            *   NODES   - NUMBER OF CIRCUIT NODES
            *   BRNCHS  - NUMBER OF CIRCUIT BRANCHES
            *   VB      - BRANCH VOLTAGE VECTOR
            *   VE      - ELEMENT VOLTAGE VECTOR
            *   IE      - ELEMENT CURRENT VECTOR
            *
            *
  2          INTEGER A,BRNCHS
  3          REAL JS,IE
  4          LOGICAL OUT,NOED,VNOUT,VBOUT,VEOUT,IEOUT,IBOUT
  5          COMMON /UNITS/ LUNIN,LUNOUT
  6          COMMON /DEBUG/ MISC
            *
  7          DIMENSION OUT(5), VN(20), A(20,50), DI(50,50), G(50,50)
  8          DIMENSION ES(50), JS(50)
  9          DIMENSION VB(50), VE(50), IE(50)
            *
 10          IF ( MISC .EQ. 3 )                                1   TRUE   1   FALSE   0
                                                                   FINAL IF TRUE
 11          WRITE ( LUNOUT , 900 ) OUT                        1
 12          ENDIF                                            1
 13          VNOUT = OUT ( 1 )                                1   INIT =  1   FINAL =  1
 14          VBOUT = OUT ( 2 )                                1   INIT =  1   FINAL =  1
 15          VEOUT = OUT ( 3 )                                1   INIT =  1   FINAL =  1
 16          IEOUT = OUT ( 4 )                                1   INIT =  1   FINAL =  1
 17          IBOUT = OUT ( 5 )                                1   INIT =  1   FINAL =  1
 18          WRITE ( LUNOUT , 910 )                           1   TRUE   1   FALSE   0
 19          IF ( VNOUT )                                     1   FINAL IF TRUE
 20          WRITE ( LUNOUT , 920 )                           1
```

**Figure 7-9** Statement probe analysis for module OUTPUT.

STATEMENT PROBE ANALYSIS REPORT

| NO. | LABEL | SOURCE TEXT | EXECUTION COUNT | |
|---|---|---|---|---|
| 21 | | DO ( I = 1 , NODES ) | 2 | INIT = 1  FINAL = 2<br>MIN = 1  MAX = 2 |
| 22 | | WRITE ( LUNOUT , 930 ) I , VN ( I ) | 2 | |
| 23 | | ENDDO | 2 | |
| 24 | | ENDIF | 1 | |
| 25 | | IF ( VBOUT .OR. VEOUT .OR. IEOUT .OR. IBOUT ) | 1 | TRUE 1  FALSE 0<br>FINAL IF TRUE 1 |
| 26 | | CALL VBCALC ( NODES , BRNCHS , A , VN , VB , VBOUT ) | 1 | |
| 27 | | IF ( VEOUT .OR. IEOUT .OR. IBOUT ) | 1 | TRUE 1  FALSE 0<br>FINAL IF TRUE 1 |
| 28 | | CALL VECALC ( DI , VB , ES , BRNCHS , NOED , VE , VEOUT ) | 1 | |
| 29 | | IF ( IEOUT .OR. IBOUT ) | 1 | TRUE 1  FALSE 0<br>FINAL IF TRUE 1 |
| 30 | | CALL IECALC ( G , VE , BRNCHS , IE , IEOUT ) | 1 | |
| 31 | | IF ( IBOUT ) | 1 | TRUE 1  FALSE 0<br>FINAL IF TRUE 1 |
| 32 | | CALL IBCALC ( G , VE , JS , NODES , BRNCHS , IB , A , IBOUT ) | 1 | |
| 33 | | ENDIF | 1 | |
| 34 | | ENDIF | 1 | |
| 35 | | ENDIF | 1 | |
| 36 | | ENDIF | 1 | |
| 37 | | IF ( MISC .EQ. 3 ) | 1 | TRUE 1  FALSE 0<br>FINAL IF TRUE 1 |
| 38 | | WRITE ( LUNOUT , 940 ) | 1 | |
| 39 | | ENDIF | 1 | |
| 40 | | RETURN | 1 | |
| 41 | 900 | FORMAT (5X,20HENTER OUTPUT. OUT = ,EL1) | | |
| 42 | 910 | FORMAT (1H1///20X,19HDC CIRCUIT RESPONSE , /<br>20X,19H-------------------- /// ) | | |
| 43 | 920 | FORMAT (5X,13HNODE VOLTAGES , //<br>5X,13HNODE  VALUE , /<br>5X,13H------ ------ ) | | |
| 44 | 930 | FORMAT (6X,I2,2X,1PE12.5) | | |
| 45 | 940 | FORMAT (5X,11HEXIT OUTPUT ) | | |
| 46 | | END | | |

Figure 7-9 *continued*

179

STATEMENT PROBE ANALYSIS REPORT

| NO. | LABEL | SOURCE TEXT | EXECUTION COUNT |
|---|---|---|---|
| 1 | | SUBROUTINE IBCALC (G,VE,JS,NODES,BRNCHS,IB,A,IBOUT) | 1 |
| | | *ROUTINE TO CALCULATE NETWORK BRANCH CURRENTS AND OUTPUT | |
| | | *RESULTS IF REQUESTED. | |
| | | *ROUTINE ALSO CALCULATES NODAL CURRENT UNBALANCES TO VALIDATE | |
| | | *SOLUTION ACCURACY. | |
| | | * | |
| | | *DESCRIPTION OF VARIABLES | |
| | | *    G      - BRANCH CONDUCTANCE MATRIX | |
| | | *    VE     - ELEMENT VOLTAGE VECTOR | |
| | | *    JS     - INDEPENDENT CURRENT SOURCE VECTOR | |
| | | *    BRNCHS - NUMBER OF CIRCUIT BRANCHES | |
| | | *    IB     - BRANCH CURRENT VECTOR | |
| | | *    IBOUT  - BRANCH CURRENT OUTPUT FLAG | |
| | | *    A      - NODAL INCIDENCE MATRIX | |
| | | *    MISC   - DEBUG OUTPUT FLAG | |
| | | *    LUNIN  - LOGICAL INPUT UNIT | |
| | | *    LUNOUT - LOGICAL OUTPUT UNIT | |
| | | *    ERROR  - CURRENT UNBALANCE VECTOR | |
| | | *    ERRTOT - TOTAL CURRENT UNBALANCE | |
| | | * | |
| | | ** | |
| 2 | | INTEGER A,BRNCHS | |
| 3 | | REAL JS,IB | |
| 4 | | LOGICAL IBOUT | |
| 5 | | COMMON /UNITS/ LUNIN,LUNOUT | |
| 6 | | COMMON /DEBUG/ MISC | |
| | | * | |
| 7 | | DIMENSION A(20,50), G(50,50), VE(50), JS(50), IB(50) | |
| 8 | | DIMENSION ERROR (20) | |
| | | ** | |
| 9 | | IF ( MISC .EQ. 3 ) | 1   TRUE 1   FALSE 0 |
| 10 | | WRITE ( LUNOUT , 900 ) IBOUT | 1 |
| 11 | | ENDIF | 1 |
| 12 | | DO ( I = 1 , BRNCHS ) | 5   FINAL IF TRUE 1   INIT = 1   FINAL = 5   MIN = 1   MAX = 5 |
| 13 | | IB ( I ) = 0.0 | 5 |
| 14 | | DO ( J = 1 , BRNCHS ) | 25   INIT = 1   FINAL = 5   MIN = 1   MAX = 5 |
| 15 | | IB ( I ) = IB ( I ) + G ( I , J ) * VE ( J ) | 25   INIT =-0.5254916   FINAL = 0.5689926   MIN =-0.8658432   MAX = 0.5689926 |
| 16 | | ENDDO | 25 |
| 17 | | IB ( I ) = IB ( I ) - JS ( I ) | 5   INIT =-0.3612320   FINAL = 0.5689926   MIN =-0.3612320   MAX = 0.5689926 |
| 18 | | ENDDO | 5 |
| 19 | | ERRTOT = 0.0 | 1 |

**Figure 7-10**   Statement probe analysis for module IBCALC.

STATEMENT PROBE ANALYSIS REPORT

| NO. | LABEL | SOURCE TEXT | EXECUTION COUNT | | |
|---|---|---|---|---|---|
| 20 | | DO ( I = 1 , NODES ) | 2 | | |
| | | | | INIT = 1 | FINAL = 1 |
| | | | | MIN = 1 | MAX = 2 |
| 21 | | ERROR ( I ) = 0.0 | 2 | | |
| 22 | | DO ( J = 1 , BRNCHS ) | 10 | | |
| | | | | INIT = 1 | FINAL = 1 |
| | | | | MIN = 1 | MAX = 5 |
| 23 | | ERROR ( I ) = ERROR ( I ) + A ( I , J ) * IB ( J ) | 10 | | |
| | | | | INIT = -0.3612320 | FINAL = 0.0000000E+00 |
| | | | | MIN = -0.5689926 | MAX = 0.5960464E-07 |
| 24 | | ENDDO | 10 | | |
| 25 | | ERRTOT = ERRTOT + ABS ( ERROR ( I ) ) | 2 | | |
| | | | | ONLY VALUE ASSUMED = 0.5960464E-07 | |
| 26 | | ENDDO | 2 | | |
| 27 | | IF ( IBOUT ) | 1 | | |
| | | | | TRUE 1 | FALSE 0 |
| | | | | FINAL IF TRUE | |
| 28 | | WRITE ( LUNOUT , 910 ) | 1 | | |
| 29 | | DO ( I = 1 , BRNCHS ) | 5 | | |
| | | | | INIT = 1 | FINAL = 1 |
| | | | | MIN = 1 | MAX = 5 |
| 30 | | WRITE ( LUNOUT , 920 ) I , IB ( I ) | 5 | | |
| 31 | | ENDDO | 5 | | |
| 32 | | ENDIF | 1 | | |
| 33 | | WRITE ( LUNOUT , 930 ) ERRTOT | 1 | | |
| 34 | | IF ( ERRTOT .GT. 0.001 ) | 1 | | |
| | | | | TRUE 0 | FALSE 1 |
| | | | | FINAL IF FALS 0 | |
| 35 | | WRITE ( LUNOUT , 950 ) | 0 | | |
| 36 | | WRITE ( LUNOUT , 960 ) ( I , ERROR ( I ) , I = 1 , NODES ) | 0 | | |
| 37 | | ENDIF | 1 | | |
| 38 | | IF ( MISC .EQ. 3 ) | 1 | | |
| | | | | TRUE 1 | FALSE 0 |
| | | | | FINAL IF TRUE | |
| 39 | | WRITE ( LUNOUT , 940 ) | 1 | | |
| 40 | | ENDIF | 1 | | |
| 41 | | RETURN | 1 | | |
| 42 | 900 | FORMAT (5X,22HENTER IBCALC, IBOUT = ,L1 ) | | | |
| 43 | 910 | FORMAT (1H0,4X,15HBRANCH CURRENTS ,/ | | | |
| | | 5X,15HBRANCH  VALUE ,/ | | | |
| | | 5X,15H------  ----- ) | | | |
| 44 | 920 | FORMAT (7X,I2,2X,1PE12.5) | | | |
| 45 | 930 | FORMAT (///5X,20HNODAL CURRENT UNBALANCE = ,1PE12.5 ) | | | |
| 46 | 940 | FORMAT (5X,11HEXIT IBCALC ) | | | |
| 47 | 950 | FORMAT (1H0,4X,30HINDIVIDUAL CURRENT UNBALANCES // | | | |
| | | 5X,30H NODE   VALUE  // | | | |
| | | 5X,30H ----   ----- ) | | | |
| 48 | 960 | FORMAT (10X,I2,2X,1PE12.5) | | | |
| 49 | | END | | | |

Figure 7-10 continued

DD-PATH DEFINITIONS

SUBROUTINE IBCALC (G,VE,JS,NODES,BRNCHS,IB,A,IBOUT)

...SOURCE TAB

| STMT | NEST | LINE | SOURCE... | |
|------|------|------|-----------|---|
| 1 | | 1 | SUBROUTINE IBCALC (G,VE,JS,NODES,BRNCHS,IB,A,IBOUT) | |
| | | 2 | C ROUTINE TO CALCULATE NETWORK BRANCH CURRENTS AND OUTPUT | |
| | | 3 | C RESULTS IF REQUESTED. | |
| | | 4 | C ROUTINE ALSO CALCULATES NODAL CURRENT UNBALANCES TO VALIDATE | |
| | | 5 | C SOLUTION ACCURACY. | |
| | | 6 | C | |
| | | 7 | C DESCRIPTION OF VARIABLES | |
| | | 8 | C G - BRANCH CONDUCTANCE MATRIX | |
| | | 9 | C VE - ELEMENT VOLTAGE VECTOR | |
| | | 10 | C JS - INDEPENDENT CURRENT SOURCE VECTOR | |
| | | 11 | C BRNCHS - NUMBER OF CIRCUIT BRANCHES | |
| | | 12 | C IB - BRANCH CURRENT VECTOR | |
| | | 13 | C IBOUT - BRANCH CURRENT OUTPUT FLAG | |
| | | 14 | C A - NODAL INCIDENCE MATRIX | |
| | | 15 | C MISC - DEBUG OUTPUT FLAG | |
| | | 16 | C LUNIN - LOGICAL INPUT UNIT | |
| | | 17 | C LUNOUT - LOGICAL OUTPUT UNIT | |
| | | 18 | C ERROR - CURRENT UNBALANCE VECTOR | |
| | | 19 | C ERRTOT - TOTAL CURRENT UNBALANCE | |
| | | 20 | C | |
| | | 21 | C | ** DDPATH  1 IS PROCEDURE ENTRY |
| | | 22 | C | |
| 2 | | 23 | INTEGER A,BRNCHS | |
| 3 | | 24 | REAL JS,IB | |
| 4 | | 25 | LOGICAL IBOUT | |
| 5 | | 26 | COMMON /UNITS/ LUNIN,LUNOUT | |
| 6 | | 27 | COMMON /DEBUG/ MISC | |
| 7 | | 28 | C DIMENSION A(20,50), G(50,50), VE(50), JS(50), IB(50) | |
| 8 | | 29 | DIMENSION ERROR (20) | |
| | | 30 | C | |
| 9 | | 31 | C IF (MISC.EQ.3) | |
| | | 32 | | ** DDPATH  2 IS TRUE BRANCH |
| | | | | ** DDPATH  3 IS FALSE BRANCH |
| 10 | 1 | 33 | WRITE (LUNOUT,900) IBOUT | |
| -11 | | 34 | END IF | |
| | | 35 | C | |
| | | 36 | C | |
| | | 37 | C CALCULATE BRANCH CURRENTS    IB = G*VE-JS | |
| | | 38 | C | |
| | | 39 | C | |
| 12 | | 40 | DO (I=1,BRNCHS) | |
| 13 | 1 | 41 | IB(I) = 0.0 | |
| 14 | 1 | 42 | DO (J=1,BRNCHS) | |
| 15 | 2 | 43 | . IB(I) = IB(I)+G(I,J)*VE(J) | |
| 16 | 1 | 44 | . END DO | ** DDPATH  4 IS LOOP ESCAPE |
| | | | | ** DDPATH  5 IS LOOP AGAIN |

**Figure 7-11**  Module text with DD-path definitions.

DD-PATH DEFINITIONS            SUBROUTINE ESCALC (G,VE,JS,NODES,BRNCHS,IB,A,IBOUT)            ...SOURCE TAB

STMT NEST LINE SOURCE...
=========================================================================================================

17    1    45       .    IB(I) = IB(I)-JS(I)
18         46            END DO
           47    C
           48    C -------------------------------------------------------------
           49    C     CALCULATE NODAL CURRENT UNBALANCE     ER = A*IB
           50    C
           51    C -------------------------------------------------------------
                                                                          ** DDPATH   6 IS LOOP ESCAPE
                                                                          ** DDPATH   7 IS LOOP AGAIN
19         52       ERRTOT = 0.0
20    1    53       DO (I=1,NODES)
21    1    54    .    .    ERROR(I) = 0.0
22    1    55    .    .    DO (J=1,BRNCHS)
23    2    56    .    .    .    ERROR(I) = ERROR(I)+A(I,J)*IB(J)
24    1    57    .    .    .    END DO
                                                                          ** DDPATH   8 IS LOOP ESCAPE
                                                                          ** DDPATH   9 IS LOOP AGAIN
25    1    58    .    .    ERRTOT = ERRTOT+ABS(ERROR(I))
26         59       END DO
           60    C
           61    C -------------------------------------------------------------
           62    C     OUTPUT BRANCH CURRENTS
           63    C
           64    C -------------------------------------------------------------
                                                                          ** DDPATH  10 IS LOOP ESCAPE
                                                                          ** DDPATH  11 IS LOOP AGAIN
27         65       IF (IBOUT)
                                                                          ** DDPATH  12 IS TRUE BRANCH
                                                                          ** DDPATH  13 IS FALSE BRANCH
28    1    66    .    .    WRITE (LUNOUT,910)
29    1    67    .    .    DO (I=1,BRNCHS)
30    2    68    .    .    .    WRITE (LUNOUT,920) I,IB(I)
31    1    69    .    .    .    END DO
                                                                          ** DDPATH  14 IS LOOP ESCAPE
                                                                          ** DDPATH  15 IS LOOP AGAIN
32         70       END IF
           71    C
           72    C -------------------------------------------------------------
           73    C     OUTPUT NODAL CURRENT UNBALANCE
           74    C
           75    C -------------------------------------------------------------
33         76       WRITE (LUNOUT,930) ERRTOT
34         77       IF (ERRTOT.GT.0.001)
                                                                          ** DDPATH  16 IS TRUE BRANCH
                                                                          ** DDPATH  17 IS FALSE BRANCH
35    1    78    .    .    WRITE (LUNOUT,950)
36    1    79    .    .    WRITE (LUNOUT,960) (I,ERROR(I),I=1,NODES )
37         80    .    END IF
           81    C
=========================================================================================================

**Figure 7-11** continued

183

...SOURCE TAB

```
STMT NEST LINE SOURCE...

 38        82          IF (MISC.EQ.3)

                                                           ** DDPATH 18 IS TRUE BRANCH
                                                           ** DDPATH 19 IS FALSE BRANCH

 39    1   83       .  END IF
 40        84          RETURN
 41        85    C------------------------------------------------------------
 42        86    900 FORMAT (5X,22HENTER IBCALC. IBOUT = ,L1 )
 43        87    910 FORMAT (1H0,4X,15HBRANCH CURRENTS ,//
 43        88                 5X,15HBRANCH   VALUE ,/
 43        89        1        5X,15H-----------  )
 44        90    920 FORMAT (7X,I2,2X,1PE12.5)
 45        91    930 FORMAT (//5X,28HNODAL CURRENT UNBALANCE = ,1PE12.5 )
 46        92    940 FORMAT (5X,11HEXIT IBCALC )
 47        93    950 FORMAT (1H0,4X,30HINDIVIDUAL CURRENT UNBALANCES //
 47        94                 5X,30H    NODE    VALUE              /
 47        95        1        5X,30H    ----    -----              )
 48        96    960 FORMAT (10X,I2,2X,1PE12.5)
 49        97        2
 49        98        END
```

**Figure 7-11**  *continued*

```
I                                 I   S U M M A R Y  - -  T H I S   T E S T I         C U M U L A T I V E   S U M M A R Y
===============================================================================================================================
TEST I  MODULE  I  NUMBER OF  I  NUMBER OF   I  D-D PATHS  I  PER CENT  I  NUMBER   I              I            I
CASE I   NAME   I  D-D PATHS  I  INVOCATIONS I  TRAVERSED  I  COVERAGE  I  OF TESTS I  INVOCATIONS I  TRAVERSED I  COVERAGE
===============================================================================================================================
  1  I
     I  OUTPUT       17              1             10         58.82          1            1             10         58.82
     I  TRCALC       19              1             15         78.95          1            1             15         78.95
     I
     I  SSALLSS      36                            25         69.44          1                          25         69.44
     I
===============================================================================================================================
```

**Figure 7-12** Coverage summary for one test case.

```
===========================================
MODULE  I TEST   I PATHS I      LIST OF DECISION TO DECISION PATHS NOT EXECUTED
NAME    I NUMBER I NOT HIT I
===========================================
OUTPUT  I  1   I   7   I   1   3   5   9  11  13  15  17
        I CUMUL I   7   I   1   3   5   9  11  13  15  17
-------------------------------------------
IBCALC  I  1   I   4   I   1   3  13  16  19
        I CUMUL I   4   I   1   3  13  16  19
-------------------------------------------
```

**Figure 7-13**  DD-paths not hit for one test case.

Part III   Automated Verification

RECORD OF DECISION TO DECISION (DD PATH) EXECUTION

MODULE SIBCALC S          TEST CASE NO.    1

DD PATH I NO. NOT EXECUTED I   NUMBER OF EXECUTIONS -- NORMALIZED TO MAXIMUM          I   I NUMBER OF
NUMBER                      I.----20.----40.----60.----80.----100.                    I   I EXECUTIONS

| DD PATH NUMBER | NOT EXECUTED | NUMBER OF EXECUTIONS — NORMALIZED TO MAXIMUM | NUMBER OF EXECUTIONS |
|---|---|---|---|
| 1 | | XX | 1 — 1 |
| 2 | | XX | 2 — 1 |
| 3 | 3 | 00000 | |
| 4 | | XXXXXXXXXXXX | 4 — 5 |
| 5 | | XXXXXXXXXXXXXXXXXXXXXXXXXXXXXXXXXXXXXXXXXXXXXXX | 5 — 20 |
| 6 | | XX | 6 — 1 |
| 7 | | XXXXXXXXXXX | 7 — 4 |
| 8 | | XXXXX | 8 — 2 |
| 9 | | XXXXXXXXXXXXXXXXXXXXX | 9 — 8 |
| 10 | | XX | 10 — 1 |
| 11 | | XX | 11 — 1 |
| 12 | | XX | 12 — 1 |
| 13 | 13 | 00000 | |
| 14 | | XX | 14 — 1 |
| 15 | | XXXXXXXXXXX | 15 — 4 |
| 16 | 16 | 00000 | |
| 17 | | XX | 17 — 1 |
| 18 | | XX | 18 — 1 |
| 19 | 19 | 00000 | |

TOTAL OF 4 NOT EXECUTED          EXECUTED 15/ 19          PERCENT EXECUTED = 78.95

TOTAL NUMBER OF DD PATH EXECUTIONS = 52

**Figure 7-14** Detailed DD-path execution count report.

set of functional test cases. The testing goal is full coverage of all DD-paths. The next step is to generate additional structurally oriented test cases that will extend the percentage of DD-path coverage. The process of generating new test cases focuses attention on the source code of the program and frequently reveals errors that would go undetected when looking only at execution results.

We will now arbitrarily focus on the module IBCALC as the target for improved testing coverage. The untested DD-paths of IBCALC have been denoted on the nothit report contained on Figure 7–13. DD-path 19 is selected as the target for the next test case because it may be at the end of a long reaching set which could provide additional collateral testing coverage. In consulting the IBCALC listing shown in Figure 7–11, we see that DD-path 19 is the false branch of a predicate controlled by the variable MISC. This DD-path will be traversed if MISC acquires a value other than 3.

RXVP80™ does provide a facility for tracing predicate variables not easily mapped into the input space of the program. This is called *reaching set assistance*. RXVP80™ provides a reaching set report that analyzes the internal logic of a module to the DD-path sequence that leads from one DD-path up to and including another path. It has been the experience of this author that the reaching set assistance is one capability of RXVP80™ that is not particularly useful. As a practical matter, automated tracing of variables is seldom required. When the AVS testing approach is applied to small blocks of software, actual experience indicates that the test inputs needed to attain the desired coverage can almost always be identified through manual analysis. When difficulties are encountered, they usually involve tracing variables across module boundaries, a capability that RXVP80™ does not provide in an automated manner.

For demonstration purposes, a reaching set analysis for the module IBCALC is shown in Figure 7–15. RXVP80™ has been asked to trace the path sequence from the beginning of the module to DD-path 19, our testing target. The report shows that DD-path 19 is reached by following the sequence that consists of paths 1, 2, 3, 4, 6, 8, 10, 12, 13, 14, 16, 17, and 19. The source code that comprises this reaching set is included on the report below the reaching set path sequence. In this case, the reaching set report is not particularly illuminating. The problem, as we shall see, is that of tracing the source of the variable MISC across module boundaries.

We have already concluded that DD-path 19 will be exercised if MISC obtains a value not equal to 3. By examining the IBCALC module listing in Figure 7–11, it can be seen that MISC enters IBCALC through the common block DEBUG. It would now be useful to determine where this single member common block is set. Recall that RXVP80™ issues a documentation report called the common matrices which provides that information. In referring to this report, previously included as Figure 7–4, we discover that the symbol MISC of the common block DEBUG is set by the module CNTRL. This is denoted on the common matrices report by the X at the intersection of the symbol row MISC and the module CNTRL. On the possibility that MISC could be an external input to the module CNTRL, the INPUT/OUTPUT statement report in Figure 7–8 is scanned for an I/O statement that involves the variable MISC. Line 47 of CNTRL is a READ statement which includes MISC as the third element of the first record read by CNTRL.

The input source that controls the predicate associated with DD-path 19 has been located. The input record will be modified so that MISC will now contain a value of two instead of three. This input change will cause the decision element to be evaluated as false and, hence, exercise DD-path number 19.

## RETEST ANALYSIS

Figures 7-16 and 7-17 show the cumulative summary and nothit reports as a result of adding this new test case to the test set. Note that the cumulative DD-path coverage has increased from 69.44 to 80.56%. The coverage achieved individually by the second test case is coincidentally identical to that of the first test case—69.44%. Obviously, this identical coverage was attained as a result of traversing several new DD-paths previously unexercised because the overall coverage has increased. It can be seen from the nothit report in Figure 7-17 that several new DD-paths have been hit as a result of executing this second test case—DD-paths 3 and 17 in module OUTPUT and DD-paths 3 and 19 in module IBCALC. Additional test cases may be contrived by using the methodology just described until the testing goals are attained.

Automated test tools are currently gaining widespread use and acceptance. They are attaining recognition as cost effective devices that provide the ability to exhaustively test software to a level that would otherwise be cost prohibitive when using manual means. The realization of benefits derived from this approach is contingent upon the proper scope of application. This procedure, when applied to large amounts of code, can become overly involved and thus probably neutralize potential positive effects. Recent project experiences indicate that maximum advantage is attained when this testing approach is applied at the individual thread level; here, reasonably small chunks of code (100 to 300 source lines) are involved. Indeed, this scope of application is consistent with the overall objective of uncovering as many errors as possible early in the implementation period rather than to risk encountering these errors at higher levels of integration.

## 7.2

## Effect on Life Cycle Costs

It is possible to view the quantitative benefits to software life cycle costs that result from the test strategy described previously. The expected benefit is modeled on the basis of the following factors:

1. An accounting of additional errors detected from a recent software project at Hughes Aircraft Company, which utilized this approach

2. A profile of the escalating relative cost to correct errors the later in the life cycle the error is discovered

```
REACHING SET ANALYSIS                    SUBROUTINE IBCALC (G,VE,JS,NODES,BRNCHS,IB,A,IROUT)

NON-ITERATIVE REACHING SET FROM DD-PATH   1 TO DD-PATH  19
DDPATHS IN REACHING SET
                        1    2    3    4    6    8   10   12   13   14   16   17   19

        SOURCE CODE IN REACHING SET

    1        1        SUBROUTINE IBCALC (G,VE,JS,NODES,BRNCHS,IB,A,IBOUT)
             2     C  ROUTINE TO CALCULATE NETWORK BRANCH CURRENTS AND OUTPUT
             3     C  RESULTS IF REQUESTED.
             4     C  ROUTINE ALSO CALCULATES NODAL CURRENT UNBALANCES TO VALIDATE
             5     C  SOLUTION ACCURACY.
             6     C
             7     C  DESCRIPTION OF VARIABLES
             8     C  G      - BRANCH CONDUCTANCE MATRIX
             9     C  VE     - ELEMENT VOLTAGE VECTOR
            10     C  JS     - INDEPENDENT CURRENT SOURCE VECTOR
            11     C  BRNCHS - NUMBER OF CIRCUIT BRANCHES
            12     C  IB     - BRANCH CURRENT VECTOR
            13     C  IBOUT  - BRANCH CURRENT OUTPUT FLAG
            14     C  A      - NODAL INCIDENCE MATRIX
            15     C  MISC   - DEBUG OUTPUT FLAG
            16     C  LININ  - LOGICAL INPUT UNIT
            17     C  LUNOUT - LOGICAL OUTPUT UNIT
            18     C  ERROR  - CURRENT UNBALANCE VECTOR
            19     C  ERRTOT - TOTAL CURRENT UNBALANCE
            20     C
            21     C
            22     C

    9       32     C  IF (MISC.EQ.3)
   10    1  33           WRITE (LUNOUT,900) IBOUT
   11       34        END IF
            35     C
            36     C  ----------------------------------------
            37     C  CALCULATE BRANCH CURRENTS    IB = G*VE-JS
            38     C  ----------------------------------------
            39     C
   12       40        DO (I=1,BRNCHS)
   13    1  41           IB(I) = 0.0
   14    1  42           DO (J=1,BRNCHS)
   15    2  43              IB(I) = IB(I)+G(I,J)*VE(J)
   16    2  44           END DO
   17    1  45           IB(I) = IB(I)-JS(I)
   18    1  46        END DO
            47     C
            48     C  CALCULATE NODAL CURRENT UNBALANCE.    ER = A*IB
            49     C
            50     C
   19       51        ERRTOT = 0.0
   20       52        DO (I=1,NODES)
   21    1  53           ERROR(I) = 0.0
   22    1  54           DO (J=1,BRNCHS)
   23    2  55              ERROR(I) = ERROR(I)+A(I,J)*IB(J)
   24    2  56           END DO
   25    1  57           ERRTOT = ERRTOT+ABS(ERROR(I))
   26    1  58        END DO
            59     C
            60     C
```

**Figure 7-15** Reaching set analysis.

```
STMT NEST LINE  SOURCE...
--------------------------------------------------------------------
          61   C-------------------------------------------------
          62   C    OUTPUT BRANCH CURRENTS
          63   C-------------------------------------------------
          64   C
27        65        IF (IBOUT)
28   1    66          WRITE (LUNOUT,910)
29   1    67          DO (I=1,BRNCHS)
30   2    68   .         WRITE (LUNOUT,920) I,IB(I)
31   1    69   .      END DO
32        70        END IF
          71   C
          72   C-------------------------------------------------
          73   C    OUTPUT NODAL CURRENT UNBALANCE
          74   C-------------------------------------------------
          75   C
33        76        WRITE (LUNOUT,930) ERRTOT
34        77        IF (ERRTOT.GT.0.001)
35   1    78   .      WRITE (LUNOUT,950)
36   1    79   .      WRITE (LUNOUT,960) (I,ERROR(I),I=1,NODES )
37        80        END IF
          81   C
          82   C-------------------------------------------------
38        82        IF (MISC.EQ.3)                        **TARGET DD-PATH BEGINNING**
          83   C
40        84   .      END IF
41        85          RETURN
          86   C-------------------------------------------------
49        98   .   END
          --------------------------------------------------------
```

**Figure 7-15**  *continued*

| TEST CASE | MODULE NAME | NUMBER OF D-D PATHS | SUMMARY -- THIS TEST: NUMBER OF INVOCATIONS | SUMMARY -- THIS TEST: D-D PATHS TRAVERSED | SUMMARY -- THIS TEST: PER CENT COVERAGE | CUMULATIVE SUMMARY: NUMBER OF TESTS | CUMULATIVE SUMMARY: INVOCATIONS | CUMULATIVE SUMMARY: TRAVERSED | CUMULATIVE SUMMARY: COVERAGE |
|---|---|---|---|---|---|---|---|---|---|
| 2 | | | | | | | | | |
| | OUTPUT | 17 | 1 | 10 | 58.82 | 2 | 2 | 12 | 70.59 |
| | IBCALC | 19 | 1 | 15 | 78.95 | 2 | 2 | 17 | 89.47 |
| | $$ALL$$ | 36 | | 25 | 69.44 | 2 | | 29 | 80.56 |

**Figure 7-16** Cumulative summary after two test cases.

```
=====================================================================================================
II MODULE I TEST I PATHS  I                                                                         II
II NAME   I NUMBER I NOT HIT I           LIST OF DECISION TO DECISION PATHS NOT EXECUTED            II
=====================================================================================================
II OUTPUT I   1  I   7   I    3   5   9  11  13  15  17                                             II
II        I   2  I   7   I    2   5   9  11  13  15  16                                             II
II        I CUMUL I   5   I    5   9  11  13  15                                                    II
=====================================================================================================
I  IRCALC I   1  I   4   I    3  13  16  19                                                          I
I         I   2  I   4   I    2  13  16  18                                                          I
I         I CUMUL I   2   I   13  16                                                                 I
-----------------------------------------------------------------------------------------------------
```

**Figure 7-17** Not hit report after two test cases.

The general influence of this exhaustive testing strategy and its projected influence on life cycle costs of this project is depicted on Figure 7–18. This figure shows the comparative effects of the testing approach that utilizes the automatic tool in contrast to the standard test approach that does not. The use of the automatic test tool results in higher error detection rates during the construct period. During subsequent periods, however, including operations, the detection rate of latent errors remains higher in the situation in which the test tool is not used. The area under both curves, that is, the total number of errors, should be approximately equal. Of course, the cost of rectifying the same error later in the life cycle is higher than it would have been were it detected earlier. The genesis of the anticipated life cycle cost benefit is explained in the following paragraphs.

The exhaustive testing approach on the Hughes software project consisted of first checking out each thread, using a set of functionally oriented test cases. It is at this point where the traditional brand of testing would conclude. Instead, additional test cases were contrived in order to achieve a DD-path coverage of close to 100%; the expectation was that this extra test effort would expose additional errors. The actual experience on this project supported this hypothesis. Because of these clearly demarcated testing phases, it was a simple matter to maintain a count of the errors detected by the extended testing. The accounting showed that an average of one additional error per thread was uncovered. The cost, in schedule time, of performing the extended testing ranged from a half day to three days per thread; the

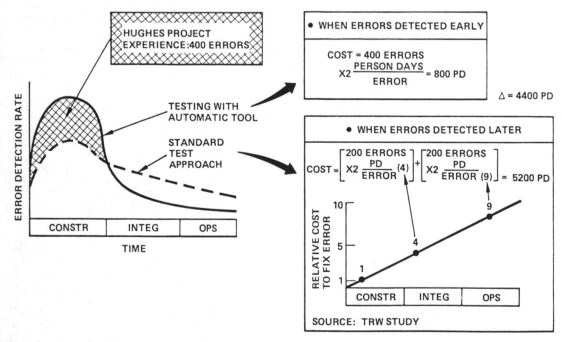

**Figure 7–18** Automatic tool cost effective in life cycle. (Michael S. Deutsch, "Software Project Verification and Validation," *Computer* (April, 1981), ©1981. Reprinted by permission of IEEE.)

average schedule cost was close to one day per thread. Normally, two persons were involved with the testing of the thread at this point. Hence, the incremental cost of the exhaustive testing effort was an average of two person-days per thread.

This project consists of about 400 threads. The incremental cost of finding and correcting the 400 additional errors exposed is 800 person days (400 errors $\times$ 2 person days/error).

In a survey performed at TRW, which seems to have become an industry standard, a profile was composed that depicted the relative cost of fixing errors as a function of life cycle stage in which they are discovered. This profile was compiled from a number of software projects at TRW, IBM, and General Telephone and Electronics. Some of the pertinent data extracted from this profile are

1. Average relative cost to fix an error during integration activity versus construct activity is 4.

2. Average relative cost to fix an error during operations phase versus construct activity is 9.

In order to model the life cycle cost benefits, we will assume that the discovery of these 400 errors would have otherwise been evenly distributed over the integration and operations periods; this is probably a conservative assumption because the type of errors overlooked during the construct activity are more likely to reappear in operations where the software would undergo its first thorough exercise. The 200 errors found during integration would cost 1600 person days (200 errors $\times$ 2 person days/error $\times$ 4) to correct under this model; the 200 errors found during operations would cost 3600 person days (200 errors $\times$ 2 person days/error $\times$ 9) to correct. Thus, the differential life cycle cost avoidance achieved by the exhaustive testing strategy is speculated to be 4400 person days (3600 + 1600 = 5200 person days less 800 person days) for this particular project.

The specific quantitative cost advantage accrued on this project or any other project as a result of this discipline is undoubtedly speculative. None of us are clairvoyant, and we have no means of precisely determining what would have occurred on a project had we done things differently. We are forced to rely on models in these circumstances, a course of action vulnerable to controversy. The form of the model that has been used or its parameters may be argumentative. But the exact magnitude of the life cycle cost benefit is not the major issue here. Rather, the key thesis is that the use of this exhaustive testing approach should reveal more errors earlier in the development cycle, and this phenomenon has been observed in actual practice. This effect provides a very positive contribution to the software project despite some quantitative uncertainty.

**Part IV**

# Verification and Validation Over the Software Life Cycle

# Organizing the Project for Verification and Validation

It has already been observed that the approach to verification and validation of modern software projects involves activities over the entire software life cycle, not just testing. The merits of this practice include a more reliable product, lower life cycle costs, early exposure of requirements inconsistencies, and early exposure of design errors. Statistics have been compiled that depict the escalating costs to correct errors as later stages of the development cycle are traversed.[1] This profile reveals that it is 10 to 100 times more costly to correct an error after the software is operational than it would have been if detected during the preliminary design period.

In this chapter, the structure of the basic software project organization is described. The responsibility for verification and validation is distributed among the organizational components that comprise the project. Each major component

[1] Barry Boehm, ''Government/Industry Software Management Initiatives—Status and Trends,'' in *Documentation from the Software Management Conference, 1978* (Jointly sponsored by AIAA, TMSA, DPMA), p. 8.

of the organization is at least minimally involved with verification and validation activities in each stage of the software life cycle. The full life cycle involvement of the project with verification and validation is explored in the following sections, beginning with an overview of the software life cycle and continuing with an account of verification and validation activities of each of the organization's components.

## 8.1
## Software Life Cycle

The growth of a software system from conception to operation traverses four phases of a life cycle:

1. Requirements definition
2. Development
3. Transition
4. Operations and maintenance

Each of these phases contains an infrastructure of one or more activities. The scope and breadth of these phases and activities is appropriately variant, depending on the size and complexity of the system. Selection of the proper life cycle sequence for an individual system is itself an exercise in verification and validation. It would be absurd, for example, to manage the development of a small office payroll system under the same sequence of life cycle events as a gigantic ballistic missile defense system. The life cycle that is described in the following paragraphs would be applicable to a large complex software system; smaller systems would follow a tailored subset of these activities.

The software life cycle may be viewed in the context of a problem solving exercise. We are constantly reminded that a problem is most difficult to solve when all its aspects are considered simultaneously. In order to simplify the problem, it is broken down into constituent elements each of which is easier to solve than the total problem considered all at once. This same philosophy is applied to system development. The system is decomposed into components that are defined and built semiautonomously. The term *computer program configuration item* (CPCI) is applied to a component of software that is individually developed and controlled. The CPCIs are eventually recomposed in successive stages until a system product is assembled, accepted by the buyer, and installed. Each activity of the life cycle establishes a baseline from which an orderly and controlled growth of the system and its intermediate products are effected.

### REQUIREMENTS DEFINITION PHASE

This phase consists of two sequential parts—the *specify* activity and the *allocate* activity. In the specify activity, the customer's operational needs are transformed into performance requirements. This includes the allocation of overall system requirements to the software system. A software system requirements specification is prepared. This specification along with supporting interface documentation, analyses, and plans are evaluated through a *system requirements review* (SRR). This activity establishes the software system requirements as a baseline that is controlled throughout the life cycle.

The allocate activity involves the allocation of software system requirements to specific CPCIs. A requirements specification is generated for each individual CPCI. These requirements and supporting analyses are evaluated in a *system design review* (SDR). The CPCI requirements specification becomes a baseline that is controlled throughout the life cycle.

## DEVELOPMENT PHASE

This phase entails five sequential activites—define, design, construct, test, and integrate. Each of these activities establishes a baseline that becomes a point of departure for the succeeding activity.

The define activity is the initial design effort. A preliminary design approach is created for each CPCI based upon the CPCI requirements specification intially drafted during the allocate activity. A partial CPCI design specification is constructed. The preliminary design is reviewed and evaluated at a *preliminary design review* (PDR). A design baseline is created that documents the efforts of the define activity. This baseline is controlled until it is superseded by the next baseline.

The design activity is the detailed design effort and entails an expansion of the preliminary design created by the previous activity. The key products of this activity are the completed CPCI design specification, CPCI test plans, and CPCI test procedures. The concluding event of this activity is the *critical design review* (CDR). A detail design baseline is established that is controlled internally by the developer.

The next event of the development phase is the construct activity. This activity encompasses software coding, checkout, and preliminary qualification testing of each CPCI. These tasks are all performed by the responsible development organization for each CPCI. The construct activity readies the CPCI for formal testing in the subsequent activity. A test baseline, consisting of the CPCI product itself, updated design specification, updated test plans and procedures, and a draft user's manual is established for the next activity.

The test activity is the formal qualification testing of each individual CPCI. This establishes that the CPCI meets design requirements and performance specifications. This testing is performed by an independent test organization using formal test plans and procedures. Support is provided by the CPCI developer. The product baseline is established by the test activity and is formally controlled throughout the rest of the life cycle.

The integrate activity is the process of interfacing the component CPCI's of the software system and establishing that the system product meets the software system level requirements. This activity is performed by an independent test organization. It may begin at the contractor's facility, but final integration concludes at the operational site. This activity establishes the integrated baseline, which includes updated versions of the items that established the product baseline.

## TRANSITION PHASE

The transition phase is accomplished by the *initial operational test and evaluation* (IOT & E) activity. Its purpose is to determine the operational readiness of the system product through on-site testing and evaluation. The IOT & E activity is directed toward exercising the system in as nearly a realistic operational environment as possible in order to establish that the system performs as intended within the operational environment. This evaluation involves heavy participation of the user's of the system. This activity establishes the operational baseline, which consists of updates to the items of the previous baseline.

## OPERATIONS AND MAINTENANCE PHASE

This phase begins routine operation of the system. It continues through the remainder of the life cycle of the system. Operations involve the use of the system to perform its assigned mission. Maintenance consists of rectifying and correcting system flaws that interfere or deter from performance of the mission. This phase may include a *follow-on operational test and evaluation* (FOT & E) activity if any liens remained from the IOT & E activity.

It should be reiterated that the life cycle which has just been summarized is a full-scale process appropriate to a large system. A system of lesser magnitude would adapt a subset of this life cycle. Cost effectiveness and risk are the major considerations in identifying the life cycle appropriate to a specific system. The selection of a proper sequence of life cycle events can be construed as a verification and validation decision. The checks and balances inherent in the life cycle sequence will have a direct influence on product quality.

## 8.2

## The Software Project Organization

The software project organization is structured along the pattern of any high technology product development organization. The arrangement of a representative software project is pictured on Figure 8-1. It is composed of both line and staff organizations (shown on the diagram as adjuncts to the project management block). The responsibility for verification and validation is distributed among all the organizational entities of the project. The exception is the project controls staff. This is an administrative function which primarily maintains current status of costs and schedules. While in a broad sense this might be considered a verification and validation function, this shall be considered beyond the scope of interest here.

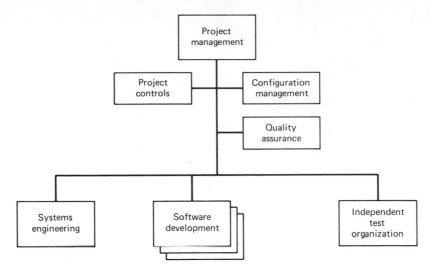

**Figure 8-1**   Software project organization structure.

The main technical tasks of verification and validation are performed by the three technical line organizations that comprise the software project—system engineering, software development, and the independent test organization.

SYSTEM ENGINEERING   This is normally the smallest of the three groups. It is responsible for prescribing the overall architecture of the system. This includes definition of system level requirements, system level design, and requirements for each CPCI. By focusing responsibility for definition and maintenance of a system's external attributes (requirements) in a single organization, it is assured that the system architecture reflects a single philosophy and a unified set of concepts System engineering defines the system architecture at an abstract level and does not prescribe a specific implementation.

SOFTWARE DEVELOPMENT   This organization designs and implements the software product in accordance with the intentions of the architects. On large projects, software development may be divided into several or more groups. Each group develops a chunk of the system, usually a CPCI. At the conclusion of thread/build testing, the development organization hands the software product over to the independent test organization for formal qualification testing.

INDEPENDENT TEST ORGANIZATION (ITO)   The ITO maintains a healthy adversarial relationship with the software development organization. It is the ITO's job to scrutinize (by testing) the software product and identify discrepancies where the requirements have not been implemented correctly. The discrepancies are referred back to the developer for rectification. The ITO also integrates the individual CPCIs to form a unified system product.

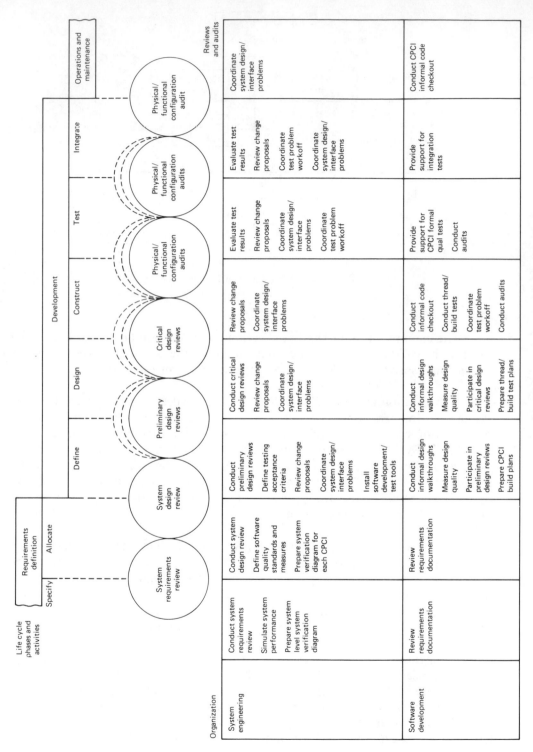

**Figure 8-2** Verification and validation activities of each organization.

| | | | | | | | |
|---|---|---|---|---|---|---|---|
| Independent test organization | Prepare system test requirements<br><br>Review requirements documentation<br><br>Prepare system integration plan<br><br>Define test software requirements | Prepare CPCI test requirements<br><br>Review requirements documentation | Review design documentation<br><br>Prepare CPCI test plans | Review design documentation<br><br>Prepare CPC test procedures<br><br>Prepare test data base(s) | Prepare integration test plans | Prepare integration test procedures<br><br>Conduct CPCI formal qual tests<br><br>Prepare CPCI test reports<br><br>Manage test problem reporting | Conduct system integration testing<br><br>Prepare integration test reports<br><br>Manage test problem reporting | Prepare test plans/procedures<br><br>Conduct maintenance retesting<br><br>Manage test problem reporting |
| Configuration management | Publish CM plan<br><br>Define functional baseline<br><br>Process change requests | Define allocated baseline<br><br>Process change requests | Define design baseline<br><br>Process change requests | Define detail baseline<br><br>Process change requests | Define test baseline<br><br>Deliver baseline for audit<br><br>Process change requests<br><br>Operate computer program library | Define product baseline<br><br>Deliver baseline for audit<br><br>Process change requests<br><br>Operate computer program library | Define integrated baseline<br><br>Deliver baseline for audit<br><br>Process change requests<br><br>Operate computer program library | Process change requests<br><br>Operate computer program library |
| Quality assurance | Publish QA plan<br><br>Review design reqmts spec<br><br>Track design review action items | Review CPCI reqmts specs<br><br>Track design review action items | Review design for compliance to standards<br><br>Monitor reqmts vs design matrix<br><br>Review test plans for compliance<br><br>Track design review action items | Review design for compliance to standards<br><br>Monitor reqmts vs design matrix<br><br>Review test plans/procedures for compliance<br><br>Track design review action items | Review code for compliance to standards<br><br>Review test plans/procedures for compliance | Witness formal qual tests<br><br>Verify documentation reflects baseline<br><br>Review test plans/procedures for compliance<br><br>Evaluate test results | Witness integration tests<br><br>Verify documentation reflects baseline<br><br>Review test plans/procedures for compliance<br><br>Evaluate test results<br><br>Monitor corrective action | Verify documentation reflects baseline |

**Figure 8-2** *continued*

The two staff functions shown in Figure 8–1—configuration management and quality assurance—are semitechnical and clerical in nature.

CONFIGURATION MANAGEMENT   This staff function is an arm of the project manager. Configuration management is responsible for establishing the initial software configuration and controlling changes to the configuration. This includes the establishment of intermediate baselines and controlling associated documentation. The configuration management function provides traceability for all changes and enforces rules and procedures for changes.

QUALITY ASSURANCE   This is also a function directly delegated by the project manager. Quality assurance furnishes an independent review and audit to ensure that each product meets contractual requirements. It is strictly an evaluation service and does not take corrective actions. Quality assurance is applied over the entire course of the software life cycle.

The verification and validation activities that occur over the software life cycle are summarized in Figure 8–2. The V & V tasks are allocated to the five performing organizations. All the organizations are at least minimally involved with verification and validation at each life cycle stage. The intended effect is that there exists a set of checks and balances on the software project between the organizations that conspire to produce a reliable software system product. The verification and validation activities of each software project organization component are examined in the following sections.

Some readers might recognize what has been presented so far as a somewhat idealized picture of the interaction of the project organization with the software life cycle. But does it really happen this way in practice? The answer is yes and no. The yes part of the answer concerns the concept that the basic discipline of the life cycle is followed:

1. The activities of the life cycle do occur, the prescribed products are produced, and baselines are established.

2. Each organization of the software project performs the specific set of tasks allocated to it.

The no part of the answer requires some elaboration.

It has been convenient to view a software development as consisting of separate and sequential activities. In reality, some crossing and recrossing of activity boundaries occur as natural functions of the human problem solving process, which is basically iterative. The imposition of this iterative phenomenon on the software life cycle is illustrated in Figure 8–3.[2] This figure, with the life cycle simplified into six phases, shows the interaction of the players (analyst, customer, programmer, etc.) with the problem solving process. The arrows entering from above represent the influence of the players on each particular phase of the problem. In our idealized model, this would be entirely a feed-forward operation. Because humans do not perform and communicate with perfection, some rework of previous phases becomes necessary. The rework may be precipitated by mistakes,

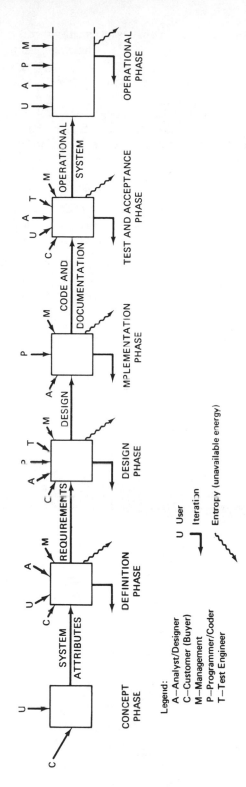

**Figure 8-3** Feedback over the software life cycle. (Randall W. Jensen and Charles C. Tonies, *Software Engineering*, © 1979, p. 559, fig. A-3. Reprinted by permission of Prentice-Hall, Inc., Englewood Cliffs, N.J.)

need for more optimization, or newly interjected ground rules that did not exist at the time the original work was done. For whatever reason, some of the effort invested in each phase is nonproductive and results in wasted energy or entropy. The net result is a partial regression back into a previous phase to revise some of the earlier work.

The costs of recycling and entropy are high and, naturally, we would like to avoid them. Because of the basic nature of problem solving, some iteration is unavoidable, but it can be controlled. Verification and validation is one of the major means to minimize the magnitude of recycling. In recognition of this iterative process, verification and validation methodologies should be selected that span life cycle activity boundaries. This will tend to lubricate the communications process and provide traceability over the activity transitions both forward and backward. An example fitting this description is the threads approach explained in Chapter 3. This technique can span from the specify activity all the way into the integrate activity.

# System Engineering Verification and Validation Activities

The key task of the system engineering organization is to prescribe the external attributes of the system. This task entails

- Specifying the software system level requirements
- Allocating software system requirements to CPCIs
- Specifying CPCI requirements
- Prescribing and maintaining the overall software system architecture, including data base

Essentially, system engineering defines the system architecture at an abstract level without committing to a specific implementation; the nature of the implementation is the job of the software developer. The development of the system architecture and specification of requirements (external attributes) are centralized in the system engineering organization in order that the system reflect a single philosophy and a unified set of concepts.

Viewed chronologically, the initial responsibility of system engineering is to establish a system with conceptual integrity[1]; it is the purpose of the system engineering verification and validation activities to preserve this integrity. A representative partitioning of system engineering verification and validation activities is delineated in the following list:

- Conduct formal design reviews
- Validate requirements
- Administer data base
- Coordinate system design and interface problems
- Review change proposals

This list is possibly not exhaustive, depending on your point of view. An extreme contention might be that all system engineering activities involve evaluative aspects; thus, the verification and validation tasks should constitute the total list of things that the system engineering organization does. Although this radical perspective is avoided, the previous list does lean somewhat liberally in that direction. The last two items on the list deal with changes to the system. Changes, whether associated with demonstrated problems or with improvements, tend initially to be viewed in a localized context. It is the job of system engineering to assess the full system impact of proposed changes and, hence, to maintain the integrity of the system concepts over the duration of the life cycle.

## 9.1

## Formal Design Reviews

At periodic points in the software development, design reviews are conducted in order to permit customers, users, and management to assess progress. These design reviews are a vehicle to force design information into the public domain for scrutiny and, hence, serve as a basic verification and validation method. The chronology of the design reviews may span several phases of the system acquisition life cycle. The specific number, format, and content of the reviews will depend on the customer, nature of the system, and contractual obligations. The following discussion centers on the design reviews prescribed by DOD.[2] Because these are oriented toward stringent design review and control standards required for critical defense systems, they are not necessarily of universal application. However, this design review schedule can be used as an initial model that may be tailored for specific application according to the nature of the individual system. The actual allocation of subjects and documents for each review is established in a systems engineering management plan

---

[1] Frederick P. Brooks, *The Mythical Man-Month* (Reading, Ma.: Addison-Wesley, 1975), p. 44.
[2] *Military Standard: Technical Reviews and Audits for Systems, Equipment, and Computer Programs* (Washington, D.C.: Department of Defense, 1976), MIL–STD–1521A.

negotiated between customer and developer on each individual project. The full set of design reviews prescribed by DOD standards in chronological order is

- System requirements review (SRR)
- System design review (SDR)
- Preliminary design review (PDR)
- Critical design review (CDR)

The association of these design reviews with life cycle phases and activities is depicted in Figure 9-1.

All of the organizations of the software project contribute to the design reviews. It is the system engineering organization that is responsible for the coordination of design review materials and for the conduct of the review itself. A brief description of each design review is provided in the following paragraphs.

SYSTEM REQUIREMENTS REVIEW (SRR)   The SRR is conducted to determine initial progress and direction of concept definition studies and convergence on an optimum and complete system configuration. Items to be reviewed include in-process results of preliminary requirements allocation and integrated test planning. The following products are normally reviewed at the SRR:

- Software system requirements specification
- System test plan
- Interface documentation

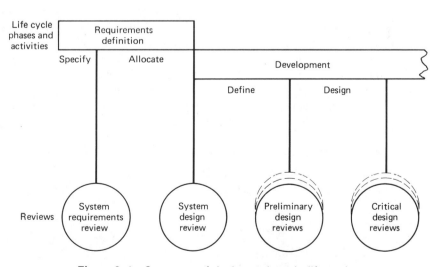

**Figure 9-1**   Sequence of design reviews in life cycle.

The system engineering organization records and publishes minutes of the review meeting. The minutes include

- Action items, including assignee and due date
- Notation of special risks or concerns identified by reviewers
- Liens against the review

SYSTEM DESIGN REVIEW (SDR)  The SDR evaluates the optimization, traceability, correlation, completeness, and risk of the allocated functional requirements, including the corresponding test requirements for the software system. The review is conducted when the definition effort has proceeded to the point that requirements and design approach have achieved a precise level of definition. This normally occurs at the end of the validation phase or early in the full-scale development phase of the system life cycle. The principal items reviewed are

- CPCI requirements specifications
- System test plan
- Computer program development plan
- Trade-off results
- Risk assessments
- Software development standards and practices
- Modifications to interface documentation

The system engineering organization records and publishes minutes of the meeting in a manner similar to the SRR.

PRELIMINARY DESIGN REVIEW (PDR)  The PDR is a formal technical review of the basic design approach for a CPCI. There would normally be one successful PDR for each CPCI. A collective PDR for a functionally related group of CPCIs, treating each CPCI individually, may be held when such an approach is advantageous. The PDR is held after authentication of the CPCI requirements specification and the accomplishment of preliminary design efforts, but prior to the start of the detail design. All development and test tools that are planned for use during program development but not deliverable under terms of the contract are to be identified. The principal items reviewed are

- Preliminary design approach (usually a partial design specification)
- User interface characteristics
- Storage and timing estimates
- CPCI test plans
- Results of trade-off studies and analyses
- Updates to system test plan
- Updates to interface documentation

The system engineering organization records and publishes the review minutes. The minutes include

- Action items, including assignee and due date
- Notation of significant comments, customer approved redirections, and points of controversy
- Notation of liens against the review, particularly with regard to the baseline materials, and a schedule of completion dates

CRITICAL DESIGN REVIEW (CDR)  The CDR is a formal technical review of the CPCI-detailed design conducted prior to the start of coding. The CDR is intended to ensure that the detailed design solutions, as reflected in the draft CPCI design specification, satisfy performance requirements established by the CPCI requirements specification. The CDR is also accomplished for the purpose of establishing the integrity of computer program design at the detailed design level prior to coding and testing. The principal items reviewed are

- CPCI design specifications
- Updated CPCI test plans
- CPCI test procedures
- Updates to interface documentation
- User interface characteristics
- Results of trade-off studies and analyses

Minutes are taken by the system engineering organization, highlighting the same types of key items as in the PDR minutes.

Upon formal approval of a design review, the pertinent documentation is released by configuration management to establish a baseline. This baseline forms a point of departure from which advanced activities can now proceed.

Formal design reviews are generally held for the main benefit of the customer and user as contractually required. Design reviews are usually effective at two levels:

- They reveal glaring conceptual misconceptions.
- They uncover some inconsistencies at the detailed level.

The first type of error typically involves a misdirected approach resulting from a misunderstanding of the mission aspects of the system; they are illuminated because it is the customers and/or users who are the mission experts. Some detailed inconsistencies are revealed as a result of a brute force effort; an army of reviewers mechanically scrutinize the design documentation. For the most part, formal design reviews should not be relied upon to redirect errant technical approaches. The technical basis of the design is frequently not challenged by the review team with the exceptions noted previously. It is the designers who have the intimate knowledge of the design; the reviewers are generally not as knowledgeable. Other means are usually more effective in objectively evaluating the design and overcoming natural biases of the designers.

## 9.2
## Requirements Validation

Here we address the issue of how it is determined that the process of translating a customer's operational needs into an explicit set of software requirements has been done correctly. This is a challenging exercise for the system engineering organization. There is, of course, no substitute for initial sound conceptual thinking. No set of validation mechanisms will rescue an effort from disaster that lacks essential soundness to begin with. We can, however, explore a set of methods and tools which balance and cross-check the requirements definition process in order to enhance the quality of the basic effort:

- Independent review
- System verification diagram
- Constructive methods
- Computer aided requirements analysis
- Simulation

These items encompass mechanisms that operate in parallel with the requirements analysis and which evaluate the results ex post facto.

### INDEPENDENT REVIEW

This is the process of getting all interested parties with approval authority (and maybe even some without) to concur that the content of a requirements specification drafted by system engineering is acceptable to them. This review cycle is informal; it happens before the formal design review is held to incorporate the specification into an approved baseline.

The review is initiated by the informal distribution of the first coherent draft of the requirements specifications. Comments are solicited from the recipients. The process is iterative. The feedback from the reviewers is considered by system engineering and factored into the next draft of the specification. The revised spec is then redistributed for review, comments are received again, and so forth. The goal is to get as much as possible of the negotiating and "horse trading" out of the way before formal approvals are sought. This process subscribes to the axiom that in any venture, not just software systems, you accomplish much more business informally than working through formal channels. A requirements specification is understandably going to stimulate much more interest from reviewers than a design specification. The requirements spec addresses the rudimentary attributes and capabilities of the system or CPCI. Reviewers of diverse backgrounds can relate to such fundamentals; the design spec, a highly technical document, attracts a lesser level of interest.

The following are the parties whose concurrence on a requirements spec is likely to be necessary either by a formal signature requirement or because of political considerations:

- The customer
- The user
- Independent test organization
- Software development organization
- Quality assurance
- Configuration management
- The project manager

The flow of this review sequence is illustrated in Figure 9-2. Some of the specialized comments/considerations/questions likely to emanate from each of these parties is annotated. This points out one of the key characteristics of this review mechanism. The reviewers all represent special interest groups, and the nature of their feedback will represent each of their special interest orientations. The positive effect that results is an intensive review with respect to each special area. The negative aspect is that the review comments are uncoordinated and almost always conflicting. System engineering must balance and reconcile the responses. Realistically, there will be some comments that are conflicting and/or unreasonable that have to be rejected. Some of these, if the author persists, may have to be referred to the project manager for resolution. Even the project manager may not be able to reconcile the problems at this point. Thus, some residual exceptions to the requirements specification may come up as issues at the SRR or SDR despite the efforts of all concerned to precoordinate and resolve these issues.

The posture of the customer in reviewing the requirements spec, as one would expect, is straightforwardly oriented toward adequacy of requirements to support the mission within the prescribed budget. The customer will frequently rely on the users for a detailed technical evaluation.

The user will expectedly evaluate the requirements primarily based on operability considerations. Classically the users will press for more capabilities than are being offered by the developer. This interjects some interesting opportunities for the application of diplomacy, compromise, and negotiation. The users will typically ask for more information on the operational features of the system than would normally be available at this stage in the life cycle. This should be regarded as constructive prompting of the developer to continue to factor the user orientation into the requirements and design.

The test organization will scrutinize the specification mainly for understandability and conciseness of presentation. This perspective is slanted toward determining the testability of the requirements and identifying what tools will be required to adequately test the system or CPCI.

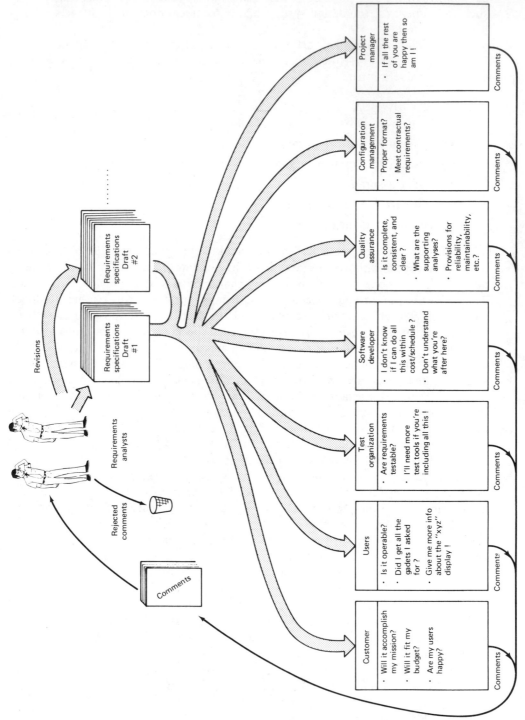

**Figure 9-2** Informal requirements review cycle.

Part IV   Verification and Validation Over the Software Life Cycle

The software developer will also be preoccupied with understandability. Because this is the organization that will eventually transform the requirements into a physical implementation, they want to understand what they are getting into. They need to develop a concise understanding of the functions and relate them to schedule and budget considerations.

Quality assurance will be concerned over whether the proper engineering analyses have been performed to support the resulting requirements. They will also be interested in the conciseness of the language and will be especially absorbed with assuring that the document deals with requirements and not design.

Configuration management will be dwelling upon certain editorial aspects of the requirements specification. They must be convinced that the content and format of the document is in compliance with contractual requirements.

The project manager's main entanglement with this review process is to attempt to make sure all the other parties are satisfied. If they are happy, the project manager will also approve. Unfortunately, in the real world it would be a rare occurrence for all of these diverse interests to be in concurrence at this point. A frequent basis of disagreement is the disparate demands of the user in contrast to the allocated schedule and budget. Not only might the user and developer be in conflict in this situation, but the customer and user may also be in antagonistic positions. This is not to imply that the user is necessarily unreasonable; many times he correctly assesses the mission needs. No neat or easy solution is offered here to break the deadlock. Obviously, a great deal of discussion between customer, user, and developer will transpire before the requirements are finalized.

Particularly for large systems, the informal requirements specification review is probably the most effective requirements validation technique at hand. When special organizational interests are at stake or threatened, intensive interest is practically automatic. Unfortunately, this same scenario does not extend to the design phase, where the affected parties are not so interested in the machinations of the implemenation.

One further point regarding reviews is worth pursuing, both formal and informal. If, after entering the development phase, the dominant theme of review comments is "What is the system doing?" rather than "How is the system doing it?" there is a major problem—the requirements are not adequately defined! At some time in the system life cycle, the requirements *will* be identified. On balance, it will be less costly to pause and resolve the requirements issues at this point. To ignore the symptoms inevitably results in costly recycling through the development phase until the correct requirements are finally identified.

## SYSTEM VERIFICATION DIAGRAM

In Chapter 3, the system verification diagram (SVD) was introduced as a tool to define a software test procedure. It was also mentioned that an ancillary asset of the SVD was its value as an informal requirements validation tool. We will now refocus on this tool in the context of its requirements validation benefits by

- Recounting the mechanics of the SVD
- Reviewing, primarily by example, the application of the SVD as a requirements validation device

The SVD is formulated from the requirements specification (either CPCI or system). It represents these requirements graphically as a sequence of stimulus/response elements. The form of a representative SVD is contained in Figure 9-3.

Each stimulus/response element, also referred to as a thread, is associated with specific requirements from the specification. Each element of the diagram is labeled with the requirement number or paragraph references. The stimulus consists of an input event and any associated conditional qualifiers of the state of the system at that point. The response is symmetrically composed of output events plus conditional qualifiers occurring as a result of the input event. An example of the generation of a thread from requirements employed in Chapter 3 is redisplayed in Figure 9-4.[3] This shows an input event—a new hostile track event—and a conditional qualifier, that the track files are not full, combining from paragraphs 3.7.1.1.4 and 3.7.3.1.5 of the specification to form the stimulus of this thread. The response is also derived from information offered by these two paragraphs. The total set of threads representing the requirements specification are concatenated with arrows which denote the flow of the thread sequence to form the SVD.

An assisting effect to the validation of the requirements occurs as a result of the discipline of the SVD procedure. The process of constructing the SVD causes the requirements to be viewed in a parallel context because of the graphic medium. Simply reading the text of the specification allows only a serial assimilation of the information. Also, the SVD procedure focuses additional attention on the requirements content that otherwise would not have occurred. The net effect is that inconsistencies, redundancies, and omissions may be revealed that would have gone undetected at this point. An effective sequence of events in applying the SVD approach would be as follows:

- Construct the SVD immediately upon availability of the requirements spec draft.
- Document errors and suspicious areas.
- Consult with customer, if necessary, and develop revisions to erroneous areas.
- Incorporate revisions into next draft of requirements spec.
- Update SVD.
- Repeat previous procedure until no more flaws in the requirements are evident.

[3] Robert Carey and Marc Bendic, "The Control of a Software Test Process," *Proceedings Computer Software and Applications Conference 1977* (New York. IEEE, 1977), IEEE Catalog No. 77CH1291-4C. © 1977 IEEE.

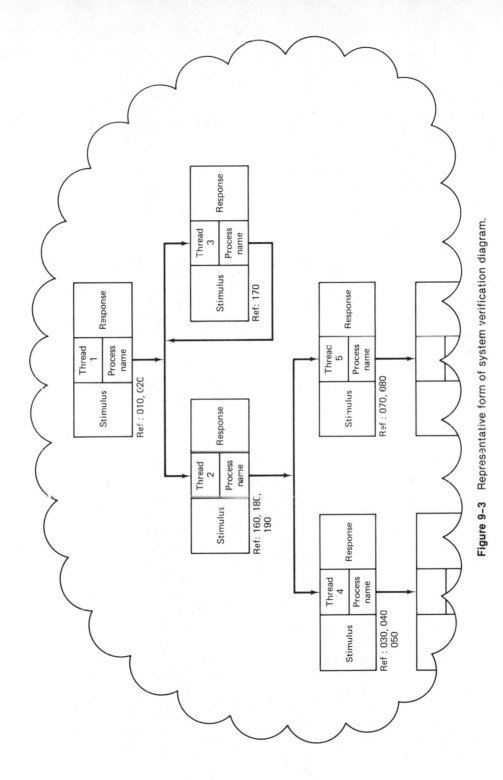

**Figure 9-3** Representative form of system verification diagram.

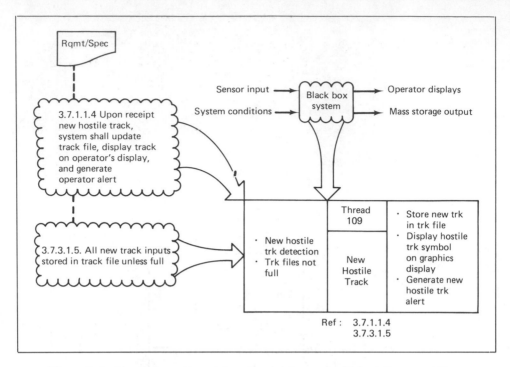

**Figure 9-4** Identifying a thread from the requirements. (Robert Carey and Marc Bendic, "The Control of a Software Test Process," *Proceedings Computer Software and Applications Conference 1977* (New York, N.Y.: IEEE, Inc.), IEEE Catalog No. 77CH 1291-4C, © 1977 IEEE.)

In order to exemplify an occurrence of a requirements flaw that would be exposed by this tool, we refer back to the hostile track thread of Figure 9-4. The conditional qualifier of the stimulus is that the track files are not full. After dealing with this thread, it is natural to expect the requirements analyst to create a parallel thread consisting of the same input event and a corollary qualifier—that the track files are full. The identification of this thread, 110, is illustrated in Figure 9-5. What is the flaw here? Inspection of paragraphs 3.7.1.1.4 and 3.7.3.1.5 provide no indication of what the system reaction should be to a new hostile track under the condition that the track files are full (assuming that there are no other spec paragraphs addressing this issue). The response to this stimulus cannot be signified on the SVD at this time. Further clarification is required, as this would seem to be a very important issue in this system. Perhaps the new track should be dropped, or maybe the new track should displace an existing track of lesser importance. The analyst may wish to discuss this point with the customer before arriving at a conclusion. In any case, the requirements spec must be revised to clear up this omission.

The system verification diagram is an informal device for the validation of requirements. Its main thrust is to represent requirements text in graphical form, and in so doing to direct the analyst's attention to possible inconsistencies, redundancies, and omissions.

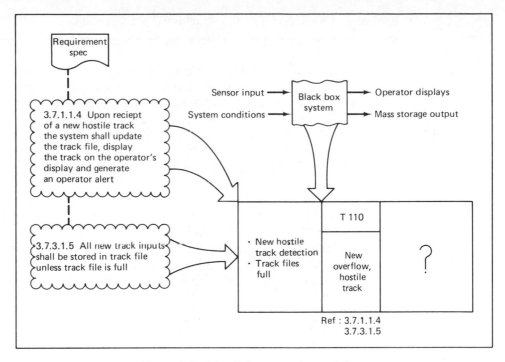

**Figure 9-5** Identifying a requirement flaw.

## CONSTRUCTIVE METHODS

A constructive approach to validation of requirements pivots on the concept that to achieve confidence in the results of a requirements analysis, one has to reason carefully about the correctness of the requirements as they are being generated. The basic underlying thesis of this observation is that some way must be found to limit the complexity of the problem being addressed until it is "intellectually manageable." There are fundamental limits of the human mental process to deal with complexity, and the level of success attained in addressing problem solutions is inversely related to the degree of complexity being confronted. By systematically decomposing a complex system problem into a number of intellectually simpler problems, we are able to construct solutions to each of the individual pieces that are more likely to be correct than if the problem were attacked in all its aspects simultaneously. This is the essence of the constructive approach.

A constructive method for preparing a requirements specification is directed toward identifying and correcting problems while still in the mental process before these difficulties become embedded in the actual product. In effect, this amounts to requirements validation in parallel with requirements analysis. The constructive method of requirements decomposition results in what is now popularly referred to as a *structured specification*. We will examine the constructive methodology of requirements analysis by

- Exploring the attributes of the structured specification
- Showing an example of the construction of a structured specification

An excellent work on the subject of structured requirements analysis is the book by Tom DeMarco, *Structured Analysis and System Specification* (cited in the bibliography). This book is strongly recommended to those who are interested in obtaining a practical working familiarity of this subject. Because it is presumed with high likelihood that the reader has not paused and gone out to buy this book, a summary of some its salient points is provided here.

DeMarco has defined the structured specification to consist of the following elements:

- *Data Flow Diagrams,* showing the major decomposition of functions, and all the interfaces among the pieces.
- *Data Dictionary,* documenting each of the interface flows and data stores on any of the Data Flow Diagrams.
- *Transform Descriptions,* documenting the internals of the Data Flow Diagram processes in a rigorous fashion.[4]

Using these tools, DeMarco further characterizes the resulting structured specification as possessing all of the following qualities:

1. It should be *graphic.* The Data Flow Diagrams should present a meaningful picture of what is being specified, a conceptually easy-to-understand presentation of the subject matter.
2. It should be *partitioned.* The processes on the Data Flow Diagrams are the basic elements into which the system is decomposed. As we shall see, this partitioning can be done in a top-down fashion so that there is a smooth progression from the most abstract to the most detailed.
3. It should be *rigorous.* The Data Dictionary will provide rigorous documentation of the interfaces; and the Transform Descriptions, a rigorous specification of process.
4. It should be *maintainable.* Redundancy is minimized and used in a controlled manner. The process of changing the Structured Specification can be tightly controlled.
5. It should be *iterative.* Portions of the Structured Specification have the characteristic that they can be dealt with separately. We can move them back and forth across the user's desk with a short author–reader cycle until they are right. The working documents that the user deals with are actual components of the Structured Specification. When he approves them, they will appear unchanged in the resultant Structured Specification.

[4] "Characteristics of the Structured Specification" is from *Structured Analysis and System Specification,* by Tom DeMarco. New York: Yourdon Press. © 1979, 1978, pp. 31–32. Reprinted by permission.

6. It should be *logical, not physical.* By eliminating elements that depend upon hardware, vendor, and operating procedure from the Structured Specification, we protect ourselves against changes to the specification caused by changes in physical thinking.

7. It should be *precise, concise, and highly readable.*[5]

Instead of pursuing further abstract description of the structured specification and its tools, an example of the creation process of a specification is now presented. We shall rely upon the dc network analysis system that was initially examined in Chapter 3. In fact, a functional requirements specification for this system was included as Figure 3-11. This is definitely *not* a structured specification. This spec will now be reconstructed in structured form. Hopefully, the higher quality of the structured configuration of the specification will be apparent.

From previous analyses for the original spec, a first-level data flow diagram has already been constructed. This diagram is redisplayed in Figure 9-6. The basic DFD consists of three functions and is labelled as the level 0 diagram. The objective is to now decompose the functions of diagram 0 into successive lower-level diagrams. The partitioning continues until a primitive level has been reached where further decomposition is not possible, or it is arbitrarily not desirable to continue. The next level data flow diagrams for functions 1 and 2 are shown in Figure 9-7. Function 3 is judged to already be a primitive process, and no further partitioning is performed.

Let us examine diagram 1 in Figure 9-7 more closely. There is no data flow

Diagram 0

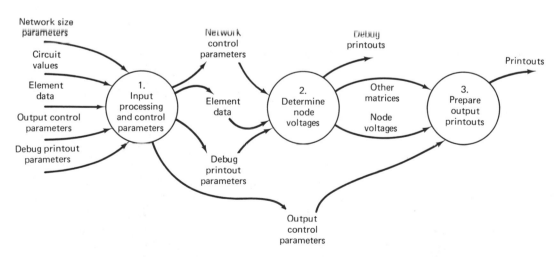

**Figure 9-6**  Level 0 data flow diagram for DC network analysis system.

[5] DeMarco, op. cit., p. 32.

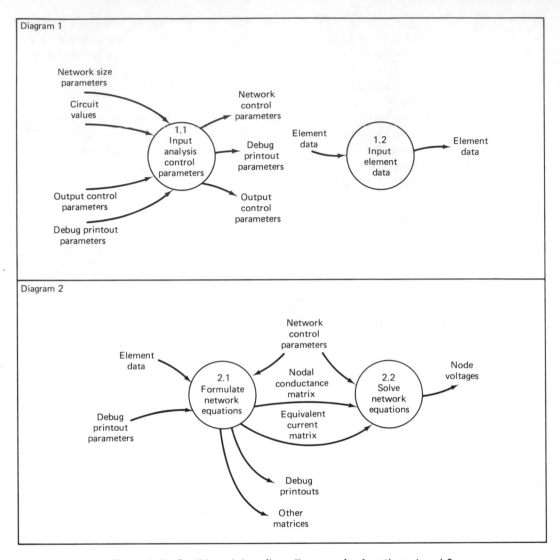

**Figure 9-7** Partitioned data flow diagrams for functions 1 and 2.

between *1.1 input analysis control parameters* and *1.2 input element data*. This disconnection is an indication of poor partitioning. The input element data function does not flow from 1.1, but it does flow into *2.1 formulate network equations*. The data flow interface between 1.2 and 2.1 is the element data file.

    The problem really emanated at the level 0 data flow diagram where the element data flow was misassociated with function 1–input processing and control parameters. Perhaps the problem should have been noticed even before the level 0 diagram was partitioned. The compound object of the name chosen for function 1 should have been cause for suspicion. Either a compound predicate or object in a function name suggests lack of cohesion and poor packaging. A repartioning is warranted here.

The revised data flow diagrams are contained on Figure 9–8. Note that the element data input flow now enters function 2–Determine Node Voltages. One of the results is that function 1 is now a primitive. Diagram 2 now subsumes the input element data function. Undoubtedly, function 2.2 can be decomposed further. We will arbitrarily not do so only because the concept involved here has already been sufficiently illuminated. The final remaining primitives for this specification are functions 1, 2.1, 2.2, 2.3, and 3.

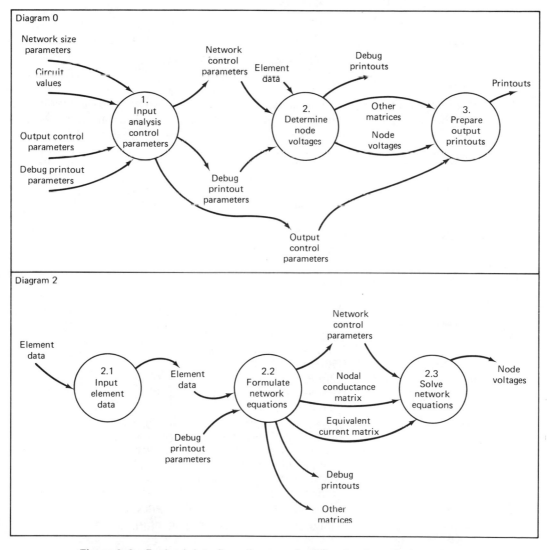

**Figure 9–8** Revised data flow diagrams for DC network analysis system.

The data dictionary, the second element of the structured specification, is now illustrated. The data dictionary defines the composition of each of the data flows depicted on the data flow diagrams. The revised DFDs in Figure 9–8 will be the baseline from which to construct the data dictionary for the dc network analysis system. All the data flows into and out of the primitive functions will be defined.

Partitioning of processes has been shown using data flow diagrams as an illustration mechanism. Data also has an infrastructure, which is described in the data dictionary. Certain symbols are used to annotate relationships between data elements. The following notations are employed:

=    means EQUIVALENT TO

+    means AND

[]    means SELECTION; select one of the items within the brackets

{}    means ITERATION; the set enclosed repeats

()    means the enclosed item is OPTIONAL[6]

These operators bring uniformity and a degree of formalism to the data definitions.

The data dictionary for the dc network analysis system is delineated in Figure 9–9. Definitions of all the data flows from the DFDs are included. In addition, cer-

---

| | |
|---|---|
| BRANCH-CONDUCTANCE-<br>MATRIC = | {RESISTANCE + CONDUCTANCE + CAPACITANCE +<br>INDUCTANCE + TRANSCONDUCTANCE + TRANS-<br>FLUENCE + TRANSRESISTANCE} |
| CIRCUIT-VALUES = | SHORT-CIRCUIT-VALUE +<br>OPEN-CIRCUIT-VALUES |
| DEBUG-PRINTOUT-PARA-<br>METERS = | DEBUG-SET-1 FLAG +<br>DEBUG-SET-2 FLAG +<br>DEBUG-SET-3 FLAG |
| DEBUG-PRINTOUT-PARA-<br>METERS-FILE = | DEBUG-SET-1 FLAG +<br>DEBUG-SET-2 FLAG +<br>DEBUG-SET-3 FLAG |
| DEBUG-PRINTOUTS = | [ DEBUG-SET-1<br>DEBUG-SET-2<br>DEBUG-SET-3 ] |
| DEBUG-SET-1 = | NODAL-INCIDENCE-MATRIX-PRINTOUT +<br>INDEPENDENT-VOLTAGE-SOURCE-MATRIX-<br>PRINTOUT + INDEPENDENT-CURRENT-<br>SOURCE-VECTOR-PRINTOUT + BRANCH-<br>CONDUCTANCE-MATRIX-PRINTOUT +<br>DEPENDENT-VOLTAGE-SOURCE-MATRIX-PRINTOUT |
| DEBUG-SET-2 = | NODAL-CONDUCTANCE-MATRIX-PRINTOUT |
| DEBUG-SET-3 = | EQUIVALENT-CURRENT-VECTOR-PRINTOUT |

**Figure 9-9**   Data Dictionary for DC Network Analysis System

[6] DeMarco, op. cit., p. 133.

| | |
|---|---|
| DEPENDENT-VOLTAGE-<br>SOURCE-MATRIX = | {TRANSPOTENTIAL + TRANSRESISTANCE} |
| ELEMENT-DATA = | {BRANCH-TYPE + BRANCH-NUMBER + INITIAL-<br>NODE + FINAL-NODE + BRANCH-ELEMENT-<br>VALUE + BRANCH-NUMBER-FOR-DEPENDENT-<br>SOURCE} |
| ELEMENT-DATA-FILE = | {BRANCH-TYPE + BRANCH-NUMBER + INITIAL-<br>NODE + FINAL-NODE + BRANCH-ELEMENT-<br>VALUE + BRANCH-NUMBER-FOR-DEPENDENT-<br>SOURCE} |
| EQUIVALENT-CURRENT-<br>MATRIX = | {EQUIVALENT-CURRENT-SOURCE-FOR-NODE} |
| INDEPENDENT-CURRENT-<br>SOURCE-MATRIX = | {INDEPENDENT-CURRENT-SOURCE-FOR-THIS-BRANCH} |
| INDEPENDENT-VOLTAGE-<br>SOURCE-MATRIX = | {INDEPENDENT-VOLTAGE-SOURCE-FOR-THIS-BRANCH} |
| NETWORK-CONTROL-<br>PARAMETERS-FILE = | CIRCUIT-VALUES + NETWORK-SIZE-PARAMETERS |
| NETWORK-SIZE-PARAM-<br>ETERS = | NUMBER-OF-NETWORK-NODES +<br>NUMBER-OF-NETWORK-BRANCHES |
| NODAL-INCIDENCE-MA-<br>TRIX = | {RESISTANCE + CONDUCTANCE + CAPACITANCE +<br>INDUCTANCE} |
| NODAL-CONDUCTANCE-<br>MATRIX = | {CONDUCTANCE-FOR-THIS-NODE} |
| NODE VOLTAGES = | {VOLTAGE-FOR-THIS-NODE} |
| OTHER MATRICES = | NODAL-INCIDENCE-MATRIX +<br>DEPENDENT-VOLTAGE-SOURCE-MATRIX +<br>BRANCH-CONDUCTANCE-MATRIX +<br>INDEPENDENT-CURRENT-SOURCE-MATRIX |
| OUTPUT-CONTROL-<br>PARAMETERS = | NODE-VOLTAGES-PRINTOUT-FLAG +<br>BRANCH-VOLTAGES-PRINTOUT-FLAG +<br>ELEMENT-VOLTAGES-PRINTOUT-FLAG +<br>ELEMENT-CURRENTS-PRINTOUT-FLAG +<br>BRANCH-CURRENTS-PRINTOUT-FLAG |
| OUTPUT-CONTROL-<br>PARAMETERS-FILE = | NODE-VOLTAGES-PRINTOUT-FLAG +<br>BRANCH-VOLTAGES-PRINTOUT-FLAG +<br>ELEMENT-VOLTAGES-PRINTOUT-FLAG +<br>ELEMENT-CURRENTS-PRINTOUT-FLAG +<br>BRANCH-CURRENTS-PRINTOUT-FLAG |
| PRINTOUTS = | NODE-VOLTAGES-PRINTOUT +<br>BRANCH-VOLTAGES-PRINTOUT +<br>ELEMENT-VOLTAGES-PRINTOUT +<br>ELEMENT-CURRENTS-PRINTOUT +<br>BRANCH-CURRENTS-PRINTOUT |

**Figure 9-9** *continued*

tain subsidiary data explanations are provided where the content of the data flow definition is not self-explanatory. One bothersome item in the data dictionary is the entry OTHER MATRICES. The title really does not convey any meaningful information. The content of this data flow does not become clear until the data dictionary is referenced to learn its content. The five component matrices of this data flow are independent items and should have been represented individually on the DFDs. This would have avoided the mystery associated with the OTHER MATRICES data flow. It is assumed that the requirements analyst will pick up this observation and revise the next draft of the specification appropriately.

The last part of the specification is the transform descriptions. There is an individual description for each of the primitive functions:

1. Input analysis control parameters

2.1 Input element data

2.2 Formulate network equations

2.3 Solve network equations

3. Prepare output printouts

These descriptions are contained in Figures 9-10 through 9-14.

In these descriptions, *structured English* has been used as a specification language. Structured English is simply an uncluttered version of basic English that uses certain controlled constructions and key words. The three basic constructs are shown below along with the reserved key words associated with each construct:

- Simple declarative sentence
- Decision construct

  IF (condition)
  THEN
  (operations if condition true)
  ELSE
  (operations if condition false)

- Iteration construction
  Option 1:

  REPEAT
  (operations while condition
  not true)
  UNTIL (condition)

```
PROCESS 1.  Input Analysis Control Parameters
    Input network size parameters
    Store in network control parameters file
    Input circuit values
    Store in network control parameters file
    Input output control parameters
    Store in output control parameters file
    Input debug printout parameters
    Store in debug printout parameters file
```

**Figure 9-10**  Input Analysis Control Parameters Transform Description

```
PROCESS 2.1   Input Element Data
    REPEAT
        Read element data for this branch
        Store in element data file
    UNTIL data from all branches input
```

**Figure 9-11**   Input Element Data Transform Description

Option 2:

```
        WHILE (condition)
        (operations while condition
        true)
```

Structured English has many variations; there is no unique version. The key words shown here and used in the transform descriptions have been carefully selected but are, nonetheless, somewhat arbitrary. The attributes of any key word set should be unambiguity, conciseness, clarity, and uniformity. Note that the indentation of subordinate operations contributes to clarity and readability.

By using this constructive approach to the preparation of this requirements specification, a product that seems superior to the original specification appearing in Chapter 3 has been produced. Perhaps one or two inconsistencies were caught along the way and redundancies have been minimized. The expectation is that the

Process 2.2   Formulate Network Equations
    REPEAT for each branch
        Compute resistance, conductance, capacitance, inductance, independent voltage source, independent current source, transconductance, transfluence, transpotential, and transresistance
    UNTIL all branches processed
    Construct modal incidence matrix, $A$
    Oonstruct independent voltage source matrix, $C$
    Construct independent current source matrix, $J$
    Construct branch conductance matrix, $G$
    Construct dependent voltage source matrix, $D$
    IF requested by DEBUG-SET-1 flag
        THEN,
        Printout nodal incidence matrix, independent voltage surce matrix, independent current source matrix, branch conductance matrix, and dependent voltage source matrix
    Calculate nodal conductance matrix, $G_n$, using equation
$$G_n = A(GD^{-1})A^T$$
    Calculate equivalent current source vector, $J_n$, using equation
$$J_n = A(J - GE)$$
    IF requested by DEBUG-SET-2 flag
        THEN,
        Printout nodal conductance matrix
    IF requested by DEBUG-SET-3 flag
        THEN,
        Printout equivalent current source vector

**Figure 9-12**   Formulate Network Equations Transform Description

```
Process 2.3   Solve Network Equations
    REPEAT for each node
        Calculate node voltage, using equation
            Vn = GnJn
    UNTIL all nodes processed
```

**Figure 9-13**   Solve Network Equations Transform Description

software development team that receives this requirements specification will do a better job of implementation because of its enhanced quality and understandability.

## COMPUTER-AIDED REQUIREMENTS ANALYSIS

Computer assistance to the requirements analysis process is in its infancy. It is on the threshold of becoming a major contributor but has yet to advance to the point of mass application. Computer-aided requirements analysis can offer benefits in three areas:

1. Automated consistency checks
2. Production of reports which allow the analyst to perform in-depth consistency and completeness checks
3. Automated documentation

Some clarification is appropriate as to what computer-aided requirements analysis is and is not. First, it is not a technique nor a methodology; it is a tool. Such a tool

```
Process 3.   Prepare Output Printouts
    IF requested by NODE-VOLTAGES-PRINTOUT flag
        THEN,
        Printout node voltages
    IF requested by BRANCH-VOLTAGES-PRINTOUT flag
        THEN,
        Compute branch voltages
        Printout branch voltages
    IF requested by ELEMENT-VOLTAGES-PRINTOUT flag
        THEN,
        Compute element voltages
        Printout element voltages
    IF requested by ELEMENT-CURRENT-PRINTOUT flag
        THEN,
        Compute element currents
        Printout element currents
    IF requested by BRANCH-CURRENTS-PRINTOUT flag
        THEN,
        Compute branch currents
        Printout branch currents
```

**Figure 9-14**   Prepare Output Printouts Transform Description

renders automated assistance to the technique of structured analysis, which manifests itself as the product called the *structured specification*. In order to effectively use a computer-aided requirements analysis tool, the system engineering organization must already be educated in the constructive methods of requirements analysis (structured analysis).

A tool that shows great promise of practical assistance to the requirements analysis process is the PSL/PSA (problem statement language/problem statement analyzer) system developed at the University of Michigan. Its utilization on pilot projects in industry has resulted in favorable reports. The capabilities of PSL/PSA will be explained in this section through an example application to the dc network analysis system.

PSL provides the facilities to express requirements in a formal language with a precise syntactical structure. The requirements specification is thus expressed in a machine-readable data base. PSA performs automated consistency checking and can output a number of documentation reports. PSA analyzes the preciseness of PSL statements by

- Checking the syntax of the statements
- Checking that the names in new statements are consistent with names already in the data base

Consistency of new PSL statements is verified by

- Identifying conflicting name types
- Identifying contradicting relationships of names

These capabilities are valuable in cross-checking the inputs of several individuals working on the problem. PSA produces reports which provide machine assistance to the analyst who is performing consistency and completeness checks of the following system aspects:

- System flow
- System structure
- Data structure
- Data derivation
- System size and volume
- System dynamics
- System properties
- Project management

The utility of PSL/PSA is demonstrated through an application to an example problem. The results are presented in the following paragraphs.

We again rely on the dc network analysis system as a demonstration vehicle. The requirements for the dc network analysis system were defined in the syntax of the problem statement language. The language provides a capability for naming objects that play a role in the system. Objects include data components, processes, and external interfaces. The most powerful aspect of PSL/PSA is the ability to define relationships between the objects. Among the relationships that may be described are system boundaries, process structure, data structure, data derivation, size, and system dynamics.

A *formatted problem statement report* for the dc network analysis system is contained in Figure 9–15. Each section of the report is denoted by an object name

```
                          FORMATTED PROBLEM STATEMENT

PARAMETERS FOR: FPS

    FILE INDEX PRINT EMPTY NOPUNCH SMARG=5 NMARG=20 AMARG=10 BMARG=25 RNMARG=70 CMARG=1 HMARG=40
    NODESIGNATE ONE-PER-LINE DEFINE COMMENT NONEW-PAGE NONEW-LINE NOALL-STATEMENTS
    COMPLEMENTARY-STATEMENTS LINE-NUMBERS PRINTEOF

 1  ELEMENT                         branch-conductance-print;
 2      CONTAINED IN:  debug-set-1;
 3
 4  ELEMENT                         branch-currents-printout;
 5      CONTAINED IN:  printouts;
 6
 7  ELEMENT                         branch-currents-printout-flag;
 8      CONTAINED IN:  output-control-parameters,
 9                     output-control-parameters-file;
10
11  ELEMENT                         branch-element-value;
12      CONTAINED IN:  element-data,
13                     element-data-file;
14
15  ELEMENT                         branch-num-depend-source;
16      CONTAINED IN:  element-data,
17                     element-data-file;
18
19  ELEMENT                         branch-number;
20      CONTAINED IN:  element-data,
21                     element-data-file;
22
23  ELEMENT                         branch-type;
24      CONTAINED IN:  element-data,
25                     element-data-file;
26
27  ELEMENT                         branch-voltages-printout;
28      CONTAINED IN:  printouts;
29
30  ELEMENT                         branch-voltages-printout-flag;
31      CONTAINED IN:  output-control-parameters,
32                     output-control-parameters-file;
33
34  ELEMENT                         capacitance;
35      CONTAINED IN:  nodal-incidence-matrix,
36                     branch-conductance-matrix;
37
38  ELEMENT                         conductance;
39      CONTAINED IN:  nodal-incidence-matrix,
40                     branch-conductance-matrix;
41
42  ELEMENT                         conductance-for-this-node;
43      CONTAINED IN:  nodal-conductance-matrix;
44
45  ELEMENT                         debug-set-1-flag;
46      CONTAINED IN:  debug-printout-parameters,
47                     debug-printout-parameters-file;
48
49  ELEMENT                         debug-set-2-flag;
50      CONTAINED IN:  debug-printout-parameters,
51                     debug-printout-parameters-file;
52
53  ELEMENT                         debug-set-3-flag;
54      CONTAINED IN:  debug-printout-parameters,
55                     debug-printout-parameters-file;
56
57  ELEMENT                         depend-voltage-source-print;
58      CONTAINED IN:  debug-set-1;
59
60  ELEMENT                         element-currents-printout;
61      CONTAINED IN:  printouts;
```

**Figure 9–15**  Formatted problem statement report.

```
 62
 63 ELEMENT                                   element-currents-printout-flag;
 64     CONTAINED IN:  output-control-parameters,
 65                    output-control-parameters-file;
 66
 67 ELEMENT                                   element-voltages-printout;
 68     CONTAINED IN:  printouts;
 69
 70 ELEMENT                                   element-voltages-printout-flag;
 71     CONTAINED IN:  output-control-parameters,
 72                    output-control-parameters-file;
 73
 74 ELEMENT                                   equiv-cur-source-for-node;
 75     CONTAINED IN:  equivalent-current-matrix;
 76
 77 ELEMENT                                   equivalent-current-print;
 78     CONTAINED IN:  debug-set-3;
 79
 80 ELEMENT                                   final-node;
 81     CONTAINED IN:  element-data,
 82                    element-data-file;
 83
 84 ELEMENT                                   indep-cur-source-for-branch;
 85     CONTAINED IN:  indep-current-source-matrix;
 86
 87 ELEMENT                                   independ-current-source-print;
 88     CONTAINED IN:  debug-set-1;
 89
 90 ELEMENT                                   independ-voltage-source-print;
 91     CONTAINED IN:  debug-set-1;
 92
 93 ELEMENT                                   inductance;
 94     CONTAINED IN:  nodal-incidence-matrix,
 95                    branch-conductance-matrix;
 96
 97 ELEMENT                                   initial-node;
 98     CONTAINED IN:  element-data,
 99                    element-data-file;
100
101 ELEMENT                                   nodal-conduct-matrix-print;
102     CONTAINED IN:  debug-set-2;
103
104 ELEMENT                                   nodal-incidence-matrix-print;
105     CONTAINED IN:  debug-set-1;
106
107 ELEMENT                                   node-voltages-printout;
108     CONTAINED IN:  printouts;
109
110 ELEMENT                                   node-voltages-printout-flag;
111     CONTAINED IN:  output-control-parameters,
112                    output-control-parameters-file;
113
114 ELEMENT                                   number-of-network-branches;
115     CONTAINED IN:  network-size-parameters,
116                    network-control-params-file;
117
118 ELEMENT                                   number-of-network-nodes;
119     CONTAINED IN:  network-size-parameters,
120                    network-control-params-file;
121
122 ELEMENT                                   open-circuit-values;
123     CONTAINED IN:  circuit-values,
124                    network-control-params-file;
125
126 ELEMENT                                   resistance;
127     CONTAINED IN:  nodal-incidence-matrix,
128                    branch-conductance-matrix;
129
130 ELEMENT                                   short-circuit-value;
131     CONTAINED IN:  circuit-values,
132                    network-control-params-file;
133
134 ELEMENT                                   transconductance;
135     CONTAINED IN:  branch-conductance-matrix;
136
137 ELEMENT                                   transfluence;
138     CONTAINED IN:  branch-conductance-matrix;
139
140 ELEMENT                                   transpotential;
141     CONTAINED IN:  depend-voltage-source-matrix;
142
143 ELEMENT                                   transresistance;
144     CONTAINED IN:  depend-voltage-source-matrix,
145                    branch-conductance-matrix;
146
147 ELEMENT                                   voltage-for-this-node;
148     CONTAINED IN:  node-voltages;
149
```

**Figure 9-15** *continued*

```
150 ENTITY                            debug-printout-parameters-file;
151     CONSISTS OF:
152                         debug-set-1-flag,
153                         debug-set-2-flag,
154                         debug-set-3-flag;
155     USED BY:        determine-node-voltages,
156                     formulate-network-equations;
157     DERIVED BY:     input-analy-control-params;
158
159 ENTITY                             element-data-file;
160     CONSISTS OF:
161                         branch-type,
162                         branch-number,
163                         initial-node,
164                         final-node,
165                         branch-element-value,
166                         branch-num-depend-source;
167     USED BY:        formulate-network-equations;
168     DERIVED BY:     input-element-data;
169
170 ENTITY                             equivalent-current-matrix;
171     CONSISTS OF:
172                         equiv-cur-source-for-node;
173     USED BY:        solve-network-equations;
174     DERIVED BY:     formulate-network-equations;
175
176 ENTITY                             network-control-params-file;
177     CONSISTS OF:
178                         number-of-network-nodes,
179                         number-of-network-branches,
180                         short-circuit-value,
181                         open-circuit-values;
182     USED BY:        determine-node-voltages,
183                     formulate-network-equations,
184                     solve-network-equations;
185     DERIVED BY:     input-analy-control-params;
186
187 ENTITY                             nodal-conductance-matrix;
188     CONSISTS OF:
189                         conductance-for-this-node;
190     USED BY:        solve-network-equations;
191     DERIVED BY:     formulate-network-equations;
192
193 ENTITY                             node-voltages;
194     CONSISTS OF:
195                         voltage-for-this-node;
196     USED BY:        prepare-output-printouts;
197     DERIVED BY:     determine-node-voltages;
198     DERIVED BY:     solve-network-equations;
199
200 ENTITY                             other-matrices;
201     CONSISTS OF:
202                         nodal-incidence-matrix,
203                         depend-voltage-source-matrix,
204                         branch-conductance-matrix,
205                         indep-current-source-matrix;
206     USED BY:        prepare-output-printouts;
207     DERIVED BY:     determine-node-voltages;
208     DERIVED BY:     formulate-network-equations;
209
210 ENTITY                             output-control-parameters-file;
211     CONSISTS OF:
212                         node-voltages-printout-flag,
213                         branch-voltages-printout-flag,
214                         element-voltages-printout-flag,
215                         element-currents-printout-flag,
216                         branch-currents-printout-flag;
217     DERIVED BY:     input-analy-control-params;
218
219 GROUP                              branch-conductance-matrix;
220     CONSISTS OF:
221                         resistance,
222                         conductance,
223                         capacitance,
224                         inductance,
225                         transconductance,
226                         transfluence,
227                         transresistance;
228     CONTAINED IN:   other-matrices;
229
230 GROUP                              debug-set-1;
231     CONSISTS OF:
232                         nodal-incidence-matrix-print,
233                         independ-voltage-source-print,
234                         independ-current-source-print,
235                         branch-conductance-print,
236                         depend-voltage-source-print;
```

**Figure 9–15**  *continued*

```
237     CONTAINED IN:   debug-printouts;
238
239 GROUP                                  debug-set-2;
240     CONSISTS OF:
241                         nodal-conduct-matrix-print;
242     CONTAINED IN:   debug-printouts;
243
244 GROUP                                  debug-set-3;
245     CONSISTS OF:
246                         equivalent-current-print;
247     CONTAINED IN:   debug-printouts;
248
249 GROUP                              depend-voltage-source-matrix;
250     CONSISTS OF:
251                         transpotential,
252                         transresistance;
253     CONTAINED IN:   other-matrices;
254
255 GROUP                              indep-current-source-matrix;
256     CONSISTS OF:
257                         indep-cur-source-for-branch;
258     CONTAINED IN:   other-matrices;
259
260 GROUP                              nodal-incidence-matrix;
261     CONSISTS OF:
262                         resistance,
263                         conductance,
264                         capacitance,
265                         inductance;
266     CONTAINED IN:   other-matrices;
267
268 INPUT                                  circuit-values;
269     GENERATED BY:   analyst;
270     RECEIVED BY:    DC-network-analysis,
271                     input-analy-control-params;
272     CONSISTS OF:
273      *                  short-circuit-value,
274                         open-circuit-values;
275
276 INPUT                              debug-printout-parameters;
277     GENERATED BY:   analyst;
278     RECEIVED BY:    DC-network-analysis,
279                     input-analy-control-params;
280     CONSISTS OF:
281                         debug-set-1-flag,
282                         debug-set-2-flag,
283                         debug-set-3-flag;
284
285 INPUT                                  element-data;
286     RECEIVED BY:    DC-network-analysis,
287                     determine-node-voltages,
288                     input-element-data;
289     CONSISTS OF:
290                         branch-type,
291                         branch-number,
292                         initial-node,
293                         final-node,
294                         branch-element-value,
295                         branch-num-depend-source;
296
297 INPUT                              network-size-parameters;
298     GENERATED BY:   analyst;
299     RECEIVED BY:    DC-network-analysis,
300                     input-analy-control-params;
301     CONSISTS OF:
302                         number-of-network-nodes,
303                         number-of-network-branches;
304
305 INPUT                              output-control-parameters;
306     GENERATED BY:   analyst;
307     RECEIVED BY:    DC-network-analysis,
308                     input-analy-control-params;
309     CONSISTS OF:
310                         node-voltages-printout-flag,
311                         branch-voltages-printout-flag,
312                         element-voltages-printout-flag,
313                         element-currents-printout-flag,
314                         branch-currents-printout-flag;
315
316 INTERFACE                              analyst;
317     GENERATES:      network-size-parameters,
318                     circuit-values,
319                     output-control-parameters,
320                     debug-printout-parameters;
321     RECEIVES:       printouts,
322                     debug-printouts;
323
```

**Figure 9-15**  *continued*

```
324 OUTPUT                                       debug-printouts;
325     GENERATED BY:   DC-network-analysis,
326                     determine-node-voltages,
327                     formulate-network-equations;
328     RECEIVED BY:    analyst;
329     CONSISTS OF:
330                             debug-set-1,
331                             debug-set-2,
332                             debug-set-3;
333
334 OUTPUT                                       printouts;
335     GENERATED BY:   DC-network-analysis,
336                     prepare-output-printouts;
337     RECEIVED BY:    analyst;
338     CONSISTS OF:
339                             node-voltages-printout,
340                             branch-voltages-printout,
341                             element-voltages-printout,
342                             element-currents-printout,
343                             branch-currents-printout;
344
345 PROCESS                                  determine-node-voltages;
346     GENERATES:      debug-printouts;
347     RECEIVES:       element-data;
348     SUBPARTS ARE:   input-element-data,
349                     formulate-network-equations,
350                     solve-network-equations;
351     PART OF:        DC-network-analysis;
352     USES:           network-control-params-file,
353                     debug-printout-parameters-file;
354     DERIVES:        node-voltages;
355     DERIVES:        other-matrices;
356
357 PROCESS                               formulate-network-equations;
358     GENERATES:      debug-printouts;
359     PART OF:        determine-node-voltages;
360     USES:           element-data-file,
361                     debug-printout-parameters-file,
362                     network-control-params-file;
363     DERIVES:        nodal-conductance-matrix;
364     DERIVES:        other-matrices;
365     DERIVES:        equivalent-current-matrix;
366     PROCEDURE;
367     REPEAT for each branch
368       Compute resistance, conductance, capacitance,
369        inductance, independent-voltage-source,
370        independent-current-source, transconductance,
371        transfluence, transpotential, and transresistance
372     UNTIL all branches processed
373     Construct nodal-incidence-matrix, A
374     Construct independ-voltage-source-matrix, E
375     Construct indep-current-source-matrix, J
376     Construct branch-conductance-matrix, G
377     Construct depend-voltage-source-matrix, D
378     IF requested by debug-set-1-flag
379       THEN,
380       Printout nodal-incidence-matrix, independent-voltage
381        source-matrix, indep-current-source-matrix,
382        branch-conductance-matrix, and dependent-voltage-
383        source-matrix
384     Calculate nodal-conductance-matrix, GN, using equation:
385                 GN = A(G D(inverse))A(transpose)
386     Calculate equivalent-current-source-vector, JN,using equation:
387                 JN = A(J - GE)
388     IF requested by debug-set-2-flag
389       THEN,
390       Printout nodal-conductance-matrix
391     IF requested by debug-set-3-flag
392       THEN,
393       Printout equivalent-current-source-vector;
394
395 PROCESS                                  input-analy-control-params;
396     RECEIVES:       network-size-parameters,
397                     circuit-values,
398                     output-control-parameters,
399                     debug-printout-parameters;
400     PART OF:        DC-network-analysis;
401     DERIVES:        network-control-params-file;
402     DERIVES:        debug-printout-parameters-file;
403     DERIVES:        output-control-parameters-file;
404     PROCEDURE;
405     Input network-size-parameters.
406     Store in network-control-params-file.
407     Input circuit-values.
408     Store in network-control-params-file.
409     Input output-control-parameters.
410     Store in output-control-parameters-file.
```

**Figure 9-15**  *continued*

```
411      Input debug-printout-parameters.
412      Store in debug-printout-parameters-file.;
413
414 PROCESS                               input-element-data;
415      RECEIVES:        element-data;
416      PART OF:         determine-node-voltages;
417      DERIVES:         element-data-file;
418      PROCEDURE;
419      REPEAT,
420        Read element-data for this branch
421        Store in element-data-file
422      UNTIL data from all branches input;
423
424 PROCESS                               prepare-output-printouts;
425      GENERATES:       printouts;
426      PART OF:         DC-network-analysis;
427      USES:            node-voltages,
428                       other-matrices;
429      PROCEDURE;
430      IF requested by node-voltages-printout-flag
431        THEN,
432        Printout node-voltages
433      IF requested by branch-voltages-printout-flag
434        THEN,
435        Compute branch-voltages
436        Printout branch-voltages
437      IF requested by element-voltages-printout-flag
438        THEN,
439        Compute element-voltages
440        Printout element-voltages
441      IF requested by element-current-printout-flag
442        THEN,
443        Compute element-currents
444        Printout element-currents
445      IF requested by branch-currents-printout-flag
446        THEN,
447        Compute branch-currents
448        Printout branch-currents;
449
450 PROCESS                               solve-network-equations;
451      PART OF:         determine-node-voltages;
452      USES:            network-control-params-file,
453                       nodal-conductance-matrix,
454                       equivalent-current-matrix;
455      DERIVES:         node-voltages;
456      PROCEDURE;
457      REPEAT for each node
458        Calculate node-voltage using equation:
459              VN = (GN)(JN)
460      UNTIL all nodes processed;
461
462 PROCESS                               DC-network-analysis;
463      DESCRIPTION;
464      This system accepts inputs describing the DC electrical
465      network, generates the network equations, and solves
466      the equations to determine the unknown voltages and
467      currents.;
468      GENERATES:       printouts,
469                       debug-printouts;
470      RECEIVES:        network-size-parameters,
471                       circuit-values,
472                       output-control-parameters,
473                       debug-printout-parameters,
474                       element-data;
475      SUBPARTS ARE:    input-analy-control-params,
476                       determine-node-voltages,
477                       prepare-output-printouts;
478
479 EOF EOF EOF EOF EOF
```

**Figure 9-15** *continued*

such as ELEMENT, ENTITY, INPUT, INTERFACE, PROCESS, and so on. Indentured beneath each object are the relationships between that object and other objects in the system. The relationships are denoted by verbs such as CONSISTS OF, GENERATES, USES, DERIVES, RECEIVES, and so forth. A structured English description of each process is detailed beneath the subheader PRO-CEDURE that is included in each PROCESS section.

Most of the problem statements enclosed in this report are direct inputs by the user. However, certain complementary relationships need only be defined once. For example, in defining the elements of an ENTITY, it is only necessary to define the component elements in a CONSISTS OF statement; the complementing relationship in the ELEMENT section that defines the entity that this element is CONTAINED IN is generated automatically by the problem statement analyzer. The syntax rules will not be belabored further; a general understanding of the problem definition can be obtained by perusing the report.

In a syntactical form, all of the elements of the structured specification can be recognized in the formatted problem statement report:

- Data flow into and out of each process
- Data dictionary
- Transform descriptions

The data flow is defined for each process using the relationships RECEIVES, GENERATES, USES, and DERIVES. Data-dictionary-type information is present in the form of object sections for each data component (ENTITY, ELEMENT, GROUP, etc.). Higher-level data components such as ENTITY or GROUP are further defined using the CONSISTS OF relationship. A transform description for each PROCESS is present under the PROCEDURE key word. Subsequent reports represent this information in more recognizable and useful forms.

It should be noted that some of the processes in the formatted problem statement report are related hierarchically. In practice, the problem statements will be developed incrementally in top-down order. As in Figure 9–15, the final set of statements will represent a history of the thought process that created them.

Even before generating the formatted problem statement report, it is useful to generate and examine the *name list report*. As shown in Figure 9–16, this report identifies the object type assigned to each name. A frequent consistency error is that

```
                          NAME LIST


   PARAMETERS FOR:  NL

   ORDER=ALPHA



        NAME                                      TYPE              SYNONYM

    1   Analyst                                   Interface
    2   Branch - Conductance - Matrix             Group
    3   Branch - Conductance - Print              Element
    4   Branch - Currents - Printout              Element
    5   Branch - Currents - Printout - Flag       Element
    6   Branch - Element - Value                  Element
    7   Branch - Num - Depend - Source            Element
    8   Branch - Number                           Element
    9   Branch - Type                             Element
   10   Branch - Voltages - Printout              Element
   11   Branch - Voltages - Printout - Flag       Element
   12   Capacitance                               Element
   13   Circuit - Values                          Input
   14   Conductance                               Element
   15   Conductance - For - This - Node           Element
   16   Debug - Printout - Parameters             Input
```

**Figure 9–16**  Name list report.

|  | NAME | TYPE | SYNONYM |
|---|---|---|---|
| 17 | Debug – Printout – Parameters – File | Entity | |
| 18 | Debug – Printouts | Output | |
| 19 | Debug – Set – 1 | XXX Undefined XXX | |
| 20 | Debug – Set – 1 – Flag | XXX Undefined XXX | |
| 21 | Debug – Set – 2 | XXX Undefined XXX | |
| 22 | Debug – Set – 2 – Flag | Element | |
| 23 | Debug – Set – 3 | XXX Undefined XXX | |
| 24 | Debug – Set – 3 – Flag | Element | |
| 25 | Debug – Set – 1 – Flag | Element | |
| 26 | Depend – Voltage – Source – Matrix | Group | |
| 27 | Depend – Voltage – Source – Print | Element | |
| 28 | Determine – Node – Voltages | Process | |
| 29 | Element – Currents – Printout | Element | |
| 30 | Element – Currents – Printout – Flag | Element | |
| 31 | Element – Data | Input | |
| 32 | Element – Data – File | Entity | |
| 33 | Element – Voltages – Printout | Element | |
| 34 | Element – Voltages – Printout – Flag | Element | |
| 35 | Equiv – Cur – Source – For – Node | Element | |
| 36 | Equivalent – Current – Matrix | Entity | |
| 37 | Equivalent – Current – Print | Element | |
| 38 | Final – Node | Element | |
| 39 | Formulate – Network – Equations | Process | |
| 40 | Indep – Cur – Source – For – Branch | Element | |
| 41 | Indep – Current – Source – Matrix | Group | |
| 42 | Independ – Current – Source – Print | Element | |
| 43 | Independ – Voltage – Source – Print | Element | |
| 44 | Inductance | Element | |
| 45 | Initial – Node | Element | |
| 46 | Input – Analy – Control – Params | Process | |
| 47 | Input – Element – Data | Process | |
| 48 | Network – Control – Params – File | Entity | |
| 49 | Network – Size – Parameters | Input | |
| 50 | Nodal – Conduct – Matrix – Print | Element | |
| 51 | Nodal – Conductance – Matrix | Entity | |
| 52 | Nodal – Incidence – Matrix | Group | |
| 53 | Nodal – Incidence – Matrix – Print | Element | |
| 54 | Node – Voltages | Entity | |
| 55 | Node – Voltages – Printout | Element | |
| 56 | Node – Voltages – Printout – Flag | Element | |
| 57 | Number – Of – Network – Branches | Element | |
| 58 | Number – Of – Network – Nodes | Element | |
| 59 | Open – Circuit – Values | Element | |
| 60 | Other – Matrices | Entity | |
| 61 | Output – Control – Parameters | Input | |
| 62 | Output – Control – Parameters – File | Entity | |
| 63 | Prepare – Output – Printouts | Process | |
| 64 | Printouts | Output | |
| 65 | Resistance | Element | |
| 66 | Short – Circuit – Value | Element | |
| 67 | Solve – Network – Equations | Process | |
| 68 | Transconductance | Element | |
| 69 | Transfluence | Element | |
| 70 | Transpotential | Element | |
| 71 | Transresistance | Element | |
| 72 | Voltage – For – This – Node | Element | |
| 73 | DC – Network – Analysis | Process | |

**Figure 9-16** *continued*

of using an object in a relationship statement without assigning it a type. Four such errors are indicated on Figure 9–16. These should be corrected before other reports are generated.

PSA furnishes a number of reports describing the data in the system and relationships between data components. The *contents report* closely resembles a data dictionary. This is shown in Figure 9–17. The data structures are depicted hierarchically. For the dc network analysis system, the content of the data structures have been defined in three levels—the ENTITY, the GROUP, and the ELEMENT. The ELEMENT is the basic unit of data that is not further divisible.

Perhaps the most important PSA outputs are those reports which describe the

```
                                        CONTENTS REPORT

ARAMETERS FOR: CONT

FILE NONCFLAG PRINT-SECURITY-INFORMATION INDEX LEVELS=ALL


  1*      1 debug-printout-parameters-file (ENTITY)
  1         2   debug-set-1-flag (ELEMENT)
  2         2   debug-set-2-flag (ELEMENT)
  3         2   debug-set-3-flag (ELEMENT)

  2*      1 element-data-file (ENTITY)
  1         2   branch-type (ELEMENT)
  2         2   branch-number (ELEMENT)
  3         2   initial-node (ELEMENT)
  4         2   final-node (ELEMENT)
  5         2   branch-element-value (ELEMENT)
  6         2   branch-num-depend-source (ELEMENT)

  3*      1 equivalent-current-matrix (ENTITY)
  1         2   equiv-cur-source-for-node (ELEMENT)

  4*      1 network-control-params-file (ENTITY)
  1         2   number-of-network-nodes (ELEMENT)
  2         2   number-of-network-branches (ELEMENT)
  3         2   short-circuit-value (ELEMENT)
  4         2   open-circuit-values (ELEMENT)

  5*      1 nodal-conductance-matrix (ENTITY)
  1         2   conductance-for-this-node (ELEMENT)

  6*      1 node-voltages (ENTITY)
  1         2   voltage-for-this-node (ELEMENT)

  7*      1 other-matrices (ENTITY)
  1         2   nodal-incidence-matrix (GROUP)
  2           3     resistance (ELEMENT)
  3           3     conductance (ELEMENT)
  4           3     capacitance (ELEMENT)
  5           3     inductance (ELEMENT)
  6         2   depend-voltage-source-matrix (GROUP)
  7           3     transpotential (ELEMENT)
  8           3     transresistance (ELEMENT)
  9         2   branch-conductance-matrix (GROUP)
 10           3     resistance (ELEMENT)
 11           3     conductance (ELEMENT)
 12           3     capacitance (ELEMENT)
 13           3     inductance (ELEMENT)
 14           3     transconductance (ELEMENT)
 15           3     transfluence (ELEMENT)
 16           3     transresistance (ELEMENT)
 17         2   indep-current-source-matrix (GROUP)
 18           3     indep-cur-source-for-branch (ELEMENT)

  8*      1 output-control-parameters-file (ENTITY)
  1         2   node-voltages-printout-flag (ELEMENT)
  2         2   branch-voltages-printout-flag (ELEMENT)
  3         2   element-voltages-printout-flag (ELEMENT)
  4         2   element-currents-printout-flag (ELEMENT)
  5         2   branch-currents-printout-flag (ELEMENT)

  9*      1 branch-conductance-matrix (GROUP)
  1         2   resistance (ELEMENT)
  2         2   conductance (ELEMENT)
  3         2   capacitance (ELEMENT)
  4         2   inductance (ELEMENT)
  5         2   transconductance (ELEMENT)
  6         2   transfluence (ELEMENT)
  7         2   transresistance (ELEMENT)

 10*      1 debug-set-1 (GROUP)
  1         2   nodal-incidence-matrix-print (ELEMENT)
  2         2   independ-voltage-source-print (ELEMENT)
```

**Figure 9-17**  Contents report.

```
      3     2    independ-current-source-print (ELEMENT)
      4     2    branch-conductance-print (ELEMENT)
      5     2    depend-voltage-source-print (ELEMENT)

    11*   1 debug-set-2 (GROUP)
      1     2    nodal-conduct-matrix-print (ELEMENT)

    12*   1 debug-set-3 (GROUP)
      1     2    equivalent-current-print (ELEMENT)
    13*   1 depend-voltage-source-matrix (GROUP)
      1     2    transpotential (ELEMENT)
      2     2    transresistance (ELEMENT)

    14*   1 indep-current-source-matrix (GROUP)
      1     2    indep-cur-source-for-branch (ELEMENT)

    15*   1 nodal-incidence-matrix (GROUP)
      1     2    resistance (ELEMENT)
      2     2    conductance (ELEMENT)
      3     2    capacitance (ELEMENT)
      4     2    inductance (ELEMENT)

    16*   1 circuit-values (INPUT)
      1     2    short-circuit-value (ELEMENT)
      2     2    open-circuit-values (ELEMENT)

    17*   1 debug-printout-parameters (INPUT)
      1     2    debug-set-1-flag (ELEMENT)
      2     2    debug-set-2-flag (ELEMENT)
      3     2    debug-set-3-flag (ELEMENT)

    18*   1 element-data (INPUT)
      1     2    branch-type (ELEMENT)
      2     2    branch-number (ELEMENT)
      3     2    initial-node (ELEMENT)
      4     2    final-node (ELEMENT)
      5     2    branch-element-value (ELEMENT)
      6     2    branch-num-depend-source (ELEMENT)

    19*   1 network-size-parameters (INPUT)
      1     2    number-of-network-nodes (ELEMENT)
      2     2    number-of-network-branches (ELEMENT)

    20*   1 output-control-parameters (INPUT)
      1     2    node-voltages-printout-flag (ELEMENT)
      2     2    branch-voltages-printout-flag (ELEMENT)
      3     2    element-voltages-printout-flag (ELEMENT)
      4     2    element-currents-printout-flag (ELEMENT)
      5     2    branch-currents-printout-flag (ELEMENT)
    21*   1 debug-printouts (OUTPUT)
      1     2    debug-set-1 (GROUP)
      2     3       nodal-incidence-matrix-print (ELEMENT)
      3     3       independ-voltage-source-print (ELEMENT)
      4     3       independ-current-source-print (ELEMENT)
      5     3       branch-conductance-print (ELEMENT)
      6     3       depend-voltage-source-print (ELEMENT)
      7     2    debug-set-2 (GROUP)
      8     3       nodal-conduct-matrix-print (ELEMENT)
      9     2    debug-set-3 (GROUP)
     10     3       equivalent-current-print (ELEMENT)

    22*   1 printouts (OUTPUT)
      1     2    node-voltages-printout (ELEMENT)
      2     2    branch-voltages-printout (ELEMENT)
      3     2    element-voltages-printout (ELEMENT)
      4     2    element-currents-printout (ELEMENT)
      5     2    branch-currents-printout (ELEMENT)
```

**Figure 9-17**  *continued*

interaction between data and processes. These are most useful in assisting the
analyst to visually identify errors. The data contents report describes in a handy
matrix form the relationships between processes and data. This report is shown in
Figure 9–18 in three parts:

- The definition of the matrix rows (data names) and columns (process
  names)
- The data process interaction matrix
- Matrix analysis messages

```
                                    DATA PROCESS REPORT

PARAMETERS FOR: DP

FILE PROCESS DPMAT DPANL DPRANL PMAT PANL

THE ROWS ARE DATA NAMES, THE COLUMNS ARE PROCESS NAMES.

   ROW NAMES                                      COLUMN NAMES

 1 node-voltages                ENTITY           1 determine-node-voltages          PROCESS
 2 other-matrices               ENTITY           2 formulate-network-equations       PROCESS
 3 network-control-params-file  ENTITY           3 input-analy-control-params        PROCESS
 4 debug-printout-parameters-file ENTITY         4 input-element-data                PROCESS
 5 element-data                 INPUT            5 prepare-output-printouts          PROCESS
 6 debug-printouts              OUTPUT           6 solve-network-equations           PROCESS
 7 nodal-conductance-matrix     ENTITY           7 DC-network-analysis               PROCESS
 8 equivalent-current-matrix    ENTITY
 9 element-data-file            ENTITY
10 output-control-parameters-file ENTITY
11 network-size-parameters      INPUT
12 circuit-values               INPUT
13 output-control-parameters    INPUT
14 debug-printout-parameters    INPUT
15 printouts                    OUTPUT


DATA PROCESS INTERACTION MATRIX

(I,J) VALUE   MEANING
-----------   -------

   R     ROW I IS RECEIVED OR USED BY COLUMN J (INPUT)
   U     ROW I IS UPDATED BY COLUMN J
   D     ROW I IS DERIVED OR GENERATED BY COLUMN J (OUTPUT)
   A     ROW I IS INPUT TO, UPDATED BY, AND OUTPUT OF
             COLUMN J (ALL)
   F     ROW I IS INPUT TO AND OUTPUT OF COLUMN J (FLOW)
   1     ROW I IS INPUT TO AND UPDATED BY COLUMN J
   2     ROW I IS UPDATED BY AND OUTPUT OF COLUMN J


        1 2 3 4 5 6 7
      + - - - - - - - +
   1  I       R I D I I
   2  I D D   R I D I I
   3  I D D R R D   R I
   4  I I R   R   I   R I
   5  I I R         I   R I
   6  I D D     I   D I
   7  I I D D   I   I R I
   8  I I D D   R   I R I
   9  I   R     D
  10  I D
  11  I I       R I R I
  12  I I       R I R I
  13  I I         R   I R I
  14  I I           R I R I
  15  I I           D I D I
      + - - - - - - - +
```

**Figure 9-18**  Data process report.

```
DATA PROCESS INTERACTION MATRIX ANALYSIS

DATA
----
element-data                    (INPUT)      (ROW   5) NOT USED BY ANY PROCESS
debug-printouts                 (OUTPUT)     (ROW   6) NOT DERIVED BY ANY PROCESS
output-control-parameters-file  (ENTITY)     (ROW  10) DERIVED, BUT NOT USED BY ANY PROCESS
network-size-parameters         (INPUT)      (ROW  11) NOT USED BY ANY PROCESS
circuit-values                  (INPUT)      (ROW  12) NOT USED BY ANY PROCESS
output-control-parameters       (INPUT)      (ROW  13) NOT USED BY ANY PROCESS
debug-printout-parameters       (INPUT)      (ROW  14) NOT USED BY ANY PROCESS
printouts                       (OUTPUT)     (ROW  15) NOT DERIVED BY ANY PROCESS

PROCESSES
---------
input-analy-control-params                   (COLUMN  3) DERIVES SOMETHING, BUT DOES NOT USE ANYTHING
input-element-data                           (COLUMN  4) DERIVES SOMETHING, BUT DOES NOT USE ANYTHING
prepare-output-printouts                     (COLUMN  5) USES DATA, BUT DOES NOT DERIVE OR UPDATE ANYTHING
```

**Figure 9-18**   *continued*

The matrix analysis messages are warnings that point out possible suspicious relationships. In this particular case, the messages result from certain peculiarities in the PSL syntax conventions and do not represent actual errors.

The inputs and outputs for each process are delineated in the process input/output report, contained in Figure 9–19. Each input or output is identified as to its specific relationship with the process. Unfortunately, PSA is not talented enough to machine produce a data flow diagram. The process input/output report is the only PSA product that represents an overall data flow, although in tabular

```
                                      PROCESS INPUT/OUTPUT

         PARAMETERS FOR: PRIO
           FILE INPUT OUTPUT DESCRIPTION NOPROCEDURE NONEW-PAGE INDEX PRINT NOPUNCH



         1*  determine-node-voltages

                                *** INPUTS ***

                      1 element-data                     RECEIVED
                      2 network-control-params-file      USED
                      3 debug-printout-parameters-file   USED

                                *** OUTPUTS ***

                      1 debug-printouts                  GENERATED
                      2 node-voltages                    DERIVED
                      3 other-matrices                   DERIVED



         2*  formulate-network-equations

                                *** INPUTS ***

                      1 element-data-file                USED
                      2 debug-printout-parameters-file   USED
                      3 network-control-params-file      USED

                                *** OUTPUTS ***

                      1 debug-printouts                  GENERATED
                      2 nodal-conductance-matrix         DERIVED
                      3 other-matrices                   DERIVED
                      4 equivalent-current-matrix        DERIVED



         3*  input-analy-control-params

                                *** INPUTS ***

                      1 network-size-parameters          RECEIVED
                      2 circuit-values                   RECEIVED
                      3 output-control-parameters        RECEIVED
                      4 debug-printout-parameters        RECEIVED

                                *** OUTPUTS ***

                      1 network-control-params-file      DERIVED
                      2 debug-printout-parameters-file   DERIVED
                      3 output-control-parameters-file   DERIVED



         4*  input-element-data

                                *** INPUTS ***

                      1 element-data                     RECEIVED

                                *** OUTPUTS ***

                      1 element-data-file                DERIVED
```

**Figure 9-19** Process input/output report.

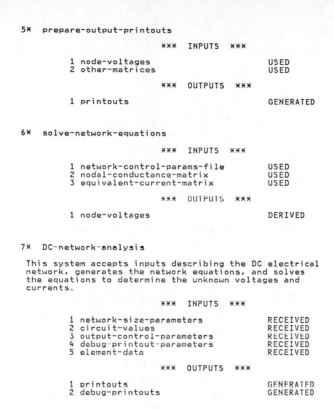

```
5*   prepare-output-printouts

                      ***  INPUTS  ***

           1 node-voltages                     USED
           2 other-matrices                    USED

                      ***  OUTPUTS  ***

           1 printouts                         GENERATED


6*   solve-network-equations

                      ***  INPUTS  ***

           1 network-control-params-file       USED
           2 nodal-conductance-matrix          USED
           3 equivalent-current-matrix         USED

                      ***  OUTPUTS  ***

           1 node-voltages                     DERIVED


7*   DC-network-analysis

     This system accepts inputs describing the DC electrical
     network, generates the network equations, and solves
     the equations to determine the unknown voltages and
     currents.

                      ***  INPUTS  ***

           1 network-size-parameters           RECEIVED
           2 circuit-values                    RECEIVED
           3 output-control-parameters         RECEIVED
           4 debug-printout-parameters         RECEIVED
           5 element-data                      RECEIVED

                      ***  OUTPUTS  ***

           1 printouts                         GENERATED
           2 debug-printouts                   GENERATED
```

**Figure 9-19** *continued*

form. A partial graphic representation of data flow is possible, such as the *process picture* shown in Figure 9–20. The data flow into and out of the input-analysis-control-paramaters process is diagrammed.

A computer-aided requirements analysis tool such as PSL/PSA is an asset to the requirements analysis process for several reasons:

1. Because the requirements must be organized in terms of objects and relationships, a better structuring of the requirements statements results.

2. Many inconsistencies can be detected automatically.

3. The problem statement language is reasonably natural and can be quickly learned.

There are some negatives associated with the tool. It is difficult to install and it consumes considerable computer resources. Its man/machine interface, command language, and overall operability are awkward but workable. A tool such as PSL/PSA can provide valuable assistance. However, the key innovation in modern requirements analysis is the structured analysis discipline, and the contribution of PSL/PSA type tools should properly be viewed in a supportive context to the basic discipline.

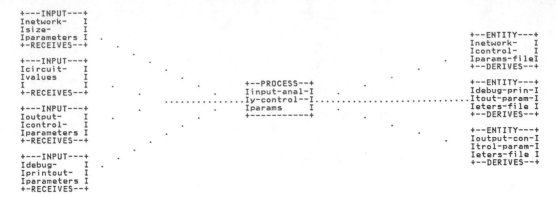

```
+---INPUT---+
Inetwork-    I
Isize-       I                                              +--ENTITY---+
Iparameters I  .                                            Inetwork-    I
+-RECEIVES--+    .                                          Icontrol-    I
                   .                                    .   Iparams-fileI
+---INPUT---+        .                                      +--DERIVES--+
Icircuit-    I         .
Ivalues      I           .                                 +--ENTITY---+
I            I   .     .     .   +--PROCESS--+   .          Idebug-prin-I
+-RECEIVES--+       .      .     Iinput-anal-I     .        Itout-param-I
                 .    .   ...............Iy-control--I..........................Ieters-file I
+---INPUT---+        .      .     Iparams      I   .        +--DERIVES--+
Ioutput-     I  .      .     .   +----------+   .
Icontrol-    I                                       .      +--ENTITY---+
Iparameters I          .                               .    Ioutput-con-I
+-RECEIVES--+             .                             .    Itrol-param-I
                   .      .                                  Ieters-file I
+---INPUT---+        .                                       +--DERIVES--+
Idebug-      I   .
Iprintout-   I
Iparameters I
+-RECEIVES--+
```

**Figure 9-20**  Process picture for input-analysis-control-parameters.

## SIMULATION

Simulation is the technique used to evaluate the performance characteristics of a system prior to its implementation. A simulator models the functional elements of a system and, usually, some part of the system's operational environment. The dynamic behavior of the system is predicted by interjecting a representation of an operational scenario or sequence of events into the system model. The performance characteristics are determined by observing the response of the system model to the scenario. The feasibility of attaining postulated performance requirements is inferred from the simulation results. Simulation is a very broad discipline. The intent here is to merely mention simulation as a validation aid for performance requirements and not to explore simulation in any degree of detail.

Simulation techniques are useful in assessing the following types of performance characteristics:

- Parameter accuracies
- System response durations to specific inputs
- CPU utilizations
- Storage utilizations
- Ability to meet operational timelines
- Man/machine interactions and responses

Depending upon the degree of sophistication desired, simulation development can be a very expensive proposition. There are available several specialized simulation languages which can ease the expense of system modeling. These include IBM's General Purpose System Simulation (GPSS), RAND's Extendable Computer System Simulation (ECSS), SIMSCRIPT, and System Analysis Machine (SAM).[7]

[7] Judith C. Enos and Richard L. Van Tilburg, "Software Design," in *Software Engineering,* ed. Randall W. Jensen and Charles C. Tonies (Englewood Cliffs, N.J.: Prentice-Hall, 1979), p. 217.

As an example of a simulation tool, the *design analysis system* (DAS), developed and used at Hughes Aircraft Company, is briefly addressed. DAS is a broad-based tool that is directed toward requirements analysis and design analysis. It interfaces with PSL/PSA through an integrated data base scheme. DAS consists of the following components and capabilities:

- Operational function diagram subsystem (OFD), which provides an interactive/graphical capability to define system operational flow and model operational scenarios
- Distributed data processing model (DDPM), to predict performance attributes such as equipment utilization, queueing statistics, and timing
- Structure chart graphics subsystem, to graphically and interactively record/modify structured design charts in a machine-readable data base
- Design quality metrics subsystem, which uses the structure chart data base to measure adherence to a set of design quality attributes

The architecture of DAS is displayed in Figure 9–21.[8]

The OFD subsystem offers the capabilities to examine system performance in response to operational scenarios. Figure 9–22 shows the application of OFD to a manufacturing center.[9] A five-step procedure is involved.

Step 1: Analyst manually depicts major processes in an information flow diagram (IFD).

Step 2: Analyst graphically inputs an operational flow diagram (OFD) for each process and specifies needed equipment, human resources, timing, and so forth.

Step 3: Analyst inputs test scenario via specification language.

Step 4: OFDs are executed by general function model.

Step 5: Performance profiles are output graphically.

The outputs are examined to determine if operational requirements are met. The sequence from steps 3 through 5 is expected to be interactive and iterative.

The *distributed data processing model* (DDPM) is employed to evaluate such trade-off alternatives as hardware selection, functional allocations, operating system, and data base management design. The DDPM consists of a number of submodels, as shown in Figure 9–23.[10] Tabular inputs to the model permit specification of system characteristics. Some of the possible outputs are device utilization, queue statistics, transaction occurrences and response times, and summary software execution results.

[8] *Hughes Software Engineering Manual* (Culver City, Ca.: Hughes Aircraft Co., 1980), Part II, p. 2–20.

[9] *Hughes Software Engineering Manual,* op. cit., p. 2–22.

[10] *Hughes Software Engineering Manual,* op. cit., p. 2–26.

89312-14R

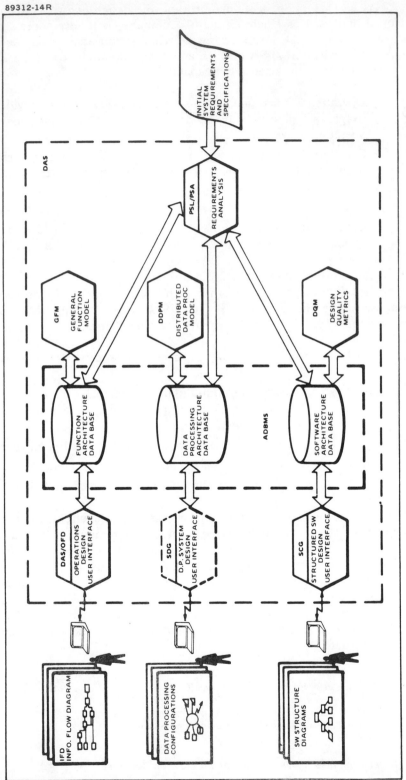

**Figure 9-21** Design analysis system (DAS) concept. (Courtesy of Hughes Aircraft Company.)

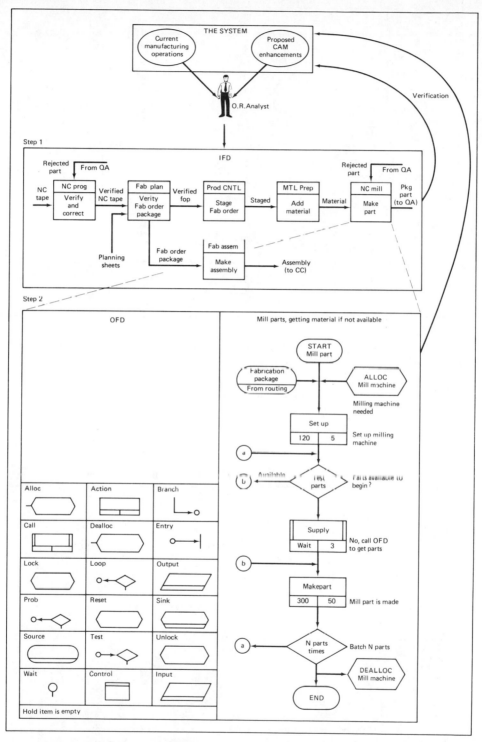

**Figure 9-22** Operations analysis of manufacturing using DAS/OFD. (Courtesy of Hughes Aircraft Company.)

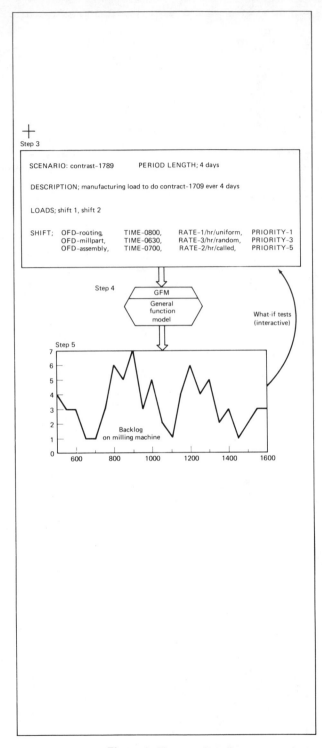

**Figure 9-22** *continued*

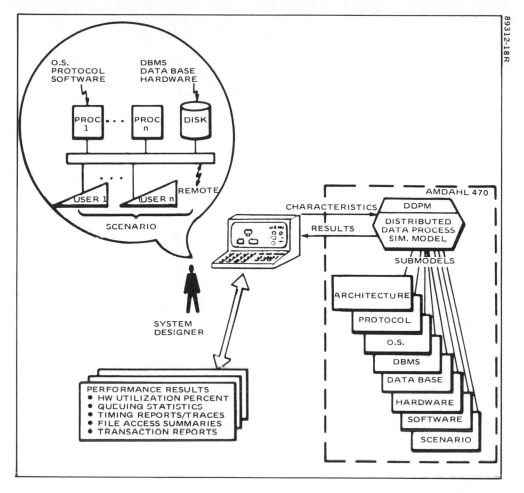

**Figure 9-23** DDPM-distributed data processing model. (Courtesy of Hughes Aircraft Company.)

The structure chart graphics and design quality metrics subsystems are described in the next chapter.

## REQUIREMENTS VALIDATION WRAP-UP

Several techniques and tools directed to the purpose of requirements validation have been explored. Although not presented in any particular order, these items do fit together synergistically if all were to be applied on the same project. The relationships between the items are parallel, sequential, and hierarchical. This configuration is represented in Figure 9-24.

The construction of the specification proceeds in parallel with simulation activities. The simulation seeks to establish the performance aspects of the CPCI or

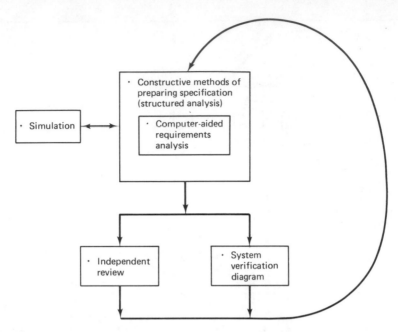

**Figure 9-24** Relationships of requirements validation methods.

system. The structured analysis discipline is used to prepare the specification. This discipline may employ a computer-aided requirements analysis tool such as PSL/PSA; the structured analysis discipline and the computer assistance tool are related in a hierarchical manner. Following in sequence after the availability of a draft specification, the independent review procedure and system verification diagram are applied as shown in Figure 9-24. The findings of these evaluation mechanisms are fed back into the process for inclusion as revisions into the next specification draft. These events iterate until the necessary levels of completeness and quality are achieved (or until the process is artificially foreclosed by management decision).

## 9.3

## Administer Data Base

In data-dominated systems, the design, implementation, and maintenance of the data base is at least as important as that of the programs. Data base is referred to in the general context; it may either consist of physical files directly accessed by the programs or a logically accessible data collection administered by a data base management system. The data base, whatever its implementation form, is a shared resource. It thus requires considerable care. Because of the centrality of the data base, only the system engineering organization is properly situated to administer it. The care and feeding of the data base is in the charge of an office of *data base administration* (DBA), a component of the system engineering organization.

The major activities of the DBA office in a verification and validation context are listed here:

- Enforce discipline and procedures of the data base
- Support the application users
- Support testing of the system

The DBA enforces standards, guidelines, and control procedures to ensure that all elements of the system are able to remain compatible with the data base. This includes issuing and maintaining accurate documentation of the data base. Because the data base is a central interface to all, or at least most, of the applications software of the system, there is a major potential for flaws in the data base to globally disrupt system operation. The enforcement activities of the DBA will include

- Coordinate changes among the applications users of the data base
- Physically implement changes to the data base only upon proper authorization
- Work with the configuration management organization to apprise users of upcoming changes

Questions from throughout the project organization will arise concerning the structure, content, access methods, and interface requirements of the data base. The DBA is best situated to answer these queries and to generally counsel users on the interface to the data base. The DBA activities in this area include

- Working with the application users to investigate and resolve interface problems with the data base
- Continually evaluate access and modification rights of various users
- Counsel users on fallback and recovery procedures in case of failure

Because testing of the system is not usually performed in the actual operating environment, a test data base must be constructed. The DBA will be responsible for collecting, installing, maintaining, and sometimes specifying the content of the test data base. DBA activities associated with testing entail

- Installing the test data base
- Collaborating with the test organization to define test cases and procedures which will fully exercise the data base
- Planning the transition from the test data base to the operational data base

The data base is just as essential to the integrity of the system as the software programs. On modern software projects, the development of the data base also follows a rigorous sequence of life cycle events. The data base will be specified, designed, and implemented in a manner not altogether different from the software programs. The same level of protections and safeguards are applied to the data base because of its central position in the software configuration.

## 9.4

## Coordinate System Design and Interface Problems

As the software project progresses through the development phase from the requirements definition phase, a number of design and interface problems will inevitably appear. As if Murphy's Law were built in, some occurrences of each of the following categories of problems will probably be encountered:

1. The requirements were misunderstood by the implementer.
2. The requirements were incorrectly implemented in the design; this is a natural repercussion of the first problem but may also happen independently.
3. The requirements were misallocated among the CPCIs.
4. Some of the requirements were unclear, ambiguous, or wrong.
5. The interface specifications were misunderstood and misimplemented.
6. The interface specifications were in some degree incorrect.
7. The system is functionally correct but does not meet performance requirements.

This list could go on *ad infinitum*. The key point is that most of the difficulties encountered during the development phase have as their origin some deficiency in the requirements analysis. The software developers are of course not perfect and will contribute their share of errors. In general, however, the vast majority of critical system problems can be traced to an inadequate requirements analysis.

As these problems surface during the development phase and subsequent phases, it is the responsibility of the system engineering organization to diagnose problem issues and prescribe solutions. In essence, the system engineering organization functions as a monitoring and consulting service during this period of the life cycle. The objective is to maintain and/or restore conceptual integrity to the system.

System engineering should formally track and maintain status reports of open-system-level issues until complete solutions have been prescribed, accepted, and implemented. Problem items are referred to system engineering from the following sources:

- Active monitoring of development by system engineering
- Design review action items
- Referral from CPCI developer

- Referral of test problem from test organization
- Problems identified by customer and/or user
- Referral from project manager

It is normal practice to report status of open technical issues to the project manager and customer at periodic review meetings. The project manager is also kept up to date at more frequent informal meetings.

A majority of the problem issues will span organizational boundaries. These problems require objective analyses and allocation of corrective actions. The system engineering organization is in a unique position to approach problem resolution from this perspective and, thus, overcome the natural biases of the individual CPCI developers. In order to successfully resolve a system level problem, the system engineer must

1. Collect the evidence—all the symptoms of the difficulty
2. Diagnose the cause from the symptoms
3. Identify the options to resolve the difficulty
4. Perform trade-offs and identify the final solution
5. Allocate corrective actions to the various organizations involved
6. Get the solution accepted

The previous sequence of events will usually involve one or more meetings called by the system engineer to confer with the CPCI developers and possibly the test organization. The system engineer must be sure not to conclude solutions on the basis of "polling the delegation." Such resolutions are prone to reflect personalities rather than objective analysis. At the same time, the valuable inputs and observations of members of these organizations should be respected and factored into the evaluation. The final solution must be imposed objectively without the appearance of being autocratic. The successful system engineer will possess both technical and diplomatic skills.

If the resolution of a matter requires changes to an established baseline, a formal change request must be submitted to a change control board. This board must approve the change request before it can be implemented. The system engineering organization supports the board by coordinating an analysis of the requested change and conveying this analysis for the board's consideration.


## 9.5

## Review Change Proposals

As has been cited previously, the key purpose of the system engineering function is to introduce conceptual integrity into the system and maintain that integrity over the full course of the life cycle. Unmanaged changes corrupt integrity. Because many proposed changes are adjuncts to the original system philosophy, they tend to blur unity and cohesiveness. Changes and their disunifying effects are inevitable and unavoidable. We can realistically only expect to minimize their negative impacts to the system image through proper management.

Changes proposed over the system life cycle may be due to

- Changing requirements for use of system
- Reduction in scope of requirements because of cost/schedule considerations
- Changes to make people in the system more efficient
- Changes to make hardware and software more efficient
- Changes to correct previous errors

The magnitude of proposed changes will vary over a broad spectrum. A good portion of them will likely have potential impacts on two or more CPCIs and will prospectively affect the activities of several organizations. The evaluation of any but the most simple changes clearly requires a coordinating agent to properly analyze the impact of a proposed change and to assure an orderly implementation if the change is approved. The system engineering organization is assigned this coordination task because of its central position in the project organization.

The change board will want to know the technical benefits and costs associated with a change proposal before approval is rendered. The system engineering function assists the change board's evaluation by performing the following review functions:

- Coordinates with user on acceptability of functional changes, changes to procedures, man/machine interfaces, and so forth
- Consults with developers on impact and feasibility of changes
- Defines components and documents impacted
- Identifies performance benefits of change
- Coordinates a preliminary schedule for implementation

The determination of whether a change proposal is approved is a management decision. This decision will likely be made on the basis of cost/benefit considerations derived from the information provided by system engineering.

After a change proposal is approved, its implementation follows a mini-life-cycle sequence of events. System engineering participates in the implementation by

- Defining the requirements changes
- Evaluating the design to assure that the requirements were understood
- Resolving any misunderstandings of the developer
- Assisting the test organization to evaluate test results

These activities are identical to those performed by system engineering in the main-stream of the project life cycle.

The verification and validation activities conducted by the system engineering organization are not particularly distinguishable from this organization's mainline functions. Many of the verification and validation tasks are surreptitious and are intrinsic to the basic activities of the organization. The topics covered in this chapter have illuminated the pervasiveness of verification and validation within the system engineering function.

A considerable portion of the space in this chapter has been allocated to requirements validation. This is in reasonable proportion to the importance of this task to the software project. Requirements definition is the most significant phase of the project in terms of its leverage on quality of the final product. The critical errors need to be caught during the requirements analysis to avoid costly recycling during the development phase. If properly performed, the cost/effectiveness ratio for requirements validation probably eclipses that of any other activity.

# Software Development Verification and Validation Activities

The software development organization(s) manufactures or constructs the software end item products. The development process involves a series of events which are listed here in approximate chronological order:

- Preliminary design
- Detail design
- Coding
- Informal checkout
- Preliminary qualification testing
- Support of formal qualification testing
- Support of integration

The main thrust of the software development activities commences with the release of requirement specifications for each CPCI. These activities conclude when the CPCI is turned over to the test organization for formal qualification testing.

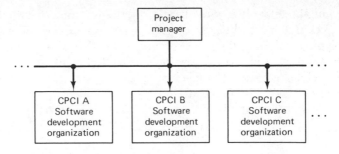

**Figure 10-1**  Development organization for each product.

Except for fairly small projects, there are multiple software development organizations partitioned by product responsibility. This is illustrated in Figure 10-1. Here, each organization is responsible for the development of a CPCI and reports directly to the project manager.

The verification and validation activities of the software development organizations are largely intermixed with and intrinsic to the fundamental product development tasks. The basic verification and validation devices employed by the development organizations are listed here:

- Team development approaches
- Constructive methods
- Computer aided design
- Walkthroughs
- Preliminary qualification testing

The methodologies and tools of these devices are discussed in the following sections.

## 10.1
## Team Development Approaches

Team development practices address the need to establish simpler communication patterns within the software development organization. The team approach permits the concentration of collective mental resources on design/programming problems. The expectation is that products of higher quality are produced under this method than that which would result from the conventional one-to-one assignment of individuals to tasks. The key features that distinguish team practices from the conventional organization are

- Continuous verification and validation
- Better integration of individual efforts

The initial team concept was IBM's chief programmer team. This team was organized such that most of the design and programming operations were performed by a chief programmer with some support from a back-up programmer. Functional responsibilities such as testing, data definition, and clerical tasks are assigned to other team members. The chief programmer team and extensions to this concept have come into widespread use.

Two variations of this team approach are utilized at Hughes Aircraft Company:

- The dual-member design team used for the design activities
- The thread integration team used for the software construction activity

Each of these team approaches is explained in the following paragraphs.

DUAL-MEMBER DESIGN TEAM  The dual-member design team approach is used to improve the manageability and productivity of software projects by moving software development from a private art to an engineering practice.[1] The concept was developed as a means of achieving a significant improvement in the productivity of the development organization.

The structure of a CPCI development organization during the design activities (when this team structure is employed) is illustrated in Figure 10–2. Improved productivity was accomplished by attacking the problem at two levels:

1. The number of elements controlled by any leader is limited to avoid the inefficiencies caused by overloading.
2. The basic element is a two-person design team, which reduces the likelihood of incorrect interpretation of requirements, hidden design flaws, and poor communications.

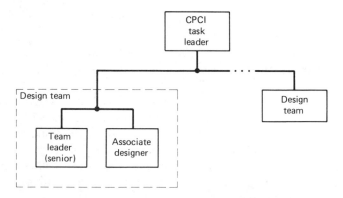

**Figure 10-2**  CPCI development organization during design activities.

[1] The dual-member design team was conceived by Dr. Randall W. Jensen of Hughes Aircraft Company.

The design team consists of a team leader and his associate. Ideally, the team leader is the senior member. The concept has shown itself to be workable, however, when both members function on a coequal basis. The two members of the design team function as a unit through the design activities to provide

- More effective use of human resources (the augmented super-designer)
- Better design due to an effective *continuous* design walkthrough environment
- Continuity in case of loss of a team member
- Fewer design errors
- Faster response to requirement changes
- Improved training atmosphere for junior designers

The mechanics of this approach do not dictate that both members perform in a continuous meeting atmosphere. The designers initially chart out (on a blackboard, for example) the top level of the design structure in a communal effort. At that point, a partition of the next lower-level design elements are agreed upon. Each design member makes a *first-cut* design of the assigned portion while working individually. The team reconvenes, perhaps the next day, to review and critique the individual efforts. Design flaws may be corrected collectively during the meeting, or an action is accepted by an individual to make certain design changes before the next meeting. This process repeats until all the identifiable design flaws are removed and the necessary level of detail is achieved. The final design product represents the collective intellectual investment of both team members.

The contrast of the utilization of personnel resources is depicted in Figure 10-3. The conventional scheme involves each designer working individually on a task in parallel with one or more other designers. The collaborative team concept replaces the parallel approach with a serial effort. The same tasks are addressed in sequence by the team. Although it would be desirable in most circumstances to generate a design as a series of sequential tasks, realism demands that several design teams function in parallel in order to generate the required design product within a reasonable schedule period.

THREAD INTEGRATION TEAM    The thread integration team replaces the dual-member design team for the software construction activity. The thread integration team fulfills the same objectives as the dual-member design team, including

- Continuous verification and validation
- Simpler communication paths
- Limited number of elements controlled by any leader
- Continuous walkthrough environment
- Better integration of individual efforts
- Insurance against loss of team member

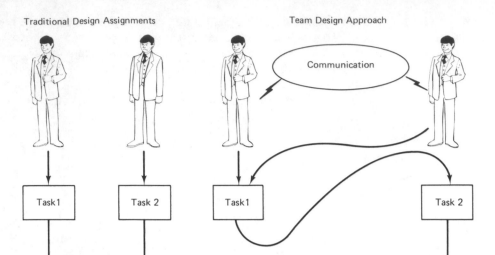

**Figure 10-3** Team design approach contrasted with traditional method. (Courtesy of Dr. Randall Jensen, Hughes Aircraft Company).

The thread integration team consists of two to five members. Two or three teams comprise a CPCI development organization at this stage of the life cycle. It would be preferable to limit the number of teams to two. Management of two parallel efforts by the CPCI task leader is viable. Experience has shown that the management of three parallel efforts within a CPCI development effort is possible but difficult.

A small integration team (two to three members) is composed of a senior programmer complemented by junior members. Each programmer is assigned a module of the thread to code. Code walkthroughs are organized by the senior member to expose the code to the public domain immediately after some informal checkout. The code walkthroughs expose each member to the *big picture* and minimizes the specialist mentality. The senior programmer is responsible for the integration of the modules into a cohesive function. As with the design team, the emphasis is on a sequential approach. Each thread is integrated before initiating activity on the next thread.

The mechanics of a larger integration team (four to five members) are similar but more complex. The larger team contains two senior members. This permits the initiation of action on a succeeding thread before complete integration of the predecessor thread. A typical scenario is illustrated in Figure 10-4. The thread developments are still largely sequential with some overlap in time. Responsibility for thread integrations alternates between the two senior programmers.

The larger thread integration team can be especially productive if the human resources involved are properly managed. This places more of a burden on the

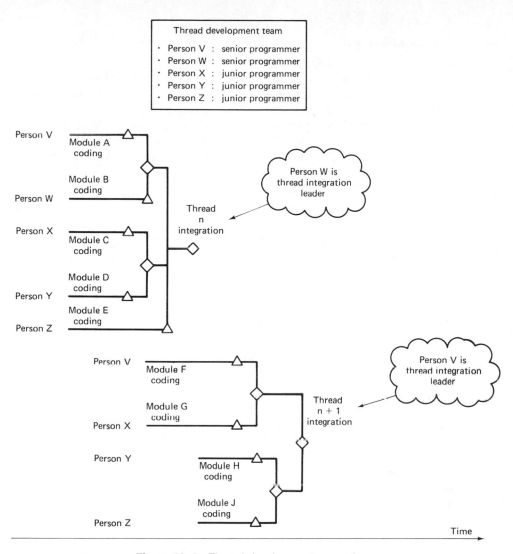

**Figure 10-4** Thread development scenario.

CPCI task leader and senior programmers. This is exactly where such burden should reside in order to insulate the junior programmers from any diversions from the technical effort.

The overall features of team development approaches include a continuous verification and validation atmosphere that is intrinsic to the basic development tasks, isolation of individual team members is avoided, and simpler lines of communication. These features result in better integration of human resources than is attained under the conventional one person per task approach.

## 10.2

## Constructive Methods

Constructive methods of design and programming introduce the element of parallel verification and validation into these development phase activities. A higher-quality product is achieved by applying certain highly organized approaches popularly known as *structured techniques*. The objective of these techniques is to reduce the complexity of the design by decomposing the problem into intellectually manageable components. The intended effects of this process are twofold:

1. A simple design intrinsically is less likely to contain design errors
2. The resulting modular architecture is easier to test

The family of structured techniques covers a broad spectrum. The two that we are immediately concerned with during the software design and construction activities are

- Structured design
- Structured programming

Structured design is a means of defining the module structure of the software architecture. It embraces the philosophy of top-down design. Top-down design successively decomposes the system into smaller and smaller elements until a certain level of granularity is achieved. Usually, the objective is to define the architecture to a level of detail where each module would consist of approximately 50 to 100 higher-order-language source lines of code. Another essential ingredient is required. The modules are defined to fit certain criteria that are characteristic of a good design. These include

- Patterning the module structure after a standard architectural model, such as input-process-output and/or a transaction center
- Subscribing to certain aspects of relationships between modules, such as maximum cohesiveness, minimal coupling, and so forth

Structured programming seeks to simplify the detailed design and code of each module. It formulates programs through the use of stepwise refinement and certain restricted control structures which result in hierarchically nested and intrinsically simple structures. The emphasis of structured programming is achieving simplicity and readability. With these attributes, a program is initially likely to contain fewer mistakes. Absence of complexity is also likely to promote more efficient programmer debugging.

A well-structured design will assist the preparation of an effective test procedure. The crisply defined module structure allows unambiguous association of individual module sets with specific requirements. With these associations firmly entrenched, testing and analysis can be performed in small digestible quantities, and excellent visibility into the status of the development is provided.

Figures 10–5 and 10–6 show the application of the structured design methodology to the dc network analysis system. Figure 10–5 is a composite data flow diagram of the system. It has been partitioned into input-central transform-output sections. The boundary between the input and transform sections is not well established, and other alternative divisions are possible. The corresponding structure diagram is contained on Figure 10–6. In addition to the module structure, the data flow between modules and between modules and files are shown. An intermediate module has been inserted in the central transform section. This has been done to distribute some of the control complexity from the main supervisory module to an immediately subordinate control module. This suggests another attribute of a well-structured design. All of the substantive computations and input/output operations are done in the terminal modules. The superordinate modules exist to provide proper control and sequencing of the terminal modules.

Figure 10–6 shows only the initial form of the structure chart. Considerable refinement and further decomposition will be necessary before the result is finalized. The detailed structure chart of the dc network analysis system that was presented in Chapter 3 reflects a good deal of refinement from the initial cut.

The structured design and programming techniques incorporate intrinsic evaluative mechanisms by avoiding complexity and error prone constructions. These constructive methods improve the testability of the system and furnish verification and validation assistance in parallel to the basic design and construction activities.

## 10.3

## Computer-Aided Design

Automated tools can assist the construction and evaluation of software design. Computer-aided design tools are not methodologies in themselves. They augment the application of design principles. We focus on the discipline of structured design that has previously been described, and show how certain automated tools aid in the structured design process. In a verification and validation context, the interaction of these tools with the design conceptualization will assist the designer in recognizing erroneous and weak areas in the design that are in need of revision.

The main tool of the structured design methodologies is the structure chart, which graphically portrays the module architecture of a system or CPCI. Structured design is an iterative procedure. An initial structure chart is refined into a more detailed version and revised at least several times before the design is finalized. Each iteration of the design cycle typically traverses the following steps:

- Designer generates structure chart
- Designer and, perhaps, associates analyze structure charts

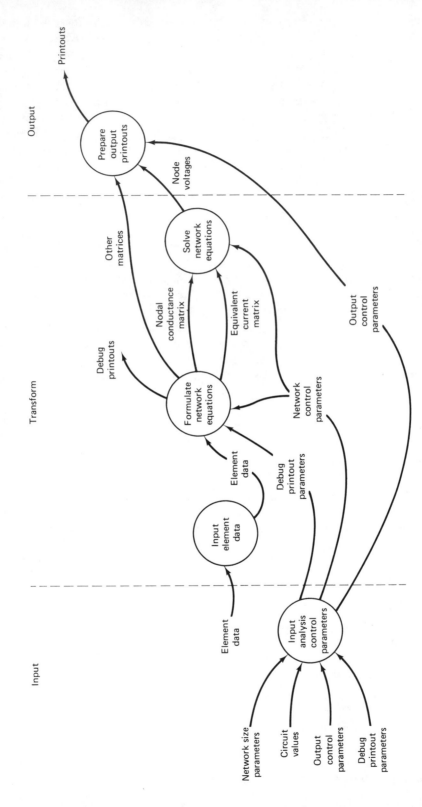

**Figure 10-5** Partitioned data flow diagram for DC network analysis system.

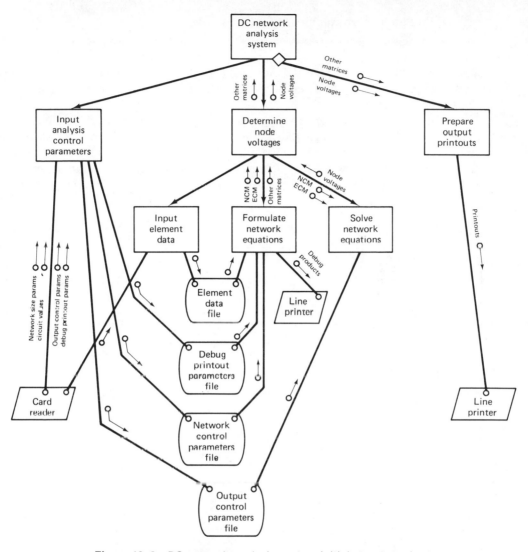

**Figure 10-6** DC network analysis system initial structure chart.

- Problem areas are identified
- Designer modifies/expands structure chart

It is precisely the iterative nature of this procedure that allows computer-aided design tools to interact effectively in the structured design process. These tools can aid in the construction, modification, and analysis of structure charts.

Two automated design assistance tools have been developed at Hughes Aircraft Company and are presently in use:

- Structure chart graphics system
- Design quality metrics system

These tools support the structured design approach by helping to enforce guidelines and consistent application of standards and procedures. Both tools are explained in the following paragraphs.

The *structure chart graphics system* (SCG) is a man/machine interactive system that allows the designer to define module structure on-line and store the resulting structure chart in a machine-readable data base. The functions and interfaces of SCG are diagrammed in Figure 10–7.[2] The designer uses a graphic terminal as an input device. The structure chart is defined in terms of its modules, data flow,

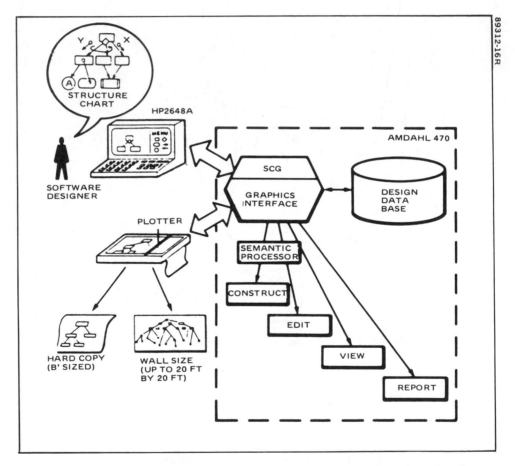

**Figure 10-7** Structure chart graphics system. (Courtesy of Hughes Aircraft Company.)

[2] *Hughes Software Engineering Manual* (Culver City, Ca.: Hughes Aircraft Co., 1980), Part II, p. 2–23.

files, and file interfaces. Sections of the structure chart can be viewed by the designer on the display. A semantic preprocessor will disallow illegal constructs, thus enforcing some of the standards of structured design. With the structure stored in the data base, CALCOMP copies of the structure chart may be requested in either page-sized charts or a wall-sized chart up to twenty feet by twenty feet.

The dynamics of the SCG man/machine interactions are depicted in Figure 10-8. The iterative nature of the use of the tool is highlighted. The four-step iterative process is explained here:

- *Step 1—Data entry*. The designer is presented with the graphically displayed structure chart or, if one has not been previously entered in the data base, a template to enter a new chart. The chart is updated as English-like commands are entered and system questions are answered.

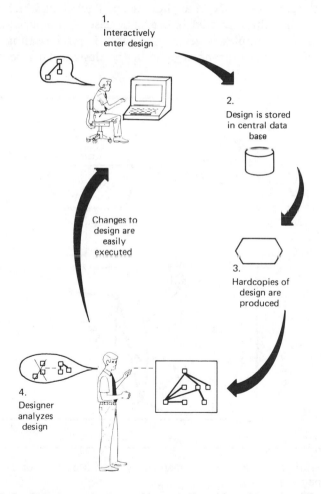

**Figure 10-8** Structure chart graphics man/machine dynamics. (Courtesy of Hughes Aircraft Company.)

- *Step 2—Internal data handling.* The structure chart is captured in a central data base where, in later steps, it may be easily modified. This saves much structure *redraw* effort. The structure data is available for access by other systems, such as Design Quality Metrics.

- *Step 3—Hardcopy output.* The designer may request drawings of the structure chart from a CALCOMP plotter in either of two sizes.

- *Step 4—Structure chart changes.* The designer analyzes the hard copy and postulates changes. The modifications are performed by returning to step 1.

The SCG system enables efficient maintenance of design structures charts and promotes compliance to structured design standards and guidelines.

The *design quality metrics system* (DQM) is an initial step to quantitatively measure levels of compliance to certain design guidelines. The DQM System is illustrated in Figure 10-9.[3] DQM applies certain algorithms which measure complexity of a structure chart entered into a data base by the structure chart graphics system. A plot of complexity versus tree depth is produced that, when examined, reveals potentially error-prone regions in the design. This permits the designer,

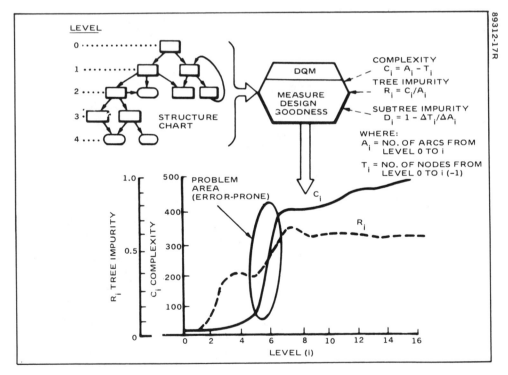

**Figure 10-9** Design quality metrics system. (Courtesy of Hughes Aircraft Company.)

[3] *Hughes Software Engineering Manual,* op. cit., Part II, p. 2-25.

upon being apprised of the complex structures, the option of modifying the design into a less error-prone configuration.

The metrics quantify the design using an algorithm based on network arcs and nodes as a function of tree depth. Several recent software projects at Hughes have shown that these metrics correlate closely with the number of errors encountered in software testing. DQM is also an iterative tool. As the design is being developed, the metrics are continuously calculated and displayed. Degree of improvement can be ascertained by comparing the values of the metrics between two successive design iterations.

These two systems, the SCG and DQM, represent pragmatic state-of-the-art computer-aided design tools. From a verification and validation standpoint, two very important characteristics of the application of these tools are

- They are iterative.
- They are man/machine interactive.

Success of the structured design methodology seems to be highly dependent upon the experience of the designer. Any organization would be expected to have only a small staff of these expert experienced designers. These computer-aided design tools, which enforce some of the rules of structured design, offer some relief from the dependence on this small cadre of craftsmen in order to produce a quality design.

## 10.4
## Walkthroughs

A *walkthrough* is an informal meeting at which the author of a design or programming product explains the details of the product to an audience consisting of other members of the team. The expected response is that the reviewing team members will assist the author in identifying errors or suspicious areas that would probably otherwise have gone undetected until some later time in the project life cycle. Walkthroughs are a key ingredient of the team approach, and this section may be viewed as a further elaboration of the team concepts discussed in Section 10.2. Walkthroughs are continuous incidents in the team development atmosphere and are not always explicit events.

There are several different types of walkthroughs. A software development organization is primarily concerned with

- *Design walkthroughs.* An individual designer presents the design to reviewers by explaining structure charts, interfaces, and file definitions. The reviewers look for flaws in the design.
- *Code walkthroughs.* An individual programmer explains the structure and flow of a small section of code to other team members.

The design walkthrough is a component concept of the dual member design team addressed in Section 10.2. The code walkthrough is intrinsic to the thread integration team concept. Walkthrough techniques may also be utilized in other areas of the project, including requirements specification walkthroughs and test specification walkthroughs.

Walkthroughs are informal and are intended to compensate for some of the shortcomings of formal design reviews. Design reviews are usually superficial, cosmetic, and at least partially politically-oriented. Informal walkthroughs are conducted more frequently and are focused entirely on technical issues.

The primary objective of walkthroughs is, of course, to find errors. The success of walkthroughs in achieving the objective will vary depending on the specific personalities involved and the intensity and dedication with which they apply themselves to the task. It can be safely asserted that walkthroughs do increase the probability of finding errors at an earlier time than would otherwise have been possible. Yourdon[4] observes that the number of errors in production systems decreases by a factor of 5 in organizations that use walkthroughs. He also notes certain other secondary advantages of walkthroughs:

- Weak areas of style such as efficiency, readability, and modularity problems are illuminated.
- The threat of a walkthrough improves the product quality of designers and programmers.
- Junior designers and programmers learn techniques from senior associates; the information can flow in the other direction also.

In essence, the objective of walkthroughs is to find errors before they become embedded in the design and code. The marginal cost of conducting walkthroughs is small in comparison to the cost of fixing errors discovered later in the project life cycle.

We can further distinguish types of walkthroughs in terms of their formality and membership. This additional categorization is applicable to both design and code walkthroughs.

- Internal continuous walkthroughs within the team environment
- Milestone walkthroughs that may include additional attendees as well as the team membership

The basic dynamics of a team approach will continuously use walkthroughs as a communications mechanism. Once the team concept has been well established within a project, it is best to allow team members to establish internal rules for their walkthrough meetings.

Milestone-type walkthroughs are more effective in a slightly more structured

[4] Edward Yourdon, *Managing the Structured Techniques* (Englewood Cliffs, N.J.: Prentice-Hall, 1979), p. 193.

atmosphere with some explicit rules. These walkthroughs are conducted when a particular product milestone has been achieved, such as the completion of design documentation for a software component or completion of testing for a thread. Inclusion of knowledgeable participants from outside the team will help to broaden the objectivity of the review. A typical list of participants for a milestone walkthrough would include

- A moderator
- The author
- Other team members
- The system engineer

The moderator coordinates the walkthrough and maintains order. The moderator may be the thread integrator, in the case of a code walkthrough, or an outsider such as a representative from configuration management or quality assurance. It is effective to have present the system engineer who defined the requirements for the subject functional area. The system engineer will be able to answer requirements issues and should probe to assure that the requirements have been properly understood and implemented correctly in the design or code.

The dynamics of the walkthrough revolve around the author of the product. The author explains the content and flow of the product to the reviewers using operational scenarios or test cases. If the walkthrough is a review of a thread test, the test results should be explained. Reviewers render constructive commentary on suspected problem areas. Interaction and questions should be encouraged during the walkthrough. If the continuity of the presentation is being destroyed, the moderator should impose restrictions and defer some of the commentary until after the presentation is concluded. Certain personality problems may be encountered, and the moderator should be sensitive to maintaining focus on the technical issues. A record of all errors detected should be made by the moderator to assure that they are followed up. It is usually better to merely note the existence of errors during the walkthrough. The nature of the solutions and scheduling of corrective action should be coordinated outside of the walkthrough because discussion of such issues may tend to disrupt the major objective of the review.

Walkthroughs are relatively inexpensive devices to identify the existence of design or programming errors before they become permanent fixtures in the product. Walkthroughs are a key ingredient of the team development approach and contribute to meaningful evaluation of the product in areas where formal design reviews are insufficient.

## 10.5
## Preliminary Qualification Testing

*Preliminary qualification testing* (PQT) is that testing performed by the development organization during the construction activity to qualify a CPCI for entry into the formal test activity. The objectives of preliminary qualification testing are

- To validate that a CPCI properly implements the requirements specification, standards and practices, and internal interfaces
- To demonstrate readiness for *formal qualification testing* (FQT)
- To provide visibility into the development prior to FQT

The threads technique explained in Chapter 3 is an approach particularly oriented toward fulfilling the objectives of preliminary qualification testing.

The PQT is an informal series of tests. All test plans, procedures, and reports are likewise informal documentation not requiring customer approval. These materials are made available for information purposes to the customer and the independent test organization. If an incremental PQT plan is followed, as described in Chapter 3, the FQT is a natural extension of the PQT activities.

Even though informal, preliminary qualification testing is guided by a test plan and test procedures. Test results are documented in a test report. These test specifications are completely controlled by the development organization.

Defined below is the basic content of a PQT plan for a CPCI. This plan is finalized before coding commences, and a first draft plan can be generated around the time of the preliminary design review.

- Test objectives
- Test description
- Test requirements
- Functional allocation of requirements to tests
- Test sequence and schedule
- Analysis requirements
- Test resources

The test objectives normally are a "boiler plate" statement of general PQT goals similar, perhaps, to the objectives mentioned in the first paragraph of this section. The test description should embrace a declaration of the testing strategy. This might include a statement of testing priorities, incremental approach, and methods of addressing risk. The test requirements are a definition of the functions and paths that must be tested. The system verification diagram (SVD) discussed in Chapter 3 provides this definition. The SVD may be explicitly furnished in the PQT plan, or it may be included by reference if the SVD was contained in the requirements specification. The functional allocation specifies the association of specific requirements with each thread and also relates the thread to the software modules which implement the thread function. A test is performed for each thread and involves the integration of the associated modules. The thread functional allocation chart delineated in Chapter 3 is a convenient device to record these relationships. The functional allocation also includes the assignment of threads to builds. The constituent threads of each build may be recorded on a form as shown in Figure 10-10 and entered into the PQT plan. The test sequence and schedule are repre-

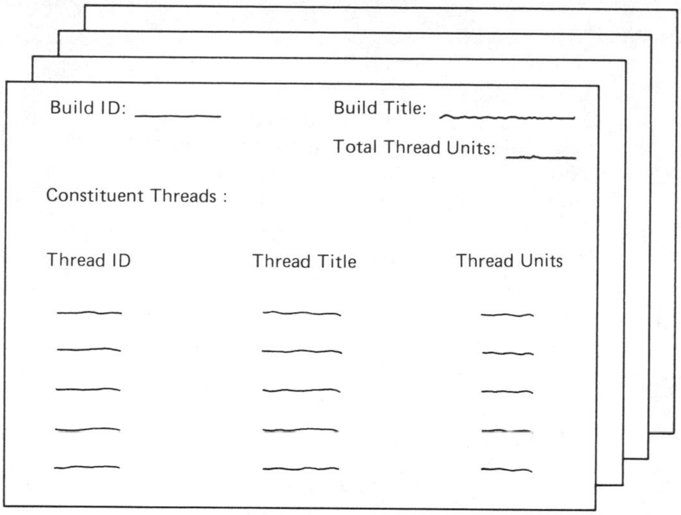

**Figure 10-10** Assignment of threads to builds.

sented by the build plan and thread production plan that were developed in Chapter 3. The analysis requirements should identify any requirements that can only be validated by analysis in lieu of testing. This section should also denote any special analysis efforts required to evaluate test results. The test resources section will specify the particular hardware, software, personnel, and data base resources necessary to conduct preliminary qualification testing.

Each thread test is given individual engineering attention. A combined test plan/procedure/report is produced for each thread test. The content of this report is prescribed in Figure 10-11. Those items prefixed by a single asterisk are filled in before the test is performed. The double-asterisked items report on the test results and are entered upon the conclusion of the test. The test goals reflect an exhaustive testing philosophy. The objective is to traverse as close to 100% of the decision-to-decision paths as is possible. The test procedure is specified in terms of stimulus/response patterns. This procession also indicates the acceptance criteria of the test results. The test cases consist of both functional test inputs defined before the test begins as well as additional cases contrived during the conduct of the test. These extra test cases extend the testing coverage to achieve the desired decision-to-decision path coverage. This thread test plan/report is intended to be concise and brief; no more than an hour or two need be invested to provide the required information. This level of brevity strikes a balance between unnecessary formality at this stage of the development and the need for some degree of orderliness.

Although informal, the thread test plans/reports are impounded by configuration management. This is done so that the performance of preliminary qualification testing can be certified at configuration audits if the matter is brought up by the customer. The PQT is the final task for which the software development

*1. Identification
  • Thread ID #                                    • Thread title

*2. Test Goals
  • Statement of function/subfunctions to be tested
  • Required testing coverage expressed in terms of
    percent of DD-path coverage (normally 100 %—if
    <100%, state why and specify mandatory DD-
    paths)

*3. Test Configuration (could be depicted graphic-
    ally)

  • IDs of new modules to          • Stubs/Drivers to
    be coded                          be used

  • IDs of already existing
    modules

*4. Expected Results and Acceptance Criteria

Stimulus  Expected Response  (Stimulus is an
_____  _____    input and/or
_____  _____    condition cre-
_____  _____    ated by input;
_____  _____    response should
_____  _____    specify accura-
_____  _____    cies expected if
_____  _____    applicable;
                             stimulus could
(Based on thread definition in  be an operator
system verification diagram.)   input with re-
                                sponse being a
                                displayed result.)

*5. Functional Test Cases
    (Specify file names and content, parameter
    input values, operator inputs)

**6. Additional Structural Test Cases
    (Definition of additional test data created after
    testing has begun to achieve required DD-path
    coverage)

**7. Test Results
  • Summary statement of results
  • Notation of any liens
  • Attach printouts from test verifying results
  • Attach RXVP80 test coverage report to show
    DD-path coverage achieved

 * Generate this info before each thread construction/test begins.
** Complete this info at conclusion of test.

**Figure 10-11**  Content of Thread Test Plan/Report

organization has prime responsibility. At the completion of preliminary qualification testing, the CPCI is turned over to the independent test organization for formal qualification testing. The software development organization performs in a
support capacity for the remainder of the testing program.

# Independent Test Organization Verification and Validation Activities

The independent test organization (ITO) is responsible for the planning and conduct of all formal testing of the software products. This embraces tests at several levels and the integration of the software components into a system product. The ITO plans a test and evaluation program over the full span of the project life cycle with the objectives that

1. All performance and maintenance requirements are met by the integrated products
2. The engineering of the test program is consistent with a low system life cycle cost

The span of responsibility of the ITO, depending on the specific project, may also include integration of the products into the configuration at the operational installation.

On the modern software project, the test organization is independent of the development organizations. There are cogent reasons for establishing the test organization as an independent entity:

- The engineering of a test program is a very major task.
- An independent test organization preserves objectivity.

The planning and execution of the test effort requires an investment of time and labor which can exceed that of the software construction. In order to assure that testing represents more than an afterthought to the construction, a parallel effort is necessary to properly engineer the test program. A group of people not involved with the implementation is more likely to do a more thorough and objective job of planning and executing the tests. The implementers would be more likely to generate a trivial series of test cases.

The scope of responsibility of the ITO is delineated in Figure 11-1. The overall test program is depicted. The testing of the software begins by the organization responsible for the development of the CPCI. The development organization codes the CPCI, assembles the CPCI, and performs incremental testing. This testing performed by the developer is known as preliminary qualification testing. At this point, the CPCI is qualified for formal testing. Control of the testing is now transferred to the ITO. The ITO performs a formal qualification test (FQT) on each CPCI. After FQT's integration testing commences, multiple CPCIs are integrated into subsystems, and subsystems are integrated to form the system product. All the integration testing is the responsibility of the ITO.

Figure 11-1 has illustrated only the sequence of test executions. Test related activities begin much earlier in the life cycle. We shall review the activities of the independent test organization over the full software life cycle in chronological order:

- Activities during requirements definition phase
- Activities during define period
- Activities during design period
- Activities during construction period
- Activities during test period
- Activities during integration period

Early planning of the testing activities is a deterrent to some costly problems that might otherwise occur later in the program. The discussion begins with the ITO involvement in the requirements definition phase.

## 11.1
## Activities during Requirement Definition Phase

During this phase, the test concepts for the overall system are established and the system test requirements are specified. The specific activities performed by the independent test organization during this phase are

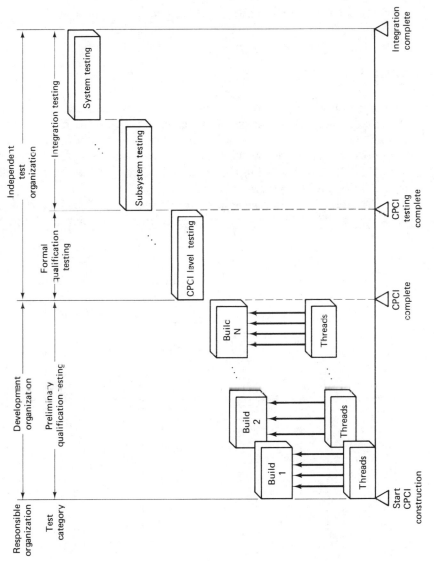

**Figure 11-1** Overview of test program.

- Prepare system test plan
- Evaluate test support tools
- Establish test and evaluation feasibility
- Participate in design reviews

Each of these activities are discussed in the following paragraphs.

## PREPARE SYSTEM TEST PLAN

The system test plan details the approach to demonstrating that the software products meet engineering and performance criteria. A draft of this plan is prepared during the requirements definition phase and is updated during subsequent activities of the life cycle. The content of a representative system test plan is shown in Figure 11-2. An explanation of the content of some of the key sections is provided in the following paragraphs.

Organizational responsibilities are defined for all organizations participating in the test activities in whatever form. These include development organizations, the

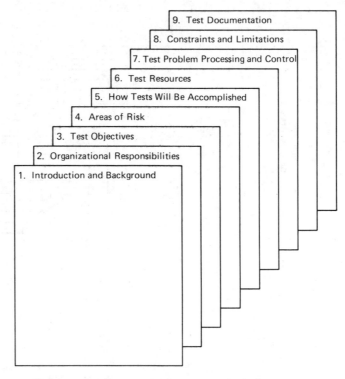

9. Test Documentation
8. Constraints and Limitations
7. Test Problem Processing and Control
6. Test Resources
5. How Tests Will Be Accomplished
4. Areas of Risk
3. Test Objectives
2. Organizational Responsibilities
1. Introduction and Background

**Figure 11-2**  Representative system test plan content.

ITO, customers, integrating contractors, user organizations, and so forth. The risk areas section delineates high-risk areas and indicates potential impacts on the test program. The need for special studies associated with areas of risk is identified. In Figure 11–2, section 5, *How Tests Will Be Accomplished,* contains the following subareas:

- Test levels
- Description of tests
- Test sequence and schedule
- Specification requirement/evaluation allocation matrix
- Acceptance criteria
- Analysis requirements

The section on test resources should include

- A description of the operational configuration
- Differences between the operational and test configurations
- Estimate of computer resource requirements for testing
- Simulation plan
- Personnel requirements for testing

Section 7 describes the process for the detection, reporting, resolution, and closure of problems discoverd during each test phase.

The preparation of the system test plan is a major undertaking. It is the architecture document for the project's overall test program. It could have a profound influence on the quality and eventual cost of the delivered system. The document addresses activities that take place during a period when delays and complications are quite costly to the project. In consideration of the potential leverage of this plan on project success, a modest investment to produce a quality plan is quite justified. An early concentration on the test and integration approach will minimize the surprises that will arise in later more vulnerable stages when the options for resolution are drastically limited.


## EVALUATE TEST SUPPORT TOOLS

It will be necessary to study the trade-off between test and evaluation efforts, development of test software support tools, modification of existing tools, and use of existing tools. It is of course preferable to be able to use existing established tools. This would constitute the lowest risk and most cost effective approach.

Should it be necessary to undertake a fresh development to obtain the desired tool capabilities, then a cost/benefit trade-off study is indicated. Basically, the issue involves the cost and risk of developing new tools versus the labor that would be required to perform the test analysis manually. Whatever the conclusion of such a study, the resulting costs and/or development efforts must be factored into the project plans.

The types of appropriate test tools will vary from one project to another. There are some types of test tools that are useful to a large number of systems. These include

- Test data base generator
- Various print routines
- Test results comparison package
- Data base diagnostic program
- Terminal activity log package
- Data base transaction log package

Some of these capabilities may be available commercially for a particular host computer. Chances are that most of them won't. Some tools are very expensive to develop. Although tool developments are likely to pay off in the long run when the cost can be amortized over several or more projects, the customer on any one project may not be willing to finance tool development when the immediate term economics are not favorable. For this reason, many organizations will allocate research and development funds for test tool development. The combination of R & D financed tools and those derived from projects have built impressive repertoires of test tools for some companies.

## ESTABLISH TEST AND EVALUATION FEASIBILITY

One of the key objectives of the test program is to demonstrate within reasonable cost that the software products meet functional and performance criteria. This feasibility is established by

- Assessment of specification requirements with regard to testability
- Establishment of evaluation methodology
- Realistically bounding the scope of the test and evaluation effort

Clearly the main thrust here is to accomplish technical goals within an affordable budget. Cost drivers such as number of tests, number of test cases, and amount of simulation must be enumerated. A balance must be arrived at between level of technical achievement and cost/schedule investment.

The results of these evaluations constitute a major portion of the test and evaluation philosophy. The system test plan serves as a vehicle to document these conclusions:

- Evaluation methodology is specified in the requirements/evaluation allocation matrix.

- Test levels where the evaluations take place are identified.
- The organizations responsible for the evaluation tasks are identified.

These items largely define the scope of the test and evaluation program.

A requirements/evaluation allocation matrix is prepared for each requirements specification and included in the system test plan. The objectives of preparing the matrices are

- Assure all requirements are tested and/or evaluated
- Assure requirements are tested and/or evaluated at the lowest test level consistent with valid results
- Establish the methods by which the requirements will be validated by the test and evaluation program
- Assure consistency of validation methodology
- Define depth and scope of the test and evaluation program early

The content of the requirements/evaluation allocation matrix includes the following information for each requirement in the specification:

1. Requirement ID or paragraph number
2. Abbreviated statement of requirement
3. Parent requirement identification
4. Method of test and/or evaluation

The method of test and/or evaluation would be selected from one or more of the following:

- *Inspection*. This consists of the physical examination of documentation, records, hardware, or software.
- *Test*. Validation is concluded from a demonstration of the actual functioning of the product.
- *Analysis*. Analytical techniques such as computer models or simulations are used to evaluate the requirement. The analytical results are compared with the requirement specification to establish satisfaction of the requirement.

If testing is the method of evaluation, the test level at which the requirement is to be validated should be specified. The test level is selected from FQT, subsystem integration test, system integration test, and so forth.


## PARTICIPATE IN DESIGN REVIEWS

There are two design reviews that occur during the requirements definition phase—the *system requirements review* (SRR) and *system design review* (SDR). The ITO presents the results of its activities at each of these reviews.

At the SRR, the ITO makes a presentation which includes the following test and evaluation topics:

- Schedules, milestones, high risk areas, and critical path areas
- Trade studies dealing with test software requirements and test bed configuration
- Review of test and evaluation methodology for system and subsystem products

The analogous presentation at the SDR will cover

- Review of test and evaluation methodology for CPCIs
- New and updated portions of the system test plan
- Review of CPCI requirement specifications for testability

Based on the findings of these design reviews, the system test plan is updated.

These ITO activities prescribed for the requirements definition phase have emphasized early planning of test activities. A modest effort expended early in the life cycle avoids some problems that might otherwise be encountered later in the program when more people are involved and the cost of complications is much higher.

## 11.2

## Activities during Define Period

In this period, during which the development organizations prepare preliminary designs, the ITO performs several parallel activities. The system test plan is updated for review at the preliminary design review. The updates will reflect assessment of new requirements and requirement changes since the SDR by

- Specifying method of evaluation
- Assigning evaluation tasks to performing organization
- Specifying acceptance criteria

The ITO prepares draft test plans for the formal qualification test (FQT) of each CPCI. The basic content of this test plan is delineated in Figure 11-3. The test description should provide a detailed description of the test and a logical flow diagram showing the elements being tested and their internal and external interfaces. The test implementation section will include descriptions of

- Baseline configuration control procedures
- Test personnel requirements
- Test simulation data requirements
- Operational data requirements

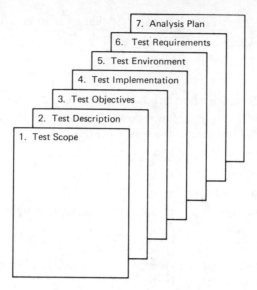

**Figure 11-3** CPCI test plan content.

The test environment should be described in terms of

- Equipment
- Software
- Documentation
- Data
- Liens and limitations

The test requirements consist mainly of a requirements/evaluation allocation matrix for the CPCI. The analysis plan will define the method for determining the pass/fail criteria for each test requirement and should address

- Test data recording
- Evaluation plan
- Acceptance criteria

The CPCI test plans are reviewed at the preliminary design reviews.

## 11.3
## Activities during Design Period

During this period, which culminates in the critical design review (CDR), the activities of the ITO entail

- Preparation of draft test procedure for each CPCI

- Preparation of draft test plans for integration tests
- Update of CPCI test plans
- Update of system test plan

These documentation products are reviewed at the CDR.

The CPCI test procedure consists mainly of the detailed step-by-step procedure required to execute the test, including

- Actions taken
- System responses
- Steps required to initiate, maintain, terminate, and restart the software under test

The test procedure will also identify any nondeliverable software and hardware that is to be employed during the test.

The ITO prepares preliminary plans during this period for each of the integration tests. The integration involves the combination of CPCIs into subsystems and the synthesis of the subsystems into the full system product. For smaller systems that contain only several CPCIs, the subsystem integration tests are an unnecessary step, and the CPCIs are integrated directly to form the system product. The integration test plan documents will follow the same content and format as that of the CPCI test plans.

## 11.4
## Activities during Construct Period

During this period, the development organizations perform preliminary qualification testing (PQT) of the CPCIs. These tests establish a test baseline prior to entry into the formal test activity. The ITO informally observes some or all of the PQT testing. Based on the PQTs, the ITO will usually refine, update, and introduce more detail into the CPCI FQT procedures.

Other activities of the ITO during this period include

- Preparation of draft test procedures for integration tests
- Update of CPCI test plans
- Update of system test plan

The construct activity culminates in the establishment of the test baseline, which forms the point of departure for the formal testing to be conducted under the cognizance of the ITO.

**11.5**

**Activities during Test Period**

During this period, the independent test organization conducts a complete and comprehensive formal test of each CPCI. The FQT is based upon a previously approved test plan procedure. The objectives of the FQT include validation that the CPCI as built satisfies all performance requirements and identification of deficiencies in product functional operation, computational performance, and compatibility with external interfaces. The ITO activities in this period will embrace

- Conduct of test
- Problem reporting and disposition
- Preparation of test report

The test activity establishes the CPCI and its associated documentation as a product baseline. The ITO activities during the test period are elaborated upon in the following text.

## CONDUCT OF TEST

This activity entails those steps involved with the actual execution of the test. In addition to supervising the test execution, the ITO coordinates the effort by means of a number of meetings:

- First pretest meeting
- Pretest meeting for each test run
- Posttest meeting for each test run
- Final posttest meeting
- Status review meetings

These meetings are chaired by a test director from the independent test organization.

The first pretest meeting occurs one or two days prior to the first test run. Its purpose is to acquaint the customer and all test participants with the test objectives and status of test materials. The meeting will include a test technical overview presentation, review of test documentation status, review of organizational support assignments, and identification of test limitations.

The conduct of most tests will involve multiple test-runs spanning several or more days. This is because the test usually consists of several separate segments or sequences. Also, as some failures will almost invariably occur, runs must be repeated until successful results are attained. Each test-run is accompanied by a pretest and posttest meeting. The pretest meeting will discuss

- Status of previously encountered problems
- Specific test objectives for upcoming run
- Specific test operator instructions

The topics covered in the posttest meeting after the test run include

- Review of new problems occurring during the just completed test-run
- Accomplishment of objectives
- Assignment of action items
- Objectives of next run

The test-runs are not always contiguous events. Frequently, it is necessary to interrupt the test sequence to allow the software development organizations the necessary time to install fixes to problems discovered during the test runs. In tight schedule situations, these activities may span two or three shifts.

A test is concluded when all the test objectives are successfully met, or when it is concluded by customer and management that certain discrepancies cannot be rectified during this test because of technical and/or economic reasons. A final posttest meeting is convened to discuss these issues:

- Problem review
- Action items on test baseline update
- Documentation status
- Conclusions/discrepancies
- Determination of test completion

If the test is concluded with discrepancies, a work-off plan for these liens is agreed upon. The vehicle for closing off the liens may be a subsequent test.

During the testing, it is common practice for the test director to brief the customer periodically on test status. The information conveyed would include accomplishments, current status, near-term activities, long-term activities, and problem status.

## PROBLEM REPORTING AND DISPOSITION

A closed-loop problem reporting/disposition system is utilized by the ITO during FQTs and integration tests to maintain a list of problems encountered. All problems recorded will either be corrected or otherwise dispositioned before the test is concluded. The problem reporting system consists of *test problem reports* (TPR) and a *test problem log* (TPL).

A TPR is written for all problems encountered during the testing. A TPR form is usually provided for ease of use by test personnel. A TPR will contain the following items:

- Subject and CPCI name
- Test ID
- Priority ID
- TPR number and date
- Organization reporting problem
- Date of occurrence
- Problem description
- Cause (if known)
- Action required/requested/assigned to
- Disposition/date

A typical test problem priority scheme is illustrated in Figure 11-4.

A test problem log is maintained, which summarizes the status and description of the TPRs. The TPL contains an entry for each TPR, consisting of

- TPR number and date
- Subject of TPR
- Status, if open
- Disposition, if closed

The TPL and TPRs are maintained throughout the test and integrate activities. They are available for review at interchange meetings and configuration audits.

## PREPARATION OF TEST REPORT

A test report is prepared for each major test to formally document the results of the test. The test report is ordinarily issued within thirty days of the completion of the test.

The overall content of a test report is as shown in Figure 11-5. The summary

| Priority ID | Description |
|---|---|
| 1 | Fix immediately—catastrophic error, test cannot proceed |
| 2 | Fix before test completion—serious error, severe degradation in performance, but can continue test process |
| 3 | Fix before system acceptance—moderate error, specification can be met |
| 4 | Fix by a specific date or event |
| 5 | Hold for later disposition |
| T | Nonrepeatable occurrence—problem will be tracked for recurrence |
| X | New problem—problem assumed to be serious but insufficient data available for analysis, investigation required |

**Figure 11-4**  Test Problem Priority Structure

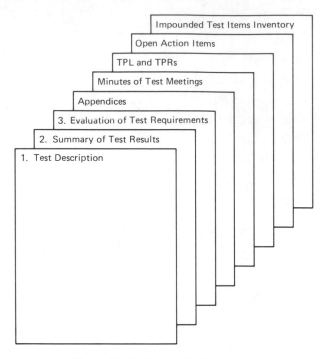

**Figure 11-5**  Content of test report.

of test results mainly describes the requirements met or not met and associated TPRs or liens. The evaluation of test requirements contains the following information for each test requirement in the test plan:

- Statement of requirement
- Data collected
- Analysis performed
- Comparison of performance against acceptance criteria
- Deviations from plan or procedure

If necessary, approved changes to the test procedure and plan should be incorporated and issued at the same time as the release of the test report.

## 11.6

## Activities during Integrate Period

The purpose of the integrate period is to combine the CPCIs into a system product and validate that the product conforms to the system requirements specification. The overall sequence of integration tests is described in the system test plan. Each individual test is prescribed by a test plan and procedure.

Each integration test is conducted by the ITO in the same manner as was prescribed for the formal qualification tests. A test problem report system is used as previously described in Section 11.5. A test report is issued for each test with the same content as in Figure 11–5.

It is not the purpose of the integration tests to revalidate requirements previously shown to conform during lower-level tests but rather to build on previous test and evaluation conduct. In certain cases, it may be necessary to revalidate CPCI level requirements. This occurs when

- Validation of certain CPCI requirements was originally allocated to one or more integration tests
- There have been major modifications invalidating previous testing
- Resolution of problems is required at the CPCI specification level

Depending on the size of the system, there may be several levels of integration tests. For example, CPCIs are first integrated into subsystems, and the subsystems are then combined to form the system.

Again, depending upon the size and complexity of the system, the ITO may either be responsible for or assist in the final integration of the system at the operational installation. If there are several development contractors, this latter job may be the responsibility of an overall integrating contractor.

The activities of the independent test organization have been explained in chronological order. The key point to be gleaned from this presentation is that the test and evaluation effort is a task of considerable magnitude and requires individual emphasis. The scope of the test and evaluation activities span the entire project life cycle. For these reasons, the test organization is an independent entity which can furnish the attention and objectivity required of the test and evaluation activities.

# Configuration Management/ Quality Assurance Verification and Validation Activities

## 12.1
### Configuration Management

The configuration management organization performs two basic functions:

1. Identifies the content of the currently approved configuration baseline
2. Provides the administrative mechanisms to process requests for changes to the current baseline

The content of the current baseline is dependent upon the stage in the software life cycle. The materials controlled by configuration management for each baseline are summarized below:

- Functional Baseline—System requirements specification
  Interface documentation

- Allocated Baseline— CPCI requirements specifications
  Interface documentation
- Test Baseline— CPCI requirements specifications
  Informal design documentation
  Test plans
- Detail Baseline— CPCI design specifications
  Test plans and procedures
- Product Baseline— CPCI design specifications
  Test plans, procedures, and reports
  Physical software product
- Integrated Baseline— CPCI design specifications
  Test plans, procedures, and reports
  Physical software product

Configuration management acts as a policeman in insisting that change procedures are followed. Because software is seemingly easier to change than hardware, more rigorous change procedures are implemented. The configuration management organization acts on behalf of the project manager, and the project manager is the final decision authority on all configuration management matters.

Configuration management establishes baselines by assigning identification numbers to all items in the baseline. Before reaching the test baseline, the baseline content will consist of documentation items; thereafter, the software physical product will be included. Once a baseline is established, only a change control board can authorize changes. Configuration management furnishes administrative support to the change control board by operating an engineering change center to accept and process change requests. The change control board is normally an informal activity that occurs before the product baseline is established by the CPCI formal qualification tests; an exception is requirement changes, which are considered by a formal change control board, including the customer. Beginning with the product baseline, full formal change control is exercised. Configuration management is responsible for releasing (not preparing) updates or new versions of documents resulting from approved changes.

Configuration management operates a *computer program library* (CPL). The CPL maintains the current software listings, the software physical media, and retains all the master documents. Several previous versions of the configuration are also retained in the event that it becomes necessary to regress because of problems with the current version. Prior to testing, the current software configuration is frozen and assigned a version number by the CPL. At the conclusion of a test, all materials are impounded in the CPL for subsequent evaluation by the quality assurance organization and other authorized evaluators.

Configuration management keeps current a listing of anomaly reports and associates these discrepancies with changes to the baseline. This provides visibility into the change authorizations for each updated version of the software configuration. Management wants to know what changes have been incorporated into the new version and the reasons for these changes.

The test plans, test procedures, design specifications, test reports, anomaly reports, and program listings are delivered by configuration management to the configuration audit. These materials are reviewed at the audit to determine if the CPCI and/or system has achieved the performance and functional characteristics defined in the requirements specification. Configuration management is responsible for the integrity of these materials, and the customer will insist on their completeness and accuracy before approving the baseline.

Configuration management is critical in maintaining order on the software project. Its tasks are mainly administrative. These tasks have included identifying the document and software content of baselines, providing an orderly change control process, and ensuring compliance to contractual configuration control requirements.

## 12.2

## Quality Assurance

The quality assurance organization functions as an independent audit and evaluation agent to review all products for compliance to quality standards. The objectives of the quality assurance function include identification of problem areas but does not include rendering of solutions. In many cases, highly technical quality assurance tasks are delegated to other organizations best able to perform them and are audited by the quality assurance organization. This is a pragmatic arrangement directed toward minimizing costs. The quality assurance function is directly accountable to the project manager.

The quality assurance program addresses completeness and consistency of documentation; design/programming tools, techniques, and methodologies; library procedures; subcontractor control; deficiency tracking and corrective action; test monitoring; evaluation of test results; and preparation for audits. The specific scope of the quality assurance function is specified in a quality assurance plan that is finalized very early in the program. The greater mass of quality assurance activities occurs in connection with testing. There are, however, quality assurance tasks that spread over the entire life cycle, as was shown in Figure 8–2.

Requirements specifications are reviewed for clarity, completeness, and consistency. Care is taken to determine that a requirements document specifies external attributes and not design. CPCI requirements specifications are examined collectively to assure that a proper and complete allocation of system requirements to CPCIs has been performed. Design documentation is evaluated to verify that all requirements can be traced to design elements.

Test plans are scrutinized to assure that each test is accompanied by an acceptance criteria, that mechanisms are provided for capturing test results, and that the overall content of the plan conforms to contractual requirements. Test procedures are reviewed to determine that the correct software versions are specified, the procedures are complete, and the test configuration, including personnel assignments, are correctly and completely specified. During the actual testing, the monitoring activities include maintaining official records of test status, assuring that test procedures are followed and recording departures, recording unexpected results, and marking and then impounding test results.

The analyses and preparation of materials for configuration audits are performed under the cognizance of the quality assurance organization in conjunction with configuration management. The types of configuration audits and their specific objectives are described in the following paragraphs.

FUNCTIONAL CONFIGURATION AUDIT (FCA) The FCA verifies that the CPCIs actual performance complies with the attributes contained in its requirements specification. Data from the test of the CPCI is perused to verify that the item has performed as required. FCAs may be conducted on an incremental basis. The FCA for a complex CPCI may be conducted progressively, with completion of the FCA occurring after completion of the level of integrated testing that may be required to validate the CPCI. The principal items provided to the customer for the FCA are the CPCI test plans, procedures, and report, plus the updated requirements specification and design specification. The CPCI test procedures and results are reviewed for compliance with the requirements specification. Requirements not validated by the CPCI test are identified, and a solution for subsequent validation is proffered (such as validation in the subsystem or system tests). An audit of the test plans/procedures is made and compared against the official test data, including checks for completeness and accuracy. Deficiencies are documented, and completion dates for all discrepancies are established and recorded. An audit of the test report is performed to validate that it accurately and completely describes the CPCI test.

PHYSICAL CONFIGURATION AUDIT (PCA) The PCA is a formal examination of the CPCI end item (the code). The CPCI is matched against its technical documentation and configuration management records in order to establish the baseline version of the CPCI. The PCA includes an audit of the design specification and an inspection of the format and completeness of the user's manual and any other manuals or handbooks due for acceptance at this time. Normally, the FCA and PCA are conducted simultaneously as part of the same meeting.

FORMAL QUALIFICATION REVIEW (FQR) The FQR verifies that the actual performance of a CPCI, as determined through testing, complies with its requirements specification and identifies the test reports/data that document the results of tests of the CPCI. When feasible, the FQR is combined with the FCA/PCA at the end of CPCI testing if sufficient test results are available at the FCA/PCA to ensure that the CPCI will perform in its system environment. Otherwise, the FQR is considered an extension of the FCA/PCA and may be conducted at the subsystem/system levels.

As a practical matter, the audit meeting is an administrative session. All of the quality and completeness checking has been performed beforehand by the quality assurance and configuration management organizations. The actual audit focuses on a check list that all of the required analyses have been done and products provided, and reviews the deficiencies.

The benefits of a quality assurance program to the software project include enforcement of discipline, an independent evaluation of products, better visibility into project status, and earlier identification of risk areas. If properly supported by project management, the quality assurance function will be a major contributor toward delivering an operable, reliable, and maintainable system.

# Verification and Validation Activities outside the Project Organization

Under nominal conditions, the software project organization will be vested with all the necessary resources to build the specified system. There are certain circumstances when the customer and/or upper-level management of the contractor find it compelling to augment the resources of the project organization with outside verification and validation assistance. The special situations which might justify such action include

- The system to be built is of unusual size and/or complexity.
- The system will consist of products provided by several developers under separate contract.
- The system already under development appears headed for disaster!

The first two items widen the scope of previous discussions. For very large systems, an individual project organization may be developing just a segment of a system. This segment will require integration with already existing segments of a system or with other segments under parallel development by other project organizations.

The response of the customer and/or management to these special situations will involve the creation of verification and validation agents that are independent of the project organization. These independent agents will take the form of

- The independent verification and validation contractor
- The independent review group

The assignment of an independent verification and validation contractor to a project does not necessarily reflect on the ability of the development contractor to do the job. It is normally a recognition that the enormity and importance of the task require the application of extra resources to boost the probability of success. In contrast, the independent review group is formed when a project is already in jeopardy of failure or clearly headed in that direction. Here, the developer may be incapable of managing the project or unable to cope with certain related circumstances and is in need of outside assistance. These two outside verification and validation activities are discussed in the following sections.

## 13.1

## The Independent Verification and Validation Contractor

The independent V & V contractor is utilized when the customer concludes that circumstances require that independent objectivity and evaluation are necessary to assure the success of a system development. This normally occurs when the system is very large, complex, or critical such that a software failure could have a catastrophic effect on life or property. The scope of the assistance rendered by the V & V contractor will vary depending on the individual system. It could range from a level of effort task as technical advisor to the customer all the way to an active technical monitoring of the development contractors including integration of the software products.

A full set of tasks for an independent verification and validation contractor might include responsibility for

- High-level requirements analysis and allocation
- Interface assurance
- Product integration
- Coordination of other contractor efforts

With the previous task description, a V & V contractor is sometimes alternatively known as the *system integrating contractor*.

The activities of the V & V contractor are depicted in Figure 13–1. The relationships between the customer, V & V contractor, and software development contractors are shown. The V & V contractor evaluates the products of the development contractors at each activity of the life cycle. During the requirements definition phase, the V & V contractor performs the following functions:

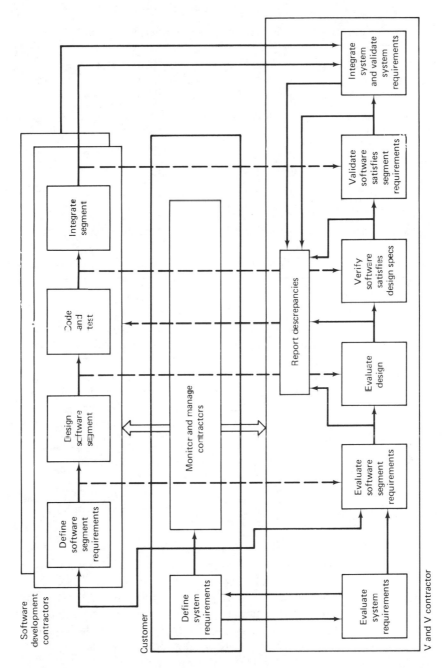

**Figure 13-1** Relationships and activities of V & V contractor.

- Evaluation of system and software segment requirements
- Management of system requirements review
- Preparation of system integrated test plan
- Preparation of interface control documents

During the development phase the V & V contractor will

- Monitor developer's performance and product status
- Support in the evaluation of designs with respect to adequacy, risk, and interface
- Review and critique test programs, plans, and methods
- Participate in formal reviews and audits
- Provide continued system and interface engineering
- Monitor developer's integration activities
- Integrate developers' products into system products

During the transition and operations and maintenance phases, the V & V contractor assists the customer by performing evaluation, engineering, and integration relative to product changes.

The relationship between the verification and validation contractor and the development contractors can be a very fragile one. The developers may understandably be sensitive to criticism, particularly of the trivial variety. The V & V contractor should be sure that discrepancies reported as a result of evaluations are substantial, relevant, accurate, and are presented in a constructive context. The customer is responsible for the direction of the development contractor. The V & V contractor may advise or suggest to the customer possible appropriate direction for the developer, but the verification and validation contractor should avoid any appearance of directing the developers.

## 13.2

## The Independent Review Group

An independent review process may begin when a program is visibly beset by technical performance, cost, or schedule problems. All programs will of course be confronted by some set of problems at various points in the life cycle. However, an independent review is called for when it appears to upper level management that the project organization is either unable or without the resources to self-diagnose and correct critical problem situations. In such troublesome situations, a wise move by customer or management may be to form an independent review group. The membership of the review group would be drawn from outside the project organization. The purpose of the review team is to

- Diagnose accurately the present status of the project
- Determine causes and causitive agents of the present difficulties
- Recommend corrective action

The steps of the independent review process from problem definition to final report are shown in Figure 13-2.[1] The independent review group must focus on a problem of limited scope in order for there to be any reasonable expectation for success. Despite possible apparent contra-indications, the project organization is still likely to be the only expert on the overall system development problem. Outside expertise will probably only be effective if concentrated on one or two key aspects

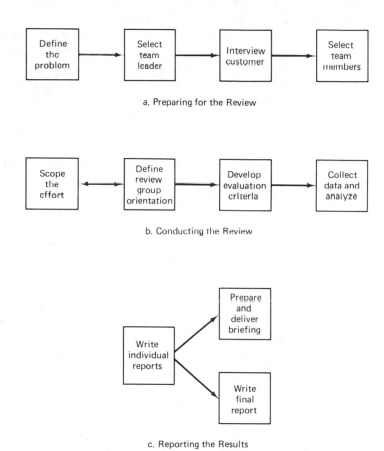

a. Preparing for the Review

b. Conducting the Review

c. Reporting the Results

**Figure 13-2** Steps of the independent review process. (a) Preparing for the review. (b) Conducting the review. (c) Reporting the results.

[1] Daniel R. Baker, David A. Herrelko, and Charles J. Grewe, Jr., *Conducting an Independent Review Group (IRG) Evaluation of C³I Software* (Hanscom AFB, Ma.: Electronic Systems Division, 1979) ESD–TR–79–251, p. 8.

of the system development. An independent review group may be formed at any stage in the project life cycle to address the following issues:

1. If the development is allowed to proceed without interference, will the software perform the required tasks?
2. What immediate actions are required before the development can proceed?
3. What overall changes in direction are necessary to deliver an effective software product?[2]

The review group should address these issues within the context of a limited set of problems. A manageable problem area might be requirements adequacy, testing methods, or machine capacity, among others.

The review group must be composed of competent membership and must reach its conclusions quickly—usually a week to a month maximum—for the review to have any influence on the project outcome. The team leader should be knowledgeable in the mission of the project, have the authority to recruit members and clear necessary paths, and possess necessary diplomatic skills to successfully interface with customer and contractor project management. The team members should be selected based on their expertise of the problems under investigation, should all have a fundamental working knowledge of software and the software development process, and should be independent of the project organization under review. The team leader will be the final authority on all matters and may frequently have to exercise that authority to avoid endless debate.

The team leader will orient team members as to the scope of the review. This may be supplemented by customer briefings which describe the mission and status of the project. The team familiarizes itself with the status of the particular problem area by scrutinizing all available materials. For example, if the problem area is requirements adequacy, the review material would consist of the requirements specifications, briefing charts from design reviews, and trade-off analysis reports. Evaluation criteria should be developed in the form of specific standards which can be quantitatively rated. Data is collected from available documentation and interviews with key personnel including those in the project organization. Dealings with the project organization should be conducted with caution. Project members will understandably be sensitive to being reviewed and possibly even hostile. Maximum diplomacy is required. The purpose of the interviews is to collect data, and aroused hostility will no doubt hinder this objective. Value judgements would be premature at this point, and conclusions should only be released through formal channels at the end of the review. The team leader should assure that results of the data analysis are objective and substantiated by statistics and examples; subjective evaluations not backed up by hard information should be rejected.

Each member of the review team will summarize his or her findings in a standard format and submit them to the team leader. The team leader will combine the individual inputs into a unified final report. Normally, this will consist of an ex-

---

[2] Baker et al., op. cit., p. 9.

ecutive summary and a detailed technical report. The executive summary outlines the review approach and states the conclusions and recommendations. The technical report recounts the review in detail and provides detailed support for the conclusions and recommendations. The team leader will likely be asked to provide a briefing of the findings of the independent review group.

The independent review process is a challenging task for all involved. It requires an extraordinary amount of work to be accomplished in a very short time. The team members must evaluate and learn at the same time, sometimes under unfriendly and even hostile conditions. The success of the effort depends upon aggressive leadership, recruitment of the right people, dedication of team members, and good organization of the effort by the team leader.

This chapter has illustrated that verification and validation activities can extend outside of the software project organization. On large, complex, or very critical systems, the customer may employ an independent verification and validation contractor to evaluate and integrate the products of the software developers. When unabated technical, schedule, or cost problems come to the attention of upper-level management, an independent review group from outside the project organization may be assembled to study the difficulties and offer recommendations for remedial action.

# Part V

# Future Trends

# Chapter 14

# Future Trends

Verification and validation is presently perhaps the most dynamic area of modern software engineering. The software engineering emphasis during the 1970's has been on introducing constructive-oriented technology, such as structured design and structured programming, with a somewhat lesser attention to advancing pragmatic verification and validation approaches. Although these constructive techniques have by no means been fully assimilated into production environments, the principles are firmly established and would not be expected to undergo any radical refinement. The same cannot be said of verification and validation technology. The environment with respect to V & V is in a state of flux. The principles of V & V have yet to be articulated as concisely as the constructive methods. We have considerable levels of activity in verification and validation research and experimentation, much of it unproven. At the same time we are having considerable difficulty in managing and implementing more mature V & V related technologies. Thus, if one accepts this assessment of the present state of affairs, there is considerable opportunity in the upcoming years for dramatic evolution of verification-and-validation-focused technologies.

It has been implied in the previous discussion that there are really two different areas of emphasis—development of new technologies and management of relatively proven technologies. For example, structured design and structured programming have matured in a pure technology sense but still represent a management challenge in introducing these techniques to actual project situations and enforcing their application. Thus, future trends in verification and validation are explored in two parts:

- Management-focused trends
- Technology-focused approaches

Although management and technology are separated here for discussion purposes, it is important to clarify that management and technology go together. The most powerful software engineering tools are those which have combined technical and management merits. A good technical approach will almost always have built-in manageability features.

## 14.1
## Management-Focused Trends

In recalling the historical progression of the software project, the need for separation of system engineering, software development, and an independent test organization developed. Unfortunately, in many instances, this resulted in the deployment of separate approaches and tools by these organizations with marginal coordination. Economics and resulting performance no longer supports the continuation of this existing arrangement. A revised, more realistic approach to software development requires an overall coordinated package of tools and methodologies covering all phases of the software life cycle. This will, of course, place more of a burden on management to achieve these results. What is needed is the continued evolution of a corps of software managers who are well educated in the elements of software physics, who are committed to modern methodologies, and who will be aggressive in overcoming inertia to assure that these approaches are implemented.

What seems to have occurred is that in the compulsion to provide individual attention to verification and validation, V & V became too detached from other activities on the software project. What remains for management to do is to review this separation and provide a more integrated role for verification and validation. This would involve reassimilating verification and validation such that each area of software engineering has certain V & V responsibilities while still maintaining the separate test organization.

In considering modern verification and validation methodologies, we include both modern testing approaches and parallel verification and validation techniques. We have referred to this latter category in previous chapters under the term *constructive approaches*. These include structured analysis for requirements definition, structured design, and structured programming. Although these constructive approaches are not pure V & V devices, they are emphasized for their parallel verification and validation value of avoiding errors and inconsistencies before they become embedded in the design and code. In taking this broad view, the supposition is that management of verification and validation essentially embraces the overall subject of software project management.

One of the more significant trends in software project management is the more precise definition of software life cycle events, associated products from each event, and the specific roles and responsibilities of each participating organization. This represents a fairly dramatic turnabout from largely *ad hoc* management practices of the past. Many companies have prepared software management manuals detailing their perception of the software life cycle. A summary of a representative sequence of life cycle phases and milestones for a very large project is shown in Figure 14-1. This figure shows the phases and activities, the review and audit sequence, and the series of specifications, plans, and reports. They key ingredient of the methodology depicted on the figure is the orderly progression of reviews and controlled baselines. A project specific computer program development plan implements the methodology shown in Figure 14-1. This plan defines the project management organization and controls, software development activities and documentation, software product assurance activities (including the test program), and computer program development resources for the project. A considerable portion of this plan addresses verification and validation activities. The government usually requires that a computer program development plan be submitted as part of the contractor's proposal for major procurements.

## 14.2
## Technology-Focused Trends

Software quality is addressed by two distinct and complementing methodologies. The first is that of assuring that quality is initially built into the product. This has been pursued using organizational methods that have been referred to as the *constructive* or *synthesis methods*. Once the product (or parts of the product) have been constructed, the second quality methodology, product analysis, becomes pertinent. Analysis is essentially test and evaluation. Testing is a diagnostic exercise and does not introduce quality into the software product per se. It provides a measure of the existing quality level. It is the follow-up activities to testing, debugging, and error correction that improve the product quality.

Present and proposed approaches for improving software quality are identified on Figure 14-2.[1] These are categorized on the figure according to their correlation with synthesis or analysis in the horizontal dimension and according to time in the vertical dimension. Those items closer to the bottom of the figure symbolize

---

[1] William R. DeHaan, *Software Testing Methodology Using RXVP80* (Santa Barbara, Ca.: General Research Corporation, 1980), RM-2333, Volume 1, p. 22.

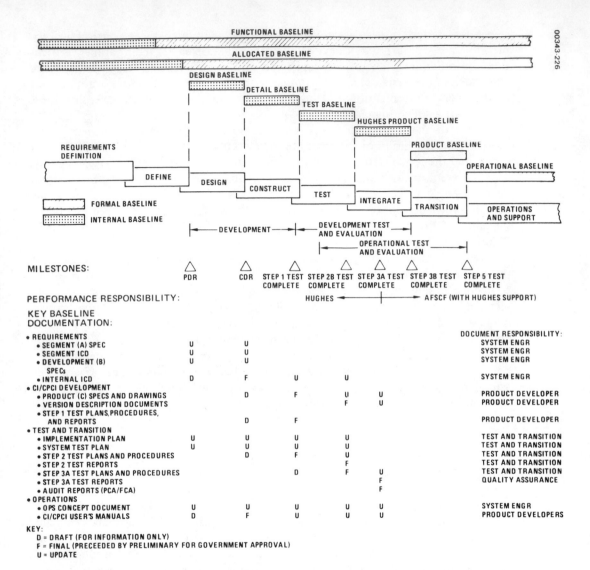

**Figure 14-1** Representative life cycle phases and milestones. (Courtesy of Hughes Aircraft Company.)

the more advanced or futuristic approaches. Figure 14–2 represents past, present, and future trends in verification and validation related technologies.

We can time register our present technology position in Figure 14–2 by associating certain of the items on the figure with specific techniques and tools that have been discussed in this book:

- AVS technology is represented by the RXVP80™ and V-IFTRAN™ tools described in Chapters 6 and 7.

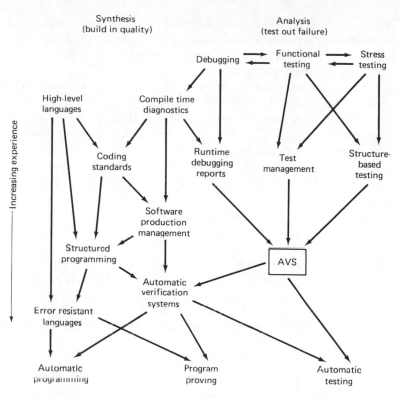

**Figure 14-2** Approaches to achieving quality software. (William R. DeHaan, *Software Testing Methodology Using RXVP80* (Santa Barbara, California: General Research Corporation, 1980), RM-2333, Volume 2, p. 22.)

- Software production management is typified by the software construction and test approach detailed in Chapter 3.
- Structured programming, referred to casually in several places throughout the book, is a state-of-the-art technique for detailed design and code construction.

Our present outer limit of pragmatic technology is thus demarcated in Figure 14-2 by the line running through structured programming, software production management, and AVS.

In addressing future tendencies typified by the items falling below the delineation identified previously, it is convenient to discuss them in two "baskets":

- Improved implementation of proven technologies
- Evolution of present experimental techniques

This first category will entail development of new tools to automate present manual procedures and also extend availability of already existing tools. The latter category will involve the possible migration of new techniques from research status to use in actual project environments.

The software development process is more accurately viewed when the technical engineering problem is considered in conjunction with the human engineering aspect of the process. The application of talented personnel should, theoretically, be a sufficient requisite on which to forecast success. However, basic human fallibilities open loopholes for errors to occur. Engineering, scientific, and management practices are frequently corrupted by human errors of consistency and omission. Computer-automated tools have been and will continue to be developed to implement existing proven technologies that are most prone to consistency and omission errors if performed manually.

Although more detailed classifications are possible, automated tools may be partitioned into two basic groups: (1) those tools that assist in the definition and design of the software, and (2) those tools that help evaluate the software, once it is built. The first group of tools performs clerical functions of checking for completeness, consistency, and omission errors during requirements definition and design activities. The usefulness of such tools depends on the ability to express requirements and software design in machine-readable form. Thus, the future utility of these tools is, to a large degree, directly keyed to progress in the development and widespread use of specification languages, program design languages, and automated documentation systems.

The RXVP80™ source text analysis system, explained in Chapter 7, is typical of the evaluation tools. This technology is already in a highly developed state, although much necessary research continues to be directed toward the automatic generation of an optimal set of test cases. Widespread use and acceptance of these tools are presently hampered by: (1) reluctance by management to forsake traditional manual methods that have been previously successful on small software projects, and (2) availability of tools only to companies that have been able to finance their development. Each of these restraints is expected to be slowly eroded in the next several years. The first problem will be overcome through an educational process, particularly with regard to cost benefits of the automated tools and the prospect of being denied contracts for large software projects if the tools are not used. The second difficulty is more acute. More companies may be willing to invest the necessary funds for automatic tool development in order to protect future business. The purchase rights to some already-existing tools are presently being marketed by their developers. A further possibility is that, for projects of which a government agency is the procurer, automatic test tools may be available as government-furnished equipment.

More extensive utilization of computer-aided requirements analysis tools such as the problem statement language/problem statement analyzer would be expected in the near term. More and more computer-aided design tools will be developed; the history of these tools to date has been that they are almost exclusively proprietary developments. Although some companies will commit the necessary research and development funds to develop computer-aided design tools, the spread of this technology will be much more restrained compared to tools in the public domain, such as PSL/PSA. The wider use and availability of structured programming languages is a certain occurrence over the next several years. Paramount in this area will be the introduction of the new Department of Defense programming language Ada.

As the more prolific usage of automated tools is expected over the software life cycle from requirements definition through testing, a more complete verification and validation of the system results. It is also expected that errors would be detected earlier in the development cycle, with such approaches leading to cost containment.

It is the forward-looking concept of some that nearly error-free programs can be constructed by applying certain organizational techniques and that the correctness of these programs can be certified in a static manner (without actual execution) by using mathematical proofs. The constructive approach to the development of programs is with us today in the form of structured design and programming. The static approach concerns program proofs, a popular subject of current research. Practical application of program proof techniques to programs of significant size may be at least a decade away.[2]

The proof concept employs the program source statements to prove mathematical theorems about program behavior. The expected program behavior is characterized by a set of assertions. The intentions of the designers are reflected in these assertions about values of variables at end or intermediate points of the programs; then, the annotated program can be converted into a theorem and the theorem proved. Program proofs are intended to place verification and validation on a more sound theoretical foundation than testing which checks the performance of programs on the limited basis of a set of sample data. Major obstacles limiting wider use of proof techniques include the difficulties in developing the assertions that are to be proved and length of the proof computations. Program proofs assume proper behavior of the application program environment (hardware, operating system, compiler, concurrent programs, etc.), often a dangerous assumption. Economic feasibility of program proofs requires further development of automatic theorem proving tools.[3]

A related subtechnology of program proofs is *symbolic execution*. This experimental technique is more likely to develop a practical implementation in the near future. Symbolic execution is a means of executing a program as a series of symbolic formulas that are verified against a set of predefined conditions or assertions. The practical difficulties involve generation of the assertions and the economics of the required computations. Because of these difficulties of use, symbolic execution does not now appear to be economically feasible for mass application to large software projects. Some selective application to critical software units would, however, be an advantageous use of symbolic execution when these soft-

[2] E. F. Miller, Jr., *Methodology for Comprehensive Software Testing* (Griffiss Air Force Base, N.Y.: Rome Air Development Center, 1975), p. 17.

[3] E. F. Miller, Jr., *A Survey of Major Techniques of Program Validation* (Santa Barbara, Ca.: General Research Corp., 1972), RM–1731, p. 58.

ware units could do irreparable harm if certain conditions are violated; an example application might be in spacecraft command and control with which certain combinations of commands could injure the vehicle. Such software would require maximum verification.

Automated assistance for test case generation is a continuing subject of current research. For example, Hsia and Petry[4] report on an experimental technique that combines dynamic testing with symbolic execution to generate test cases that will fully exercise all execution paths. The symbolic execution provides a formula for each execution path that can be mapped into the input domain. Andrews[5] has experimented with an adaptive testing technique that automatically generates new test cases based on feedback from results of the prior test set in order to incrementally stress test a simulated ballistic missile defense software system.

Presently, a good environment does not exist for the introduction of new verification and validation approaches. A consolidation of present technology is needed to fill a gap between technology and the ability of management to efficiently apply what already exists. This consolidation is a necessary step to provide a firm baseline for the introduction of advanced methodologies.

[4] P. Hsia and F. E. Petry, *An Assessment of Software Quality Assurance* (Huntsville, Al.: University of Alabama, 1979), Final Report—Contract DASG60–78–C–0088.

[5] D. M. Andrews, *Using Assertions for Adaptive Testing of Software* (Santa Barbara, Ca.: General Research Corporation, 1979), Technical Memorandum 2270.

# Bibliography

BROOKS, FREDERICK P., JR., *The Mythical Man-Month*. Reading, Ma.: Addison-Wesley, 1975.

CAREY, ROBERT, AND MARC BENDIC, "The Control of a Software Test Process," in *Proceedings Computer Software and Applications Conference 1977*. New York: IEEE, 1977. IEEE Catalog No. 77CH1291-4C.

DEMARCO, TOM, *Structured Analysis and System Specification*. Englewood Cliffs, N.J.: Prentice-Hall, 1979.

HETZEL, WILLIAM C., ed., *Program Test Methods*. Englewood Cliffs, N.J.: Prentice-Hall, 1973.

JENSEN, RANDALL W., and CHARLES C. TONIES, *Software Engineering*. Englewood Cliffs, N.J.: Prentice-Hall, 1979.

TEICHROW, DANIEL, and ERNEST A. HERSHEY III, "PSL/PSA: A Computer-Aided Technique for Structured Documentation and Analysis of Information Processing Systems," in *IEEE Transactions on Software Engineering*. SE–3, No. 1, January 1977.

WEINBERG, VICTOR, *Structured Analysis*. Englewood Cliffs, N.J.: Prentice-Hall, 1980.

YOURDON, EDWARD, *Managing the Structured Techniques*. Englewood Cliffs, N.J.: Prentice-Hall, 1979.

YOURDON, EDWARD, *Techniques of Program Structure and Design*. Englewood Cliffs, N.J.: Prentice-Hall, 1975.

YORDON, EDWARD, and LARRY L. CONSTANTINE, *Structured Design: Fundamentals of a Discipline of Computer Program and Systems Design*. Englewood Cliffs, N.J.: Prentice-Hall, 1979.

# Glossary of Terms

**Assertion**  A statement of conditions or relationships between variables that should exist instantaneously at a particular point in a program.

**Automated Verification System (AVS)**  An automated test assistance tool that measures the performance of software under test and the effectiveness of test cases.

**Baseline**  The data processing resources produced by each phase of the software life cycle. These resources are controlled until superseded by a more current baseline. The data processing resources of the baseline consist of both documentation and the software physical product.

**Bottom-Up Integration**  The process of building up a software system beginning with components at the bottom levels of the software hierarchy.

**Build**  A significant partial functional capability of a software system. A build consists of several or more threads.

**Build Plan**   An overall calendarized graphical view of the sequence of software construction/test events, including the sequence of the builds, relationships of the builds to each other, the allocation of threads to builds, and the sequence of the threads.

**Change Board**   A committee with the authority to approve changes to an established baseline. *See also* **Baseline.**

**Computer Program Configuration Item (CPCI)**   The lowest-level software entity subject to discrete formal identification, documentation, change control, and testing.

**Computer Program Library (CPL)**   A controlled repository for the current software listings, the software physical media, and current documentation.

**Configuration Management**   An administrative function that is responsible for identifying the content of the currently approved configuration baseline and that provides administrative support for control of changes to the baseline. *See also* **Baseline.**

**Data Base Administration**   A component of the system engineering organization that designs, builds, and enforces the discipline and procedures of the data base.

**Data-Dominated System**   A software system characterized by large volumes of data residing in time delayed storage and by the complexity of the data structures.

**Debugging**   The process of locating and correcting errors that were revealed by testing.

**Decision-to-Decision Path (DD-path)**   The sequence of software source statements lying between the outcome of a decision up to and including the next decision. The DD-path is the basic logical segment of a program's control structure on which testing coverage is measured.

**Developer**   *See* **Software Development.**

**Driver**   A dummy software component that simulates the activity of the software component immediately superordinate to the present component under test. Extensively used in bottom-up integration.

**Dual-Member Design Team**   A team consisting of a senior designer and associate employed to improve the quality of design by providing a continuous verification and validation atmosphere.

**Execution Order Integration**   The process of building up a software system by integrating all components in the software hierarchy associated with a function or thread in the order of the execution of the components. *See also* **Thread.**

**Formal Qualification Testing (FQT)**   A formal test of a computer program configuration item performed by the independent test organization and documented by a formal test plan, procedure, and report of results.

**Incremental Integration**   The process of building up a software system by adding only a single new entity at a time to a previous baseline.

**Independent Review Group**   A review team assembled from outside the software project organization to assess current status and make recommendations for corrective measures. The use of such a review group should not be a normal practice and is employed only when it appears that the software project organization will not successfully complete the program without outside assistance.

**Independent Test Organization (ITO)**   The organization in the software project which formally tests the computer program configuration items and integrates the CPCIs to form a unified system product.

**Independent Verification and Validation Contractor**   An organization independent of the software project organization usually employed on very large, complex, or critical projects for which independent objectivity and evaluation are judged to be required for the success of the project. The scope of activities will vary according to the project but could include high-level requirements analysis, interface assurance, product integration, and coordination of other contractor efforts.

**Integration**   The process of combining and testing software units, usually computer program configuration items, to form a unified system product.

**Maintenance**   Modification of software after initial delivery. Modifications may be needed to fix latent errors, to respond to changing user requirements, to compensate for deficiencies in other parts of the system, or for other project specific reasons.

**Module**   The smallest unit in the software system architecture, consisting of a sequence of program statements that in aggregate perform an identifiable service.

**On-Line Debugging System**   A debugging device that allows the programmer to perform debugging on-line from a terminal device during program execution using symbology native to the source language in which the program was written.

**Phased Integration**   The process of building up a software system in phases, in which integration is treated as a single phase and all components of the system are combined in a single step.

**Preliminary Qualification Testing (PQT)**   The testing performed by the responsible development organization to qualify a computer program configuration item for entry into the next increment of testing.

**Program Proof**   A method to validate proper program behavior by treating the program and assertions of proper program behavior as a mathematical theorem and proving correctness of the theorem.

**PSL/PSA**   Problem statement language/problem statement analyzer. A computer-aided requirements analysis tool developed at the University of Michigan. Provides the facilities to express requirements in a formal language, performs automated consistency checking, and produces documentation reports.

**Quality Assurance**   An organization of the software project that functions as an independent audit and evaluation agent to review all products for compliance to quality standards.

**Regression Testing**   A retesting of previously established capabilities, usually performed when a new function is added to a system to ensure that the in-place capabilities are unaffected. Also performed when a change is made to a system.

**Reliability**   A term awkwardly applied to software and generally referring to a measure of software quality. Various more specific but unreconciled definitions of software reliability exist.

**RXVP80™**   A commercial automated verification system that assists in the evaluation, testing, and documentation of software by providing static analysis, test instrumentation, test coverage analysis, and automated documentation capabilities.

**Software Development**   The organization in the software project responsible for implementing the software product in accordance with the requirements defined by the system engineering organization. Also known as the *developer*.

**Software Life Cycle**   A series of phases and activities beginning with requirements definition and concluding with operations and maintenance through which a software system evolves. Embedded in the life cycle are a series of configuration management baselines which form the basis for orderly and controlled growth and change of the software resources.

**Structured Analysis**   A method for performing requirements analysis and generating a requirements specification that is readable and understandable by using certain graphical communications tools and simplifying organizational techniques.

**Structured Design**   A method of defining software architecture using top-down decomposition, according to certain rules, to define modules and other guidelines for design goodness.

**Structured Programming**   A method for detailed design and programming of the logic of a software module which reduces complexity and enhances readability. It is characterized by the use of only certain simple logical constructs.

**Structured Specification**   A requirements specification generated by using the structured analysis technique and consisting of data flow diagrams, a data dictionary, and transform descriptions. *See also* **Structured Analysis.**

**Stub**  A dummy software component that simulates the functioning of the next component subordinate to the component presently under test. Extensively used in top-down integration.

**Symbolic Execution**  A means of executing a program as a series of symbolic formulas that are verified against a set of predefined conditions or assertions.

**System Engineering**  The organization in the software project responsible for prescribing the overall architecture of the system, including definition of system level requirements, system level design, and requirements for each computer program configuration item.

**System Verification Diagram (SVD)**  A graphical representation of software requirements as a series of stimulus/response pairings. Each stimulus/response pairing is also known as a *thread*.

**Testing**  The controlled exercise of the program code using sample input cases with the objective of exposing errors.

**Test Problem Report (TPR)**  A written report of an anomaly observed during testing that is formally logged and followed up for correction or other disposition.

**Thread**  An identifiable, operationally useful function that is individually testable. Each thread is associated with specific software modules that implement its function. Each thread is defined by a stimulus/response element in the system verification diagram.

**Thread Integration Team**  An implementation team employed during software construction and testing consisting of one or two senior members and several associates. The objective of the team is to improve the quality of the software product by establishing a continuous verification and validation atmosphere.

**Top-Down Integration**  The process of building a software system beginning at the top of the software hierarchy and integrating all components at a given level before progressing to the next lower level.

**Validation**  An activity that ensures that the software end item product contains the features and performance attributes prescribed by its requirements specification.

**Verification**  An activity that ensures that the results of successive steps in the software development cycle correctly embrace the intentions of the previous step.

**Walkthrough**  Informal meeting at which the author of a design or programming product explains the details of the product to other members of the team. The audience critiques the product.

# Index